THE FAMILY TODAY
AND TOMORROW

THE CHURCH ADDRESSES HER FUTURE

CONTRIBUTORS TO THIS VOLUME

The Reverend
Benedict M. Ashley, O.P., Ph.D.
Professor of Moral Theology
Aquinas Institute of Theology
St. Louis, Missouri

Clayton C. Barbeau,
M.A., M.F.C.C.
Psychotherapist
San Francisco, California

The Reverend Monsignor
Carlo Caffarra
President of the John Paul II
Institute for Studies on
Marriage and Family
Rome

Janice Plunkett D'Avignon, Ph.D.
Adjunct Professor of the
School of Education of
Boston College and
St. John's Seminary,
Brighton, Massachusetts

Robert A. Destro, B.A., J.D.
Assistant Professor of Law,
Catholic University of
America
Member United States
Commission on
Civil Rights

The Reverend Monsignor
Charles J. Fahey, M.S.W., M. Div.
Director of the Third Age
Center and Marie Ward Doty
Professor of Aging Studies
Fordham University
New York, New York

Paul C. Glick, Ph.D.
Adjunct Professor,
Sociology Department
Arizona State University
Tempe, Arizona

William C. McCready, Ph.D.
Associate Professor, School
of Social Service
Administration and
Director of the Cultural
Pluralism Research Center,
NORC
University of Chicago
Chicago, Illinois

Mario J. Paredes, M.A.
Executive Director
Northeast Regional Pastoral
Center for Hispanics
New York, New York

Edmund D. Pellegrino, M.D.
Director, Joseph & Rose
Kennedy Institute of Ethics
and John Carroll Professor of
Medicine and Medical
Humanities
Georgetown University
Washington, DC

The Reverend
Steven L. Preister, M.S.W.
Executive Director, National
Center for Family Studies
Catholic University of America
Washington, D.C.

The Most Reverend
John H. Ricard, S.S.J., D.D.
Auxiliary Bishop of Baltimore
Baltimore, Maryland

Beth J. Soldo, Ph.D.
Senior Research Scholar
Center for Population
Research
Georgetown University
Washington, D.C.

Paul C. Vitz, Ph.D.
Associate Professor
of Psychology
New York University
New York, New York

THE FAMILY TODAY AND TOMORROW

THE CHURCH ADDRESSES HER FUTURE

THE POPE JOHN CENTER

Nihil Obstat:
 Rev. Robert F. Coerver, C.M., S.T.D.
 Censor Deputatus

Imprimatur:
 The Most Rev. Edward J. O'Donnell, D.D., V.G.
 Archdiocese of St. Louis

June 21, 1985

The Nihil Obstat and Imprimatur are a declaration that a book or pamphlet is considered to be free from doctrinal or moral error. It is not implied that those who have granted the Nihil Obstat and Imprimatur agree with the contents, opinions, or statements expressed.

Library of Congress Cataloging in Publication Data
Main entry under title:

The Family today and tomorrow.

    Contains addresses given at a Workshop for Catholic Bishops in Dallas, Tex. in Feb. 1985.
    Includes bibliographies and index.
    1. Family — Religious life — Congresses. 2. Family — United States — Congresses. 3. Catholic Church — Doctrines — Congresses. I. Pope John XXIII Medical-Moral Research and Education Center. II. Workshop for Catholic Bishops (1985: Dallas, Tex.)
BX2351.F355   1985   261.8'3585   85-12245
ISBN 0-935372-17-2

Contents

v

This book presents the content of the workshop conducted for 235 bishops of North and Central America and the Caribbean by the Pope John Center in Dallas, TX., Feb. 4-8, 1985. The Knights of Columbus generously funded this workshop as well as the four previous ones in Dallas in 1980, 1981, 1983, and 1984. We congratulate the Knights and their Supreme Knight, Mr. Virgil C. Dechant, for their vision and magnanimity in underwriting these programs which permit Catholic bishops, not only from the United States but from other nations and cultures, to study together the profound issues facing the Church today.

The Pope John XXIII Medical-Moral Research and Education Center was founded in St. Louis, MO., in 1973. It moved to its present headquarters in Boston, Massachusetts, on July 1, 1985. The Center's staff has developed it as a research and education center responding to emerging ethical issues in health care from the perspective of the Judeo-Christian tradition and Catholic teaching. The many publications of the Center, listed at the back of this volume, and its monthly newsletter, *Ethics and Medics,* indicate the wide range of research and education the Center has undertaken in its young life span.

This fifth workshop the Center conducted for bishops developed as a logical sequel to the first four workshops. The first three had dealt with specific issues as the titles of the published proceedings indicate: *New Technologies of Birth and Death,* (1980), *Human Sexuality and Personhood,* (1981), and *Technological Powers and the Person,* (1983). The fourth workshop dealt with the fundamental and exceptionless moral norms which the Church teaches and applies to specific issues. The published volume from that workshop is entitled, *Moral Theology Today: Certitudes and Doubts.*

The planning committee for this fifth workshop realized that medical-moral issues within the Church demand a proper interaction of the medical, scientific, and technological communities with the Church and the people. This interaction depends considerably on the healthy functioning of families, and of the Church through families. In fact, the family, that basic unit within which human life is brought forth and nurtured, is the focus of the Church's work. Hence the title and theme of this workshop was, "The Bishop and the Family: The Church Addresses Her Future."

The Church's worldwide concern for the family has been well-known, especially since the 1980 Synod of Bishops studied marriage and the family. Hence the planning committee invited The Most Reverend Archbishop Albert Bovone, the Secretary of the Sacred Congregation for the Doctrine of the Faith in the Vatican, as a special observer and participant in the workshop. The committee also invited Monsignor Carlo Caffarra, President of the John Paul II Institute for Studies on Marriage and the Family in Rome, to deliver the keynote address of the workshop. His address appears as the Prologue in this volume.

The thirteen other speakers at the workshop who are listed at the beginning of this volume each contributed from his or her particular expertise. We are pleased to publish here the final, footnoted versions of their lectures plus their responses in the discussion chapters which they kindly reviewed and edited for publication.

We are grateful to The Reverend Thomas Lynch and the Commission on Marriage and Family Life of the United States Catholic Conference for the use of the first draft of their paper on the necessity of a family perspective in the ministries of the Church in Chapter 4. The second draft of this paper is scheduled to appear this August of 1985.

We have titled this volume, *The Family Today and Tomorrow,* because we sincerely believe it offers a reliable and realistic view of the family and the future directions of family life. We are happy to provide this volume for the use of the bishops who attended the workshop and for the much larger audience of readers, both clergy and lay, who are concerned with family life and family stability.

Hence we repeat our gratitude to the Knights of Columbus for their indispensable financial assistance. We are grateful to His Holiness, Pope John Paul II, for the message which he sent to the bishops at the workshop. We are also pleased to include the greetings from The Most Reverend Thomas J. Welsh on behalf of the Pontifical Council for the Family, from Supreme Knight Virgil C. Dechant of the Knights of Columbus and from Mr. John E. Curley, Jr., President of the Catholic Health Association.

We wish to thank The Most Reverend Daniel E. Pilarczyk, Archbishop of Cincinnati and Chairman of the Board of the Pope John Center, for his wise assistance and guidance. We are especially grateful to the members of the Board of the Pope John Center for their continuing encouragement. The bishop members of the Board, The Most Reverend Daniel A. Cronin, The Most Reverend John S. Cummins, and The Most Reverend Adam J. Maida, served on the planning committee along with Mr. Frank J. Schneider, another Board member, and His Eminence Bernard Cardinal Law, Archbishop of Boston and our former Board Chairman. We are likewise grateful to the Catholic Health Association staff for their cooperation in the workshop and this volume.

This volume would not have appeared without the cooperation of the entire Pope John Center staff which joined in conducting the workshop. Father William M. Gallagher, President of the Pope John Center, cheerfully directed the planning committee in its deliberations and the workshop itself. Father Edward Bayer assisted particularly with the manuscript of Monsignor Caffarra's keynote address and his discussion dialogue. Father Larry Lossing designed the cover and assisted with the page layout of this book. Mr. Timothy Cooper of the Pope John Center did copyreading for the entire volume. Miss Tina Sgroi typed the several versions of chapters 5, 10, and 15, while Mrs. Jo Anne Probst handled communications with the authors and Mrs. Charlene Renda assisted whenever needed.

This volume probably would not exist without the vigorous leadership our present Holy Father, Pope John Paul II, has given in support of the historic Catholic understanding of marriage and the family. Therefore we gratefully dedicate this volume to His Holiness. *Ad multos annos!*

June 22, 1985   The Reverend Donald G. McCarthy,
                                                          Editor

To my Brother Bishops
from North and Central America
and the Caribbean

I am very happy to send greetings to you as you assemble at another Workshop organized by the Pope John XXIII Medical-Moral Research Education Center. As I greet you in the name of our Lord Jesus Christ, I also wish to thank the Knights of Columbus whose continued generosity has again made possible your coming together from widely scattered dioceses of Canada, the Caribbean, Central America, Mexico and the United States. You gather as Pastors and Teachers of the Church, filled with an eagerness to deepen your knowledge and love of the truth, grateful for the opportunity to pray and reflect together, within the unity of the universal Church, in communion with the Successor of Peter.

In 1980, the Synod of Bishops convened in Rome to consider the Role of the Christian Family in the Modern World. The topic for that Synod was chosen in direct response to numerous requests from around the world for a concerted, detailed study of the problems facing the family today and of the mission of the family in the Church and in society. In response to the Synod and drawing upon the many insights and suggestions of the Synod Fathers, I issued, the following year, the Apostolic Exhortation *Familiaris Consortio.* Your Workshop in Dallas is, in a certain sense, a continuation of the work accomplished by the 1980 Synod, an eloquent expression of your desire as Bishops to help assist families to fulfill their irreplaceable role in the life and mission of the Church.

I was pleased to learn of the topic of this year's conference,

"The Bishop and the Family: The Church Addresses Her Future". For it indicates that you are convinced of the serious responsibility which Bishops are expected to exercise on behalf of the family, and it shows your desire to carry out your mission with the greatest possible effectiveness. As I pointed out in *Familiaris Consortio:* "The person principally responsible in the diocese for the pastoral care of the family is the Bishop. As father and pastor, he must exercise particular solicitude in this clearly priority sector of pastoral care" (No. 73). I am confident that the presentations and discussions of this Workshop will help you in your own pastoral care of the family and enable you better to inspire and guide the priests, deacons, religious and all those who assist you in this work.

In the course of these days, you will undoubtedly examine a number of current trends affecting family life, such as the challenges faced by parents in educating their children to maturity in Christ, the problems confronting aliens and migrant families, the difficulties of aging family members, the pressures in society which contribute to family disintegration, the moral evils which threaten conjugal love and human life from the moment of conception, and the many other emerging areas of special concern. At the same time, you will consider how the family shares in the life and mission of the Church, in particular in the twofold role of promoting love and unity and of fostering and protecting human life. Since the family is called to be a community of persons united in love and pledged to fidelity, it is the foundation of the unity and stability of society, and in a primary way it builds up the Kingdom of God in this world. Furthermore, as I stated in *Familiaris Consortio:* "The fundamental task of the family is to serve life, to actualize in history the original blessing of the Creator — that of transmitting by procreation the divine image from person to person" (No. 28).

As you know, at my weekly General Audiences during the past several years, I presented a catechetical series of talks on the theology of the human body and the sacramentality of marriage, including within it a confirmation and further analysis and development of the teaching of Paul VI contained in *Humanae Vitae.* A major factor which prompted me to undertake this catechesis was pastoral concern for the family and the conviction that the Pope and Bishops can best serve the family by carrying out faithfully their role as teachers of the faith, by enlightening families with the word of God and the authentic teaching of the Church. That is why I willingly extend my support to this Workshop and to other similar initiatives aimed at helping Bishops more effectively to teach and preach the Good News. I am close to you in the special role that you exercise as Bishops in *"proclaiming with joy and conviction the Good News about the family,* for the family absolutely needs to hear ever anew and to understand ever more deeply the authentic words that reveal its identity, its inner resources and the importance of its mission in the City of God and in that of man" (*Familiaris Consortio,* 86).

The title of your meeting aptly indicates that when the Church concerns herself with the family she is concerning herself with her own future. With this same conviction, I said to the United Nations General Assembly, six years ago: "I wish to express the joy that we all find in children, the springtime of life, the anticipation of the future history of each of our present earthly homelands. No country on earth, no political system can think of its own future otherwise than through the image of these new generations that will receive from their parents the manifold heritage of values, duties and aspirations of the nation to which they belong and of the whole human family. Concern for the child, even before birth, from the first moment of conception and then throughout the years of infancy and youth, is the primary and fundamental test of the relationship of one human being to another" (No. 21). Our pastoral efforts as Bishops to care for the family in our day are a concrete way in which we contribute to the future of the Church and of all humanity.

May the Holy Spirit, then, dear Brothers, abide ever more fully in your minds and hearts, "the Spirit of truth who comes from the Father" (Jn 15:26), the One who has been sent to guide us to all truth (cf. Jn 16:13). And I invoke the grace and peace of our Lord Jesus Christ upon you and your people, especially upon all the families to whom you minister by Word and Sacrament.

From the Vatican, January 16, 1985

Joannes Paulus PP. II

GREETING FROM THE PONTIFICAL COUNCIL FOR THE FAMILY

The Most Reverend Thomas J. Welsh, D.D.

I am grateful for the opportunity to speak briefly about the nature and purpose of the Pontifical Council for the Family.

We met most recently in Rome after the New Year and I bring you greetings from Archbishop Eduard Gagnon, our Pro-President.

The Council was created by Pope John Paul II in May, 1981, to succeed the former Committee for the Family because of his "desire to give an ever more adequate response to the expectations of the Christian people, as gleaned by the Episcopate of the entire world and expressed in the recent (1980) Synod of Bishops which dealt with the family."

The Pontifical Council for the Family has the task of providing the pastoral care of the family. Its composition reflects that task. There are three levels of membership:

a) *Presidency Committee* of six bishops under Archbishop Gagnon, who succeeded the late Cardinal Knox. India, Africa, Canada, South America, Poland, Germany and the United States are represented — five year terms.

b) *Members* — Twenty married couples from around the world — five year terms: meet once a year in Rome for a week.

c) *Consultors* — About twenty-five experts in various related fields.

"The future of humanity passes by way of the family." That is the eloquently stated judgment of the Holy Father. It is found in *Familiaris Consortio,* the landmark apostolic exhortation which is the fruit of the Synod of 1980 as distilled by the Holy Father. That he truly believes that the future of humanity passes by way of the family can be seen from his emphasis: the Synod, *Familiaris Consortio,* the Pontifical Council for the Family, the Institute for the Family which he created at the Lateran University, and his very long series of audience talks on human sexuality, marriage and *Humanae Vitae.*

The Pontifical Council for the Family is the specific agent of the Holy Father to help us all, bishops especially, provide pastoral care for the family. The competence is pastoral, not jurisdictional. The assembly last May, for example, with a lot of homework done before hand, studied the world-wide picture of marriage preparation and the Pontifical Council for the Family is now working with the Institute to see if some basic model can be developed.

The most universal conclusion of the assembly was that *remote* preparation for marriage/parenthood needs much more attention. We speak a lot about the "domestic church" but it is hurting very much.

Related to that — you will be receiving shortly from the Pontifical Council for the Family a summary of observations gleaned from its participation in the United Nations International Conference on Population held in August of 1984 in Mexico City.

The secular press obscured to some extent the fact that the Holy See was able to get a recommendation passed that abortion would not be used as a method of "family planning." The United States also dropped a bombshell at the Conference by announcing that it would no longer aid the programs using abortion as a means of family planning.

But the tremendous influence of the International Planned Parenthood Federation and the greatly increased use of sterilization for family planning in some Catholic countries ought to alert us even more that the family everywhere is in danger. Just as pro-choice really means pro-abortion, so family planning doesn't mean family, really, since it is now understood to include individuals and is mostly planning to have no or very small families.

I have been very edified by the talent and dedication of the assembly members: from Canada, Bernard and Huguette Fortin; from Mexico, Roberto and Elizabeth De La Fuente; and from the United States, Richard and Barbara McBride and Virgil and Ann Dechant.

I appreciate this opportunity. I encourage you to visit the Pontifical Council for the Family in Rome and ask you to let us help you and I ask you to help us.

There are few priests and fewer bishops whose vocation did not flower in a Catholic family.

GREETING FROM THE KNIGHTS OF COLUMBUS

Supreme Knight Virgil C. Dechant

It hardly seems possible that a year has passed since I last enjoyed the privilege of saying a few words on behalf of the Knights of Columbus to this unique gathering — to what I referred to last year as "The Dallas Experience."

The Order of the Knights of Columbus is a proud participant in this workshop, not so much for any expertise we can bring to the proceedings but, insofar as we are able — through the blessings the good Lord and His Mother shower upon us — to provide the wherewithal to make it possible.

In past years the topics were these: *Moral Theology Today: Certitudes and Doubts, Technological Powers and the Person, Human Sexuality and Personhood, New Technologies of Birth and Death.*

I must admit to having been somewhat intimidated by the presentations and discussions. I know, however, that the information offered, the give-and-take of the question-and-answer sessions and the opportunities for leisurely conversations have enabled the bishops to go back to their dioceses with the most up-to-date thinking available on these complicated but very vital questions. I have no doubt that the next few days will result in the same objective being met.

Personally, I have three reasons for looking forward to this year's sessions on "The Bishop and the Family: The Church addresses Her Future."

First, over the last several years I have made a concerted effort to return the Knights of Columbus — our 1.4 million members in 8,000 councils in the United States, Canada, Mexico, the Philippines, Puerto Rico, Guatemala, the Dominican Republic, the Virgin Islands, Panama, and other areas of the Caribbean — to return our organization to its original concept: to be a family organization. More and more we have been involving our wives and children in council activities; we are striving to keep the wives and children of deceased Knights as part of our "extended family" through the "Outreach to Widows" program; we are affirming and holding out as examples to others our outstanding families through the "Family of the Month/Family of the Year" program. Those bishops who were present at our annual convention over the last several years have witnessed the success of this last-mentioned effort.

Second, Ann and I were honored two years ago to be named members of the Pontifical Council for the Family by the Holy Father. What we learn here during these days will be of great benefit as we participate in the Council's deliberations.

Finally, as the father and mother of a family (although our last son will be married this year), we still feel the need to keep aware in a personal way of the many issues and dilemmas confronting young — and perhaps not so young — families today.

In closing, I pray with you that the Holy Spirit will inspire these sessions and that the Holy Family — Jesus, Mary and Joseph — will watch over us, protect us and see us safely home.

GREETING FROM THE CATHOLIC HEALTH ASSOCIATION

John E. Curley, Jr.

In addition to speaking to you as the head of the Catholic Health Association of the United States, I would like to represent myself this evening as the head of a family.

My wife Terry and I have six children, ranging in age from 16 to 24 years of age. They are a delight, and we love them dearly. But they have not always lived up to our expectations for them.

We wanted them to be strong, to be achievers. They, like us, are imperfect. Perhaps they are learning humility.

We wanted them to be healthy, to do great deeds. They, like us, are infirm. Perhaps they will do better deeds.

We wanted them to be rich and famous, to be happy. They, like us, are more comfortable with less. Perhaps they will be wise.

We have wondered if they would exercise power and seek praise. They, like us, are weak. Perhaps they will feel the need of God.

We have wanted all things for our children so that they might enjoy life. They, like us, have life. Perhaps they will enjoy all things.

Our children are nothing that we expected, but everything that we had hoped for.

Almost despite ourselves, our unspoken prayers were answered.

My wife and I often wonder: has our parenthood provided us with a very special glimpse of God?

On behalf of CHA, and on behalf of my family, I pray that this workshop on "The Bishop and The Family" brings you a very special glimpse of God.

The Ecclesial Identity and Mission of the Family

The Reverend Monsignor Carlo Caffarra

Our reflection will be divided into two fundamental parts. In the first part, I will try to demonstrate the identity of the family, and, in the second, its mission.

1. IDENTITY OF THE FAMILY.

When I speak of the identity of the family, I mean that which constitutes its *truth,* that is, the specific *characteristics* and specific *nature* which make the family different from any other social grouping.

But I realize that we must immediately tackle what today is one very serious problem. Indeed, our whole reflection will depend on the solution to this problem: Does there *exist* such a "truth" about the family? *Are* there such "specific characteristics and a specific nature" of the family? *Is* there a truth and a nature which remain unchanged for the family within *every* culture? Or must we not rather think that the family is a creation of the *culture itself*, — that *society* assigns the family whatever characteristics and nature society sees fit?

Not only from a theological point of view, but also from a philosophical one, we must begin to tackle this problem by pointing out that, when one speaks of the "truth of a thing", one must not intend by this expression first of all what *man* thinks about that thing. For the "truth of a thing" is rather what *God* thinks about it. We can cite in this connection the profound text of St. Thomas, which I shall give in Latin and paraphrase in English:

> *Prior est comparatio ad intellectum divinum quam humanum, unde etiam si intellectus humanus non esset, adhuc res dicerentur verae in ordine ad intellectum divinum. Sed si uterque intellectus, quod est impossibile, intelligeretur auferri, nullo modo veritatis ratio remaneret.*

> We must see a thing first as God understands it, not as man does. For even if no human intellect at all existed to see the truth about things, things would still be true as far as the intellect of God is concerned. But if *both* kinds of intellect — human and divine — should cease to exist — which is, of course, plainly impossible — then only could one say that there is no truth.[1]

Note the beginning of this text: "*prior est comparatio ad intellectum divinum quam humanum*" — we must see a thing first as God understands it, not as man does. This means: what each *thing is*, what each *reality is*, — its *truth* — depends on the idea that *God* has of it. The truth of any reality comes from God's idea of it and depends on the project God has in mind for it. And this, God's project for it, remains unchangeable. If, therefore, there is — as there is — a divine project for the family, there also exists a truth or identity of the family.

2

On the other hand, it is equally certain that we can observe also that the family *changes* in its structure, in the various world cultures, and even within the same culture with the passing of time. This mutating of the family is caused, in the final analysis, by two factors: the *knowledge* and the *liberty* of human persons.

Mutation — change — in the family is caused by *knowledge* or, better, lack of knowledge. For man does not always achieve *complete* knowledge of God's design for the family. His knowledge is often partial. At one period, man may know *more* about what the family is; at another period, *less*.

Change in the family is caused also by human *liberty*: even when man knows the design of God, he must freely consent to carry it out. But he can, of course, also refuse to carry it out. The family, seen as necessarily a structure of *persons*, that is, freely self-determining agents, is consequently the place in which the proposal of God and the liberty of man *meet*. And from this meeting we can derive two important consequences.

The first consequence of this meeting of God's proposal and man's liberty: Not every carrying out of the institution of the family has the same value, but its value depends on its greater or lesser faithfulness to God's design. In other words: we can and must give an *ethical* judgment, that is, a judgment on the *goodness* and *badness* of the institution of the family as it is found in any given case or era, according to the concrete way in which family life is being carried out. It is necessary and obligatory that we possess the criteria for making this judgment.

The second consequence of the meeting of God's proposal and man's liberty: The fundamental criterion, in order to work this judgment out as to how good or how bad the family is in any concrete realization is not and cannot be deduced from the *de facto* situation in which the family finds itself, or from the relevant statistics, or from the consent of the majority, but only from the *truth*, that is, from *God's design* for the family. Without *this* reference — God's design — every ethical judgment becomes, in reality, impossible.

Having clarified in which sense, then, one can and must speak of the *truth* about the family, — truth in the sense of God's design for the family — we must ask ourselves what *path* we must take in order to discover this truth of the family's identity. In the light of the Apostolic Exhortation *Familiaris Consortio* and of the catechesis of John Paul II at his Wednesday audiences over the past five years, it seems to me that we can point out the path to take: namely, the experience — the "essentially human experience" — which man, illuminated by Revelation, has of his own self, and — reciprocally — the light of Christ insofar as it reveals to man, in an internal way, this "essentially human experience" which man has of his own self.

I must pause here for a moment in order to explain this very important point. When I speak of the "essentially human experience," I mean that knowledge which man has of his *own self,* a knowledge which allows man to know his *human* identity, his truth as a *human* person, — in other words what it is, *in truth,* to be a human person.

It is obvious that this definition of the "essentially human experience" presupposes an affirmation which we cannot take time to demonstrate exhaustively here and now: that is, the very *capacity* of man to reach, by means of his own knowledge, a *truth* about himself, a truth which is not subject to the changes of history, a truth which is not relative to any culture and which is always and everywhere valid. To demonstrate this capacity of man to know the truth about himself, it is sufficient for our purpose here and now to think just a little about what happens inside each one of us when we live "an *ethical* experience", that is, the experience of an "unconditional ought-to-be," an experience of that which is an *absolute imperative* upon one as a human person. Each one of us, in that moment of "an ethical experience," sees what is good and what is evil *in relation to his or her being a human person.* How could such a *clear vision* of good and evil be possible if we do not know what *man* is? As Plato put it:

> Could we know what is the art of *improving* man himself if we did not know *who we are?* . . . If we know *ourselves,* at least there is a possibility that we will know the care we must take of ourselves. Otherwise we will *never* know that.[2]

The "essentially *human* experience", then, is a necessary foundation for "an *ethical* experience". This "essentially human experience", however, is not *enough* in order to know the design of *God* for the family, and to know that design in its *entirety* — and therefore to know the true *identity* of the family. This experience must be illuminated by the *light of Christ*. We must therefore ask ourselves, first of all, what *is* this illumination which Christ alone casts on our "essentially human experience", and secondly, *why* is such an illumination *necessary*?

First: What is this illumination of Christ on the "essentially human experience"? Pascal it was who wrote that "Man infinitely exceeds man". This means that man in himself is a mystery so great and profound that man — his own self — is the *only* created reality which he himself cannot understand entirely. This greatness and this profoundity of the mystery-which-is-man consists in the fact that the human person feels himself as *aimed* in the direction of an end, a goal, a destiny which *infinitely exceeds his powers:* "Man infinitely exceeds man" — precisely! For the goal towards which inherently he is aimed, the destiny for which he is made, is *communion with God* which is reached in the *vision of God*. This orientation, inherent to man, is part of his very make-up, moulds him, so to speak, and penetrates every dimension of his person. Man is an enigma to himself — the light of Christ solves this enigma. Christ fully reveals man to man, in that Christ shows him the fundamental *meaning* of his existence. This is precisely the illumination which Christ alone casts on the "essentially human experience": the revelation to man of what man, from the depths of his being, *waits for* and *cries out for:* total *communion* with the *Father.*

Second: Why is this illumination of Christ *necessary*? It is *necessary* because — as the faith teaches us — man was created *in Christ* and, consequently, Christ Himself *is* the *truth about man.* As one Italian theologian wrote, "the freely chosen design of God — what we call the mystery — is the humanity *of* God and our humanity *in* God: Jesus Christ and the Church, — together with the universe *in* Christ, and *for* the Church and *with* the Church. *This* is the design decided upon by God, in its unity and essence . . . Outside this one unitive and original design there is only "non-being", "the abstract."[3] To try to capture the truth about man without giving full weight to this "one unitive and original design" centered in Christ and the Church is to produce a merely theoretical ("abstract") concept of man as, in reality, he has *never existed* (a non-being").

In the believer there is, therefore, a kind of circulation, a constant going back and forth, between the "essentially human experience" and the light of Christ: *in* the light of Christ, man understands his own self more and more profoundly, and, reciprocally, the most profound consciousness of his own self, reached only in this light of Christ, allows him to receive the light of Christ more and more deeply into himself.

Having stated therefore in which sense we are speaking about the identity or truth of the family — namely, *God's* design for it — and which path brings us to the uncovering of that identity or truth — namely, the path of the "essentially human experience" of our own selves, an experience which needs the light of Christ — we are now able actually to uncover this identity of the family. It is obvious that we set out from the pre-suppositions: 1) that only marriage containing the elements of *unity* and *indissolubility* can form the basis of the family; and 2) that the *family* community is an expansion of the *husband-wife* community. In fact, we can uncover the identity of the family by beginning precisely with the following question: In what does this very expansion of the *husband-wife* community into a *family* community consist? What does this expansion consist of in its *specific* identity and nature? How, precisely, does the husband-wife community get *transformed* into a family community?

The answer is so obvious and simple that it might make us wonder if beginning with this question in order to uncover the identity of the family is perhaps *too* simple to put us on the right track: for the answer is the *child*. It is the *child* who transforms the husband-wife community into a family community, and it is therefore the act of *procreation* which expands the husband-wife community so that it becomes a family community.

We must go to the very depths of the arrival of this new existence, this new event, this new *human person* who brings about the transformation of the husband-wife community. We must go to

6

this new event as the event which indeed founds the family-community. Just as the husband-wife community's origin lies always in a meeting between the enterprise of God and the marriage consent of man and woman — a meeting between God and the couple to be married — so also in the family community, its origin lies again in a meeting between God and the married couple, — between the divine act of *creation* and the human act of *procreation*.

A) *The divine act of creation.* At the origin of the first instant of existence of every single human person there is present always a *creative act of God.* This is a truth of faith taught by the Church. But even our reasoning powers can comprehend this statement. Because the human spirit constitutes him or her as a unique and irreplaceable subject — a thinking and acting individual — the human person cannot himself be the fruit simply of some inevitable necessity or chance. The human person cannot be the result merely of the impersonal, mechanical working of purely material natural laws. When in the universe a *human being* appears, *someone* appears (and not simply *something*), — someone essentially different from and superior to the infra-personal world. Someone appears who is destined for immediate and direct communion with God. This cannot happen without God's *knowing* it and *wishing* it. God knows this person *into* existence: He wills this person *into* existence. In other words, He *creates* him.

Not only this, but, as we have said already, this new person is created in view of *Christ*, for the sake of *Christ,* by reason of *Christ*: in order to become a son or daughter in the *only-begotten* Son of the Father by participating in that divine life which, by nature, is proper, among all human beings, only to Jesus.

B) *The human act of procreation.* In the light of what we have just said, we can comprehend, then, the innermost nature of the *conjugal act of procreation.* This conjugal act is the *place where* God's divine act of *creating* takes place. The conjugal act, then, is human cooperation in a most profound divine activity.

The procreative capacity inscribed in human sexuality is ordered intrinsically to be a capacity to *work with God as Creator.* This is the reason why this act *is* — as it *must* be — inseparably connected with the *unitive* capacity of this same human sexuality:

only an act of authentic human *love* is worthy of cooperating with God's creative activity. The husband-wife community becomes the family community when this meeting takes place between creative divine love and procreative human love. It is precisely this *meeting* that determines the *truth,* the *identity* of the family. We must now turn to showing this.

The fact is that the human person owes his existence to the creative act of God, and that the married couple can only posit the *conditions* in order for this act of God to take place. (*Generatio* — said the ancients — *est opus naturae non personae:* Begetting a child is a working of nature, not of human effort.) This means that, always, the child is a *pure gift* given to the married couple by God Himself. God entrusts to them what is the most precious gift in all the universe: a human person. What, then, should be the couple's attitude, — an attitude adequate to this pure gift, the child?

St. Augustine wrote: *"Secretum Dei intentos debet facere, non adversos"*.[4] The mystery (the *secretum*), the gift hidden in God's mind for man should make us *"intentos",* that is, alert for that gift, — conscious, receptive, and active in receiving that gift — and not *"adversos",* that is, oblivious, distrustful, resentful of the gift. The married couple are involved with a *"secretum Dei"* — the gift hidden in the mind of God — because they are involved in an act which is *creative* and therefore *His* act. The right and adequate attitude, then, is one of receiving this gift according to God's intention. We have uncovered, then, the first and most fundamental dimension of the identity of the family, its deepest truth. For the family is the place, the holy temple, in which God completes His greatest act *ad extra,* the creative act. Even more precisely: the family, as such, constitutes itself this sacred place, the space for God's creation, a new human person. Moreover, this economy or divine arrangement, for creating new human persons is carried through even in the economy, that is, the divine plan, of redemption: for even the Eternal Word was made flesh inside a human family.

But, now, we must understand even *more* profoundly what this acceptance of the child as a gift made by God the Creator means. For whenever this gift is given it is not a *thing* being given, but a *person*. From this very simple observation derive some very important consequences.

The first and most immediate consequence is that the gift does not bring into existence a piece of "property", but only a "trust". (Obviously, I do not use these terms in their strict financial or juridical meaning). In other words, the new human person is given to the parents for the sole purpose of being guided to the fullness of his/her personal being, — to bring to realization, through personal acceptance, the plan which God has for every person who comes into existence.

In this way, the human person is begotten, not simply in one instant, but *continuously* and *progressively* in cooperation with the creative God of love. This continuous and progressive begetting is the *education,* the *upbringing* of the child. God Himself precisely as *Creator, preserves* in existence the person whom He has created (*conservatio est continua creatio* — for God to preserve His creatures is simply for Him to *continue* the act of creation). In the same way, therefore, a married couple also *beget continuously* the new person whom they once *pro*created (*educatio est continua procreatio*). There remains constantly, then, a profound, intimate rapport and resonance between the activity by which the Lord *continues* to create, and the couple *continue* to procreate, the new human being. The Lord in His activity of continuous creating (that is, preservation) is leading the new human person to that creature's destiny, to the purpose for which He has created the new person; and the couple in their activity of human upbringing are also leading the new creature to make God's plan his or her own — to consent more and more faithfully to what God has provided.

As I have said earlier, God's Providence establishes a purpose — indeed the *only ultimate* purpose — and He has revealed it to us: to have every person participate, that is, live in the divine sonship of *Jesus,* the Word Incarnate, the Son Who *alone* is the eternally *begotten* Son of the Father. In Jesus Christ alone our authentic communion with God, and our authentic communion with other human beings, is re-established, and re-established precisely in the *Church.*

Every human person is created in light of *this* purpose designated by God, and for *no other* purpose. Every human person is given to parents precisely so that, through the parents, the new human person can be led to this achievement of the person's *destiny,* — to the full realization of the person's very self. Obviously, only baptized parents can be conscious of this reason for God's having given them this child. But God's reason is there, whether the parents are conscious of it or not.

The first consequence, then, of God's plan in giving a child to the parents is that the child is not a piece of property, not something owned. The child is a *trust,* that is, a person *entrusted* for a particular reason, — *God's* reason.

The second consequence is simply that the parents must lead the new human person into the *family* of the sons and daughters of God, that is, the *Church.* They must lead the child into this family through Baptism and, then, through bringing the child up in the faith and Christian life of the Church. To this second essential dimension of the identity, the truth, about the Christian family, we now turn our attention.

As a result of that primeval event which we call Original Sin, human persons are born as "children of wrath", and need to be saved, to be begotten *again,* to be conceived *again,* — to be "born *again*". The life-story of any human person works itself out, then, along the lines of his being begotten into life in a two-fold way: first, by being conceived as a "living soul", as are all human beings, through the *human* begetting which is the well-spring of the human family (though "falling short of the glory of God", as this family does because it is under sin); and, second, by being conceived as a "living soul" through the *divine* begetting which is the well-spring of the *new* human family which is re-created in the glory of God, the new human family which constitutes the Body of Christ, and is the Church. Where the two kinds of giving life — human begetting and divine begetting — meet and intersect, the worldwide human family enters into the Church and the Church enters into the worldwide human family, generation by generation. The Christian family asks the Church for Baptism for its child. Precisely by asking for this Baptism, the Christian family itself brings about this joining and intersecting of the human and the divine, —

10

of the human begetting and the divine begetting of human persons. In this way, the family becomes the *place* in which God completes His redemptive work: God not only creates the human person, but He creates him or her *again* in the spiritual begetting. St. Thomas, precisely in the context of baptism, speaks of *parental care,* even *prior* to Baptism, as a *"quodam spirituali utero"*⁵ — the loving care of parents is a kind of spiritual womb, — the place where life comes to be. Christian parents beget the new person into the spiritual life in this spiritual womb of their *parental care,* that is, in the spiritual, Christian *upbringing* they give.

If, then, we at this point wish to express in a short synthesis the identity of the Christian family, we can say: the family is the place in which God has the new human person become a holy temple in which that new human person celebrates God's act of creating and redeeming him or her.

Before finishing this first part of my reflection, I should like now to say something about what *destroys* the family identity just described. For there are actions which by their very nature are an attempt to kill the truth about the family.

As we have seen, the "beginning", the founding-event, of the family-community is the wondrous and mysterious meeting and merging of the *creative* power of God and procreative capacity of the married couple. What on man's side destroys this meeting and merging of the human and divine? In what way can a man and a woman be *opposed* to this founding-event, this meeting between God's creative power and their procreative capacity? It is obviously *contraception.* Contraception breaks this merging of God's power and the couple's capacity. Precisely in *contraception* the man and the woman do their utmost to *prevent* God from being *Creator.* Precisely in this lies the grave intrinsic malice of the contraceptive act, and precisely for this reason, above all others, contraception destroys the identity of the family, its deepest truth.

But note well! This indictment of contraception must *not* be understood only in its obvious, immediate meaning. For the obvious, immediate meaning is that contraception prevents *procreation* and, therefore, the bringing forth of a *family*. It is a rejection of a capacity God has *created* in man — the capacity of procreation. It is also the rejection of another *created* being — the child.

11

This rejection of certain *created* beings is the obvious and immediate meaning of what we have just said about contraception. But the matter is much deeper than simply the rejection of two *created* entities. For what is really and more fundamentally at issue, in the final analysis, is that a man and a woman, in the contraceptive act, *arrogate* to themselves power which belongs only to *God the Creator:* power over the *appearance of new life.* Contraception thus makes them competitors with God for His rightful freedom to call forth a new human being. It is a way of saying that God should not be God.

This is the way in which a man and woman break the rapport and resonance between the creative love of God and family-community: they reduce this family-community simply to a reality created by man. As you can see, contraception changes completely the very definition of the family. For the family, by definition, it is true, is the work of human beings, but only in collaboration with the creative act of God and under His sovereign authority.

But as far as destroying the identity of the family is concerned, there is an act morally more serious than contraception itself. For God completes His artistry of creating the new human person by entrusting this new being to an openness and acceptance on the part of the couple, and primarily of the woman who conceived it.

God says to each of us: "It is good that you should be!" And each one of us comes into existence at the very moment God pronounces these words, this welcome.

But for the total completion of God's creative act, someone else too has to say: "It is good that you should be!" That must be the exclamation also of the man who begets the child, but especially of the *woman* from the very instant she realizes that she has conceived. And so in this human welcoming the new human person becomes one among us. And what prevents this from happening? We all know: *abortion.* Abortion is the one act which, more than any other act, destroys the truth of the family — totally! A human being is rejected precisely in the very moment in which he/she should find an unconditional welcome — forever! A woman withholds acceptance from another human being in his or her very moment of *origin*! I believe there *is not* and *cannot be* any other act more destructive of the identity of the family. When a human being is no longer safe even in the womb of the woman who conceived him or her, then the human being is no longer safe *anywhere*: the very well-spring of creation is polluted. Only Satan could devise an act so profoundly hostile to the whole of creation. Contraception, then, and even more so abortion are two acts which attempt to kill the deepest truth of the family.

Last but not least, the identity of the family is destroyed when the family refuses to be that *"uterus spiritualis"* — that spiritual womb of which St. Thomas spoke: in other words, when the family declines its human and Christian parental care.

I am going to close now by saying something which, strictly speaking, is outside any charism of authority I may have as a priest. For I am going to attempt a word of edification — of building up — for our bishops, our fathers-in-Christ who, more than any others, are the builders of us all, of the temples which form themselves into the great temple of God, His Church. Our readers will, I am sure, forgive my daring. And so, I say it. It is a serious duty of the bishops as pastors — more than it is anyone else's duty — to uphold God's right, God's sanctity and God's glory, when, above all, He creates a human being. The family, therefore, is the first temple in which God sanctifies His Name and reveals His Glory. It is one of the gravest duties of all pastors, but especially of our bishops, to uphold the sanctity of that temple, to prevent its profanation: to do whatever they possibly can so that God may glorify Himself in that temple, the family. When, then, Bishops above all, as the pastors of the Church, are not clear in their teaching on contraception, or on abortion, or on the right of the family to bring their children up and educate them, they become accomplices in the profanation of God's first temple.

2. MISSION OF THE FAMILY.

In the light of all that I have said in the first part of this chapter about the true identity of the family, I would like now, in this second part, to reflect on the mission of the family. The concept of mission is closely connected with the concept of identity. Moreover, one of the most important characteristics of all the great figures in the plan of salvation designed by God is that these great figures (such as Jeremiah and Paul) identified *themselves* with their mission. The mission of the family, then, can only be understood in the light of its identity.

In short, we can say that the mission of the family essentially consists in serving life in its beginning and in its growth. With such a formulation we insist above all then on the "object" of such mission — what the mission deals with. The object of this mission is *the life of the person,* both in the moment in which that life first takes shape and in the expanse of time during which it continues to take shape. The "object" of the family's mission, then, is the *human person* in his or her origins and as he or she thereafter comes to be. We must now penetrate into this "object" in order to grasp its essential dimensions.

We can start off with a question; In what does the birth of a human person consist, from the beginning up to its full growth? It is obvious that we do not ask such questions from a biological, or physiological, or sociological or any other such merely empirical point of view, but from the point of view of a philosophical and theological *anthropology,* that is, a coherently systematic understanding of what, ultimately, it means *to be human.*

A) Let us start from the point of view of *philosophical* anthropology. Plato's famous — and difficult — passage in *The Republic* is well-known. This, one of the greatest of all philosophers, says that there is a perfect parallel between, on the one hand, the way in which *the sun in the sky* enables the human *eye* to *see* and, on the other hand, the way the *"idea of good"* enables the human *spirit* to *understand.* As the sun's light makes things visible to the eye and thus allows the eye to see, in the same way "the idea of good" makes things intelligible to the intellect, and thus allows the intellect to understand. I have reflected at length on this passage, and it guided me to the answer to our question: What does being born consist of for a human person, from the very beginning right up to full growth?

The human person, as a created person, is somehow criss-crossed with two interior and highly active forces, forces very much in contrast to each other. On the one hand, the human person is a "subject", that is, the person exists "in his or her own right", "in himself or herself" (*sui iuris,* the Roman jurists used to say). The human person is an *"unum"*, an individual who cannot

14

be communicated to another being in the sense that he or she cannot become part of another being or be merged into another being, so as to disappear into the identity of another being. This ontological make-up of the person-as-such is made clear by the fact that the person is "spirit", and the "spirit" can exist *only* in this way: in *itself*. The person can never become a secondary reality of some other being, — can never become what the Scholastics would call an *"accidens."* The first interior force we observe in ourselves, then, is a force which drives us to affirm and maintain this uniqueness and distinctness of ours — our individuality.

Nevertheless, on the other hand, if we further attentively observe our internal spiritual forces and energies and dynamisms, we see that they are always attracted also toward an *"object",* toward things or persons *distinct* from our uniquely subjective, individual selves.

Our thinking is always a thinking of something; our will is always a will about something: by thinking and willing, the individual as "subject" moves to some entity outside himself or herself. In the "subject" a *centripetal* pull — a pull always to return to one's self, to what one is — criss-crosses with a *centrifugal* pull — a pull to move out from one's self to another, to what one is not. In the balancing out of these two forces, the outcome of every human person's existence is determined. To be with oneself without closing in on one's self in an empty individualism, and, at the same time, to be with the other without losing one's self: this is the constant human challenge.

Now, in light of these two contrasting human dynamics — the centripetal and the centrifugal — let us analyze one of the deepest human experiences: love: In what precisely does love consist? When can we truly say we love another human person? First of all, when we want the good of that other person, not because it is *our* good, but because it is *his* or *her* good, and, mostly, the good which is his or her own *deepest* good and the *origin* of all other goods: that person's very being and existence. Love means we want the other person to *exist* and to *be* what he or she *should* be. In wanting this, we are lifted out of ourselves by the ontological goodness of the being and existence of the other person.

Does such ecstasy, — such "standing back from one's self" — entail the *loss* of one's own self? Or, to the contrary, does it more deeply allow one to *find* one's own self? By willing another being and the good of that other being and, most fundamentally, the very existence of the other being, one who loves understands 1) that this decision to love is the only response adequate to the value of the person loved; and 2) that only in this way — by loving — is one immersed also in the deepest truth of one's *own* self. "In the sincere gift of self man finds himself", teaches *Gaudium et Spes*. The solution to the challenge we mentioned earlier — to achieve the proper balance of our own internal centripetal and centrifugal forces — lies in the truth of love: in willing the good of each being in existence in a way adequate to the value of that being (the *"ordo bonorum"* of St. Augustine), a human being goes out of himself without losing himself.

In the final analysis, what makes possible such a venture, such an "exodus" from the self, which brings us into the promised land of one's own identity as a self, — the promised land of one's own truth? What makes possible the beginning of such journey? What gives birth to such a vision of things? What enables us to see each being, each reality, as a gift with a dignity of its own? The eye begins to see only when light appears; man begins to understand himself and any other entity only when he "sees" that everything is *good*. The *light* of the *good* allows him to see this.

Let us go back, then, to the question from which we started: In what does the birth of the human person consist? Perhaps we have found the answer. The human person is "born" in the *truest* meaning of the word when the person sees that everything is *good:* then and only then is the person able to love.

But how is this vision of the goodness of all reality made possible? The first "other" person whom a new human person knows, the first person different from one's own self, the first distinctly "other" person with whom the new person enters into relationship, is the woman who conceives him or her. If this "other" welcomes him or her and says "How good it is that you are!", then the new human person enters the world of being as one who is waited for, wanted, that is, loved!

From such an experience, the new human being's own personal self emerges; he becomes himself in the embrace of a mother, an embrace which expresses to him, in a human way, God's creative act. And such an experience extends then to other persons. We now understand, perhaps, the depth of the service of the family to the life of the human person.

I cannot attempt in a short synthesis to express this depth of service which the family offers in this way. The first and fundamental mission of the family is that of *originating* the human person, — of *begetting* him or her. This begetting consists of leading the human person into the order of being, of existing realities, — into that universe of values in which the new person will be able to fully be himself, — able to be in the truth of love. In sum: to beget the human person is to lead him or her into the truth of being, into what it means to exist, into what a *wonderful thing* it is to exist. This is what sound *philosophical* anthropology can offer in answer to our question: In what does the *human birth* of a person consist from the beginning up to his or her full growth?

B) Now we will try to answer the same question from the point of view of *theological* anthropology, the anthropology contained in the truths of faith. From this point of view, the human person is born — in the deepest sense of the word — when he or she attains to that complete actualization of the self planned by God in Christ. In a word: to be "in the form of Christ".

As I have already said, the human person's new birth in Christ consists of Baptism, which is the originating configuration to Christ. From this aspect of Christian faith, the task or mission of the family consists in seeking Baptism from the Church, so that the new human person can begin to be in Christ. But the new birth in Christ gives only an *embryonic* life in Christ which must then be *developed*. The mission of the family is to lead the new human person through to the *fullness* of maturity in the Christian life.

On the one hand, parents are primarily responsible for this maturity; and this responsibility of parents has to be recognized by the Church. On the other hand, maturity of life in Christ will be proportionate to the child's involvement in the Church, for which the ordained pastors are primarily responsible. The new human person becomes entirely himself or herself in Christ thanks to the *harmony* of these two ministries — "parents" and "pastors".

17

CONCLUSION

Our meditation on the identity and the mission of the family shows us the exact "place" that this family-community has in the economy of creation and Redemption. We could say that the family is the place of origin, — the origin of man in all the truth of himself as a personal being called to live in Christ.

From this derives a consequence of great importance: the Church and in particular the pastors of the Church must have a particular regard for the family. Why? Because, in the family and from the family, the human being is born, and in a certain sense the Church itself is born. The family, this cradle of the human person, requires, then, an absolute respect and veneration. For man is the most precious creature in the world: for his sake all the visible universe was created; and, above all, man is important because it is God Himself who both creates and saves every human person. Concern for the family, then, is the first and most important expression of the Church's concern for man.

But what does it mean for the Church to care for the family? It means to *defend* it and to *promote* it: to defend it in its *identity,* in its human and Christian *truth;* to promote it in its *mission of service* to the life of the human person. The destiny of humankind will depend in great part on the care the Church takes of the family during the upcoming years.

Notes

1. *Quaestiones Disputatae de Veritate,* 1, 2 c in fine.
2. Plato, *Alcibiades,* I, 129a.
3. I. Biffi, *Theology and a Theologian, St. Thomas Aquinas,* ed. Piemme, 1984, p. 16, emphasis added.
4. *Tract. in Jo.* 27,2: CCL36,270.
5. *S.Th.* 2, 2, q.10, a.12, Resp. C.

PART I:
THE FAMILY TODAY

OVERVIEW
OF PART I

The first four chapters of this Part I offer a rich and well-documented analysis of the family today. The fifth chapter contains the dialogue between the Bishops who attended the Workshop and several of the authors. Dr. McCready did not participate in the dialogue because he had given his presentation at the opening of the Workshop and was unable to stay for the dialogue.

In his chapter, however, Dr. McCready set the state for discussing the family today by outlining "Three Ages" of the family. We in the U.S. and Canada experience the third age, the post-industrial period, which was preceded by the agricultural and the industrial age. Dr. McCready characterizes the present age as one of pluralism and speculates on the Church's response to this.

Dr. Glick, on the other hand, concentrates exclusively in Chapter 2 on statistical information about family life in the U.S. His synthesis of the wealth of available data reflects his 30 years of work with the U.S. Bureau of the Census. This chapter offers an expert and current overview of marriage and divorce patterns, family living arrangements, and family economics.

In Chapter 3, Dr. Beth Soldo focuses on the often unnoticed impact of increasing longevity on the family. She uses the concept of family life-cycle in discussing the three, four, and even five living generations of the family. She conveys substantial optimism about family loyalty by citing the fact that over 90% of all disabled elderly in the community rely in whole or in part on family members for chronic caregiving, although the family is neither compelled or compensated for this task.

Father Steven Priester trains his attention, in Chapter 4, on the systems approach to the family as an alternative to the extreme individualism of American society. He calls for Church leaders to adopt this approach in a conscious way by family impact studies in reviewing Church activities and policies.

In Chapter 5 the dialogue on pastoral concerns for the family pursues specific questions in greater depth. Concern for aging family members emerges as a major issue.

Chapter 1

The Three Ages
of the Family

William C. McCready, Ph.D

INTRODUCTION

The three ages of family that we will be referring to during this discussion concern the stages that the family has passed through during its development as the principle social unit with which societies are constructed. Typically these are described as the agricultural, industrial and post-industrial phases. However, for reasons soon to be explained, we will refer to the "age of community", the "age of institutions" and the "age of pluralism." While families in modern Western nations may already be in the pluralistic age, many in the Third World are in the communitarian age. These ages, unlike the phases of agriculture and industrialization, also lend themselves to a more synthetic analysis of the contemporary state of the family. In other words, contemporary families can be seen to have some of the qualities of those from the previous ages. The characteristics are not mutually exclusive.

What is the purpose of thinking of family in this way? Is it not sufficient to deal with the explicit needs of real families, especially given that these needs are very compelling in this day and age? What is the benefit to be gained from abstracting and describing and classifying families when in fact we want to help them grow and develop? We humans are natural model makers. We excel at finding adaptive solutions to the problems that surround us because we make plans and representations of the world around us. These plans and models are the tools of our trade, they are the ways we cope with the fact that we are neither the strongest, nor the swiftest nor the hardiest of breeds. Models and abstractions are the very essence of policy formulation. Having models for understanding the changes that surround us is essential for formulating effective policies to deal with those changes. One of the problems facing policy-makers is that they are living in the midst of the conditions for which they must create policies. Understanding the scope and impact of social changes is most necessary for the development of sound policy, be it religious or social. We hope to place the 'family' within the context of social change in such a way as to illuminate the religious issues facing families today. Within each of the three ages we will be discussing the topics of religion, social change and family structure and in the conclusion we will point toward some synthetic trends and estimate what the characteristics of the next age of the family might be.

THE FIRST AGE: THE AGE OF COMMUNITY

One of the earliest social changes to effect the family was the change from a nomadic hunting society to a more stable agricultural society. While hunting societies are communitarian in a sense, they are not communities that regenerate themselves in the way that farming communities do. In order to create an agricultural society, people must stay on the same land for many years. If they do move, it is a slower pace than nomadic peoples. Nomads tend to have their social structure built into their pattern of encampment while agricultural peoples tend to have their social structures embedded within their day to day ways of living — their culture.

The family was essentially an economic unit during this phase, since agriculture was a labor-demanding way of life. However, the tendency for humans to form permanent pairbonds was probably more the result of our sociobiological makeup than the economic conditions. Pairbonding was a generalized human phenomenon and not limited to stable agricultural societies. It stems from the extreme vulnerability of the human infant and the need for almost constant attention during the first months of life. It was most likely the economic nature of agriculture however that gave our pair-bonding the *form* that it did, the *primary group.* This is typically a pattern of one male and one female with several children, although different cultures have modified and elaborated upon this form.

The early division of labor between men and women was probably due to the biological differences in childrearing responsibilities, although a few cultures are exceptions to the rule in which women tend to raise the children and men tend to raise crops. Social scientists disagree as to the exact nature of this division. Some focus on the biology of procreation and others on the social status ascribed to work. It has been pointed out by many researchers that men tend to do that which is most valued in societies, but it is unclear as to whether men do it because it is valued, or it is valued because men do it.

Theology during this agrarian age of community reflects the gospel as seen through the eyes of the people living in this stable, cohesive social system. This is a time when religious communities can spring forth from a style of social organization which they themselves parallel. Shared authority in this environment is not very productive. Agricultural work required leadership to organize the heavy physical labor and male-oriented paternalistic style of leadership quite common. Even the religious communities of women adopted this type of organization as being the most efficient for the time. Faith was closely connected to personal experiences because the most meaningful aspect of one's life occurred in the close environment, the field, the home, the village — not in a See far away away nor in Rome nor even within the nearby abbey or parish house or convent. Those were the homes of the 'religious managers' of the day and what went on there was not for vulgar eyes. Popular faith flourished in the daily lives of people because the gospel truths were apparent and relevant to their most important needs and issues — particularly the issue of what happened when we die, given the short life-span at that time.

Second, conditions in the age of community were such that seldom did men and women have any time at all together after their last child had left the home, simply because one of them would be dead. There were so many conceptions, because in a time of high infant mortality it was the only way for the race to survive, that inevitably one partner would expire before the last child was independent. In such a content, and in a time when life was vulnerable to all manner of disease, the issue of what came after life here on earth was paramount in the culture which made it a fertile ground for faith.

Social changes during this time are not perceived from inside the community, they come from the exterior and force their way in. Some communities could adapt to new ways and others could not and this generally determined which survived and which did not. Adaption became part of man's cultural survival kit and was to surface again and again as an important aspect of man's future.

Familial relationships during this time were ascribed rather than achieved. The conditions of one's birth had a great deal to do with the conditions one found oneself in at the end of life. Hard work was necessary as a way of life, but did not necessarily bring much in the way of rewards. Adult relationships were much less common than we are accustomed to today due mainly to the short life-span. The fact that most people worked near where they lived made the socialization of the young a very different matter than we see now. It was more automatic and less arranged. Children saw before them what was happening in the adult world and joined it much sooner. In many ways, during this time, there was not the state we think of as childhood at all. Children were little adults and were not protected as innocent nor were they particularly beloved or treasured. If they survived until they were old enough to be useful, they were treated as full adults — if not, well that was the way of things.

One of the facts we should remember about this age is that we have little data about it and therefore we have to be careful about being too analytical. It was different and we have some notions about how it was different. It was probably not better, although its simplicity now can seem very attractive to those of us caught up in the seemingly overwhelming complexities of contemporary life.

THE SECOND AGE:
THE AGE OF THE INSTITUTION

Just as the discovery of agriculture and horticulture spawned the age of community, the discovery of corporate bureaucratic organization spawned the age of the institution. The technologies that were being invented required new ways of human organization because they needed to be built in parts by people with different specialties and talents. All these differences required a leader to get them organized and leadership became synonymous with authority within the bureaucratic structure. Military experiences were among the first examples which proved the value and efficiency of a hierarchical authority structure with higher levels controlling lower levels and a reverse system of accountability, lower to higher, being installed. Guilds and religious organizations followed suit and soon the paternal authority of the community, which had been based on the closeness of the workers and the leaders in a cohesive environment, began to be replaced by a bureaucratic leadership of the institution which separated leaders from followers by layers of delegation, responsibility, technology, and rules and regulations.

Those within the institution, the professional and the bureaucrats (which was not always a negative word), began to develop their prime affiliation to the institution and not to their community, and their authority became generated by their knowledge of the workings of the institutions rather than by their overall performance or their connectedness to the world outside the institution. In order to maintain succession and order and transitions from one leader to the next, life within the institution became rule-bound and very dependent upon propositional thinking rather than more imaginative and creative thinking.

27

Religion took on new forms and practices during this time as well, many of them linked to the changes in authority styles. Growth and expansion replaced reflection upon experiences as the prime activity of religious institutions became the watchword and the higher in the institution you were the better member you were thought to be. The ecclesiology was one of membership and belonging to the Church at this time. Propositional forms of religion, dependent upon the rules, was the preferred form because it so easily demonstrated the power and intensity of one's faith. The better you followed the rules the better your faith — it made it very easy to know where you stood at all times!

Society during this age was perceived as orderly and controlled and technology was around to solve any problems. Planning became a profession and was thought to be both necessary and infallible when it came to preparing for the future. (Note that during the age of community, people focused on their death as the future, while now during the age of institutions people prepare to go on forever, provided they plan for it well enough.) Social changes of considerable magnitude can be easily missed in this environment because we become locked into our past plans and analyses and cannot take in new information. Changes such as the persistence of communitarian ways of organizing; new forms of religious identity; new family structures — all can come as surprises in this age because we lull ourselves into thinking that we are in control and that we know what is going to happen. We also lull ourselves into thinking that technology and planning are our friends, only to have them run amok and fail us at the last moment. (In the case of our nuclear weaponry they may even be the proximate cause of our last moment.) Perhaps most damaging is the perception that the important social changes are the ones that effect the institution. We begin to see institutional changes as being identical to social changes and they are not. They can be the same but they need not be.

For example, right now the institution of the Church in this country is changing in that people are no longer as close to it nor do they listen to it as they once did nor do they participate in its life as they once did — however, other evidence, such as that from the CARA Values study, indicates that people's values are as religious as ever, they just don't perceive their society as being that religious. It is as though we were saying to ourselves that everybody we knew was religious, but everybody we don't know probably isn't. Yet if everybody in the sample says that, where are all the people who are not supposed to be so relegous?

The family can frequently find itself in conflict with institutions in this environment. The institutions are large and more dominant and can easily tend to their own needs rather than to those of families. Institutions are economically more important and families tend to see themselves as living in the shadow of many institutions, including the Church, without being able to exert an influence on them unless families enter coalitions and engage in confrontational activities which they tend to be disinclined to do. Institutions tend to see families as part of themselves, so we often hear language describing families as part of the Church. This reinforces the propositional imagery so beloved by institutions and communicates the families' membership status very clearly. Yet, few families would view themselves as part of the Church in the same way that their Church views them as part of herself.

Take for example the many 'programs' that have emanated from the institution over the past few years concerning the family and family ministry and the role of the family in the Church — most of them have placed greater burdens of activity on the family with very little help from the institution. Families are being asked to do more with less and less help. As the professional cadre within the institution, priest and sisters and brothers primarily, declines over the next 15 years, this situation will get much worse. (Projections are that we may have less than 25,000 priests in the country by the year 2000.) The Church has placed some of its hope for getting through this scenario on lay ministers, although it is not clear what that means. To many it seems as though it means lay people taking on quasi-clerical roles, and it is unlikely that that will be a long-term phenomenon. Perhaps the most perplexing change to hit during the age of institutions has been the realization that the age of community did not exactly fade away, but instead has exploded into many diverse communities which are the base for the third age of the family — the age of pluralism.

29

THE THIRD AGE: THE AGE OF PLURALISM

The North American experiment, which is still very experimental, has given rise to a new kind of pluralism which combines social pluralism with democratic forms of self-government based on popular choice. Pluralism simply refers to the fact that people from many diverse backgrounds and heritages and life-styles live in proximity to one another and deal with one another while respecting and tolerating their differences. In such a social environment, rules become less important than identity — propositions lose their organizing power and imagination and myth and story gain strength. People begin to deal with each other on the basis of sharing themselves and their backgrounds and their conditions, rather than on the basis of institutional memberships and what rules they abide by and who their leaders are.

One of the factors that has brought about this new age is the facility with which information and perceptions can be exchanged. The immediacy of the other's story is a new force in our history of social organization. Diversity is increased when we experience so much of it and pluralism of ideas is expanded when we can exchange them so freely. The immediacy of experiences, both our own and others, is raw material for our reflection mechanism. We want to understand experiences and their meanings. We want to understand others. We turn to our institutions for assistance in this, and if the institution is still one that is propositionally based, the answer is likely to be that we ought not be experiencing whatever it is that is before us. Yet we know our own experiences, and increasingly begin to respect them as well as the experiences of others as legitimate bases for reflection and for moral and philosophical judgements. In this environment it is very difficult to persuade people of the credibility of moral absolutes. The arguments that have always gone on behind the closed study doors are now out in the public domain where educated people can see and consider their merits and flaws. We can never go back to the previous age. Once the window has been opened, the fresh air will remain in the room even if the window is closed again.

Religion and faith still exist in the age of pluralism, what has changed is the way in which the institutions and their people are related. It does not seem useful, to me, to make the pluralism of ideas the enemy. Rather, like the ages that have gone before, this one places new demands upon us and faces us with new challenges. Absolutes and rules and propositions are not the appropriate languages for the day. The questions need to be rephrased in terms of examining the connections between people's experiences and their faith traditions. People now are learning from both, not just from one. Experience has been legitimated because it is such an inextricable part of identity, of who we are. This is in part the legacy from the age of community. People have learned that what they know from their experiences in community, especially the community of the family, is important and valid and needs to be reckoned with by them and by their institutions.

People have also accepted the new ecclesiology which challenges them to be the Church, not just to belong to the Church. However, in the age of pluralism when people consider themselves as being the Church they run into an institution that in many ways still tells them that they are only members in a club and that the important thing is how you behave according to the club rules. The disjunction between the two, between the challenge to be and the injunction to belong, is rapidly becoming painfully clear to all too many Catholics. One of the most critical aspects of life in this new age is the transmission of the religious tradition from this generation to the next and then to the next. This may well be the greatest challenge facing us as people today. Socialization is something that still happens within the family, but institutions, such as schools and churches, are also important. A failure to socialize the next generations will mean a very different life for the institution.

Families in pluralistic societies have taken on many new challenges. More adults in families are working than ever before which means that there is less time for voluntary activity. Divorce and remarriage are increasingly common and, while they do not appear to be threatening the existence of the family, they do appear to be instrumental in the changing popular definition of what is a family and what is its appropriate role in the institution of society. Families are still essentially religious if we examine data from such studies as the NORC General Social Survey, the Survey of Young Catholics and the CARA Values Study, but they are being burdened with more and more responsibilities in a complex society. Much of the family ministry programing which has been produced recently does not seem to understand this. Instead of producing new insights of the way in which the tradition speaks to contemporary experiences, we have been asking families to volunteer for activities for which they have not time. Under the name of family ministry we have all too often increased their burden rather than lightened it. One result is that we tend to deal only with those families who have extra time and who tend to agree with the institution's perspective on the various issues of the day. Families are too often considered to be the consumers of these programs and are seldom consulted in their design. The credibility of the Church to speak regarding matters of familial importance, such as sexuality, intimacy and the meaning of our life together, has been dealt a very damaging blow by the ways in which institutional positions have been announced, promulgated and enforced. The message keeps coming through loud and clear that this is a propositional matter and that the experiences of families and of women and men in intimacy are not legitimate sources for religious reflection. Nothing continues to be more damaging for our collective future than this. Nothing jeopardizes the future generations of Catholics in this society more than this.

CONCLUSION: WHAT WILL THE NEXT AGE BE?

We have tried to place the family in the social context of the changing ages from community to institutions to pluralism. These parallel the development of agriculture, industrialization and the post-industrialization technologies, but they focus more clearly on the social nature of those developments. Rather than considering these "ages" to be discrete and dialectically related to each other we have treated them synthetically, searching for those characteristics which each one leaves to the next. Each age builds on the one before and the most recent one, pluralism, contains many of the elements of the previous ones. The family exists within this context and understanding the context is required in order to understand the family. Whatever the next age is, it too will be a synthesis of its predecessors. As far as the family and religion is concerned, the future will depend upon how well the identities and imaginations and experiences of the past and present are passed along to the children. This discussion has presented some of the issues related to that process. It is a process going on all the time, inexorably. The task for organized religion is to understand the process and to bring the tradition to bear on the experiences of the people and vice-versa. Trying to change or direct the process is futile, only the people and the spirit can do that.

The task of those who mind the institution is to be *aware* of the changing context and to respect it for what it is; an important voice in the human story. That is the "Christ-life" being lived by people who are taking seriously the challenge to *be* the Church. No longer mere members of club — they now struggle to discover what *being Church* means in their lives. They need your prayers, your help, and your respect, much more than *your answers.*

Chapter 2

Social Change
And The Family

Paul C. Glick, Ph.D.

In writing on this subject in 1977, I made the observation that "Everyone is highly conscious of many aspects of change in family life, and yet the central core of family life continues very much the same as it has existed for many generations" (Glick, 1978). That statement is still true today. Most of the very substantial changes in American marriage and living arrangements of the past two decades had already occurred by 1977, but during the intervening eight years, most of the recent changes have continued to move in the same direction at a decelerated pace. And my guess is that those trends are more likely to go on at a slowing rate than to become very sharply reversed during the next decade.

This chapter will present recent information on modifications in family lifestyles in the United States since 1960 in the context of concurrent changes in a wide variety of social and economic variables. Attention will be focused on marital and fertility patterns, family living arrangements, participation in work and leisure-time activities, family economics, and dependency at the youngest and oldest ages. The concluding section will deal with some of the social implications of the recent changes as they appear to the author.

MARRIAGE AND DIVORCE PATTERNS

Declining marriage rates

Much of the attraction for early marriage and relatively large families, that had been so prevalent during the 1950s and into the 1960s, had greatly diminished by 1970. This development was not the consequence of any one or two simultaneous social changes but many of them, some of which tended to offset others. Among the most influential factors had been, and still are, the sharp increase in the educational level of young adults, especially women, and the closely associated rapid increase in the employment of women outside the home. Also, there were the expansion of the women's movement, the war in Vietnam, the increasing use of effective means of family limitation both before and after marriage, and more recently the problem of finding room in the labor market for the huge cohort of young adults who were born during the baby boom. Under these circumstances, young adults tended to replace the earlier high value on settled family relations with the pursuit of activities that would further the realization of their own potential for personal satisfaction.

In this setting the marriage rate took a downward turn, especially soon after 1970. Between 1970 and 1981 (the last year with detailed marriage statistics available) the first marriage rate, the remarriage rate after divorce, and the remarriage rate after widowhood — all three — declined by about one-fourth for both men and women. More specifically, the rate of first marriages per 1,000 never-married men went down from 72 to 54; the rate of remarriage per 1,000 divorced men went down from 205 to 151; and the rate of remarriage per 1,000 widowers went down from 41 to 31.

Corresponding decreases for women were from 83 to 65, from 133 to 66, and from 10 to 7 (U.S. National Center for Health Statistics, 1974a and 1984b). One of the reasons why the first marriage rates are consistently higher for women than for men is the fact that never-married women are more likely than never-married men to enter marriage with a person who had been previously married.

Changes in marriage and divorce during the 1970s caused the proportion of all marriages that were remarriages to increase from 24 percent in 1970 to 34 percent in 1981. Meantime, the proportion of all remarriages that followed divorce (rather than widowhood) rose from about 80 percent in 1970 to 90 percent in 1981.

During the rest of the 1980s, the population in the period of life when most first marriages occur will be diminishing, while the population in the period when most divorces occur will be approaching a peak. Therefore, the demographic basis has been established for a still further increase during the next several years in the proportion of all marriages that will be remarriages (Glick, 1984b).

As the first marriage rate has been falling, the proportion of young adults who were delaying marriage — or deciding never to marry — has been growing steadily. As a consequence, twice as large a proportion of women 20 to 24 years of age in 1984 as in 1960 had never been married — 57 percent versus 28 percent (U.S. Bureau of the Census, 1980 and 1984b). And among women who did marry, the median age at first marriage went up almost two years between 1970 and 1981 — from 20.6 years to 22.3 years (U.S. National Center for Health Statistics, 1974a and 1984b).

These findings seem likely to forebode an increase in the proportion of today's young adults who will never marry. Current statistics show that only four percent of the women in middle age (45 to 64 years old) had never married, but projections imply that three times that large a proportion (12 percent) of young adult women (25 to 29 years old) may never marry (Glick, 1984a). Perhaps there was more pressure on the older women to marry and more pressure on the younger women not to marry. If the projection turns out to show too few women leaving the state of singlehood, it will be because of a sharp reversal of the current downward trend in first marriage, a somewhat dubious prospect.

Rising divorce rates

Just how large the recent upturn in divorce has been depends on the method used to measure it. Most of the approaches yield increases that imply a doubling or tripling of divorce since 1960, or even since 1970. The divorce rate per 1,000 married women bounded upward from 9.2 in 1960 to 14.9 in 1970 and to 22.6 in 1981. Thus, the rate in 1981 was 1.5 times the rate in 1970 and 2.5 times the rate in 1960 (U.S. National Center for Health Statistics, 1974b and 1984a). According to Carlson (1979) and estimates by the present author, the divorce rate has risen in every age group during the last decade; but the proportion of all divorces that occurred among those 25 to 39 years of age increased substantially, while the proportion occurring at younger and older ages decreased. Ages 25 to 39 include the range in which most divorces occur, especially second divorces.

Since 1971, the median age at divorce, for all divorces combined, has varied between 32 and 33 years for men and between 30 and 31 for women. For divorces after first marriage, the median age at divorce is about three years younger than these overall figures, and the median age at second divorce is about three years older, according to unpublished Current Population Survey data for 1980. The same source shows that the median interval between first marriage and divorce is about seven years, but that the median interval between second marriage and redivorce is about five years.

While the divorce rate has been rising, the proportion of the adult population classified as currently divorced has gone up much more rapidly than the proportion classified as currently separated. Thus, the divorced population constituted only three percent of the total over 15 years of age in 1970 but seven percent in 1983, thereby having more than doubled in 13 years. During the same period, the separated population rose only from 1.8 percent of those 15 and over to 2.4 percent, or by only one-third (U.S. Bureau of the Census, 1975 and 1984b). Evidently more of the adults with disrupted marriages are now going through with divorce proceedings and are accordingly becoming eligible to remarry.

Adults who have *ever been divorced* are a far larger proportion of the total adult population than those currently divorced, because many have meantime remarried. Moreover, those who will *ever be divorced* are a still larger proportion. To illustrate: Recently published estimates indicate that about 22 percent of the ever-married persons 25 to 34 years old in 1980 had *already* been divorced after their *first* marriage. However, projections show that 49 percent of the ever-married persons will *eventually* end their first marriage in divorce. In addition, about 20 percent of those 30 to 39 years old in 1980 had *already* ended their *second* marriage in redivorce, and chances are that 58 percent will *eventually* end their second marriage with a second divorce (Glick, 1984a). These estimates and projections imply that the lifetime divorce experience of young adults today is likely to be somewhere close to three times as common as that of their parents or grandparents who are now between 65 and 74 years old.

Most of the adults who obtain divorces eventually remarry, but the remarriage rate has been declining, as documented above. Among persons 65 to 74 years old in 1980 who had previously ended their first marriage in divorce, about four of every five had eventually remarried. But among young adults of today, the chances are that closer to three-fourths of those who become divorced will ever remarry (Glick, 1984a). The falling remarriage rate is an important contributor to the cumulation of divorced persons who have not remarried.

FERTILITY PATTERNS

Now that the baby boom and the baby bust are behind us, the birth rate has been in a period of relative stability during the last decade, and most demographers do not expect to see it change very much during the next decade. The amount of the decline in natality since the peak of the baby boom in the late 1950s varies according to the measure that is used. The "crude" birth rate per 1,000 population dropped from 24 to 18 between 1960 and 1970, and then hovered around 15 or 16 from 1972 until 1984. For the 12 months ending in October, 1984, it was 15.5. The general fertility rate (per 1,000 women 15 to 44 years old) has declined in a similar manner. A convenient way to describe the change in this measure is to show that it declined between 1960 and 1974 from 118 to 68, and then it varied between 65 and 69 after 1974; the rate for 1983 was 68 (U.S. National Center for Health Statistics, 1984c and 1984d).

The total fertility rate is perhaps the easiest measure to relate to everyday living. This rate tells one how many children women are having in a given year. It implies that, if women in that year were to have children during their lifetime at the same rate as women of successively older ages (up to 45) in that year, the average woman would have the number of children indicated by the resulting rate, called the total fertility rate for that year. Specifically, the total fertility rate hit a peak of 3.8 children per woman at the height of the baby boom in 1957. By 1970, it had fallen to 2.5 children and by 1974 to 1.8 children, the level at which it remained until 1982 (the most recent date with information available), except for a rate of 1.7 in 1976. Thus, women today are having only about one-half as many children, on the average, as their mothers were having at the peak of the baby boom.

Much interest has been expressed in the recent rise of the birth rate for women 30 to 34 years of age. These are women who are approaching the age when they must have those postponed children if they are ever to do so. Placing this rise in perspective, it is useful to note that at the peak of the baby boom for this age group, 1955, the birth rate per 1,000 women 30 to 34 was 116. By 1975 it had declined to a low point of only 52, or less than one-half the peak level. Since 1975, the corresponding rate has climbed by about one-sixth, to 61 by 1981 (the latest year available). But this level for 1981 is still considerably lower than the 1970 rate of 73 per 1,000 women 30 to 34. Moreover, this recent increase in childbearing among women who have been postponing having children has been concentrated among those who are having their first or second child. Therefore, this lone area of rise in fertility is not contributing to an upsurge in large families.

The birth rate for *unmarried* women moved generally upward during the last decade as more young adults postponed marriage for either their first or a subsequent time. This trend was determined by whites, because the trend was generally downward for blacks (from a very high level, about three times that for whites). The proportion of all births that were born to unmarried mothers is more often cited. It shows that only five percent of all births in 1960 were to unmarried mothers but that the figure rose to 11 percent by 1970 and all the way up to 19 percent in 1982. By 1982, fully 57 percent of all black births were to unmarried mothers as compared with "only" 12 percent for whites.

The number of legal abortions rose sharply from 745,000 in 1973 to 1,554,000 in 1980 and constituted an increase from one-fifth to two-fifths as large a number as the number of live births (U.S. Bureau of the Census, 1983a, the very valuable *Statistical Abstract*). Since 1980 the increments in the number of legal abortions have been decreasing, so that by 1982 the number was only slightly higher (1,574,000) than it had been in 1980 (Henshaw, et al., 1984). In the meantime, as the number of legal abortions rose, the number of illegal abortions declined sharply during the early 1970s (Glick and Norton, 1979).

FAMILY LIVING ARRANGEMENTS

Declining size of household

The average size of the American household has been continuing its historic decline during recent decades. When the first decennial census of the United States was taken in 1790, the average household consisted of 5.7 persons. One hundred years later it was about one person smaller, at 4.8 persons in 1890. It lost another person during the next 50 years, to 3.7 in 1940. Now, a little over 40 years later, the average size of household is yet another person smaller, at 2.7 persons in 1984 (Glick, 1957; U.S. Bureau of the Census, 1984c). But probably few, if any, alive today will ever see the average size of household dwindle down to only 1.7 persons.

Through past decades, the primary cause of the declining size of household has been the longtime downward trend of the birth rate. This trend was interrupted for a couple of decades by the unprecedented baby boom of the period from roughly 1945 to 1965.

Meantime, several other factors have been involved, including the increasing proportion of the population that survives to old age and maintains small households after their children leave home, the rising divorce rate that has contributed to the expanding number of one-parent and one-person households, and the rapidly increasing number of couples living together without being married (called POSSLQs, partners of opposite sex sharing living

40

quarters). Between 1960 and 1983, one-parent households bounced up 141 percent, one-person households by 173 percent, and unmarried couple households by 300 percent. During the same period the traditional family of father, mother, and young children declined four percent (Glick, 1984b). Throughout the last two decades, those one-parent households maintained by a father remained close to one-tenth of all one-parent households. And, because of the especially high rate of births to black unmarried mothers, about two-thirds of the never-married mothers keeping up a home with their young children in 1983 were black mothers (U.S. Bureau of the Census, 1984a).

One-person households are most often maintained by adults in late middle age or old age, but the rate of increase among one-person households during recent decades has been far faster among those *below* middle age, especially among men. Between 1960 and 1983, the number of men under 45 who were living entirely alone went up by 400 percent; the corresponding figure for women was 350 percent (Glick, 1984b). These persons consisted largely of young adults experiencing independent living before marriage or noncustodial parents with a former spouse in charge of a one-parent family.

Unmarried couples living together were all of 3.6 times as numerous in 1980 as in 1960, having increased from less than one-half million to 1.6 million (Glick and Spanier, 1979; U.S. Bureau of the Census, 1984b and 1984c). Unmarried couples without children outnumber those with children by a ratio of two to one, and those maintained by men likewise similarly outnumber those maintained by women by a ratio of two to one. By 1984, there were 2.0 million unmarried-couple households, constituting about four percent of all households. But so far in the 1980s, the rate of increase in unmarried-couple households has been gradually declining.

Despite the sharp increase during recent years in the number of small families of various types, the fact deserves stressing that the great majority of *household members* live in homes managed by a married couple (73 percent in 1983). Nearly two of every four people live in traditional families of father, mother, and young children, and another one of every four are in homes with a married man and woman but no young children. The remaining one-fourth of the household population is distributed among one-parent households (8 percent), one-person households (8 percent), unmarried-couple households (2 percent), and all other households (9 percent) (Glick, 1984b).

Living arrangement of children

Nearly all young children (97 percent in 1983) live with one or both parents, but the proportion living with *two* parents has gone down from seven of every eight in 1960 to six of every eight in 1983 (Glick, 1984b). Meantime, the proportion living with only one parent has more than doubled, from nine percent to 22 percent. The most rapid gains since 1960 have occurred among children living with a divorced parent (up 300 percent) and among those living with a never-married parent (also up 300 percent). Back in 1960, there were more young children living with a widowed mother than with a divorced mother, but by 1983 there were two and one-half times as many living with a divorced mother as with a widowed mother.

Other sidelights on the living arrangements of children include the fact that lone fathers have custody of about one-third more boys than girls, whereas lone mothers have custody of about the same number of boys as girls (Glick 1974b). Another sidelight is the fact that currently about one child of every nine (11 percent) under 18 years of age is living with a natural parent and a stepparent; this means that close to one of every six or seven children under 18 living with *two parents* (11 percent versus 73 percent) is living with a natural parent and a stepparent, according to estimates by the author. To round out the picture, 58 percent of all children under 18 in 1983 were living with two parents both of whom were in their first marriage; and the final four percent were living with their two natural parents one or both of whom had remarried before these children were born.

FAMILY WORK AND LEISURE

As mothers have obtained more education, more of them have been employed outside the home. By 1984, over one-half (61 percent) of all mothers of children under 18 were in the labor force

(U.S. Bureau of Labor Statistics, unpublished Current Population Survey data). Labor force participation rates in 1984 ranged widely, from 84 percent for divorced mothers with children of school age to "only" 40 percent for never-married mothers of children under 3.

One of the main concerns for working mothers is the problem of finding — and affording to pay for — satisfactory baby sitters. Illustrative facts about the care of children under five years old of employed mothers in 1982 are as follows: 31 percent of the mothers had their children cared for in their own homes, 40 percent in another home, 15 percent in a group care center, and nine percent by the mother while working; six percent gave no report (U.S. Bureau of the Census, 1983a).

Families usually alternate their activities between work and recreation. Information about what people do when they recreate is available from a survey made in mid-1983 by the Gallup Organization. A representative sample of the population was asked which of a long list of leisure-time activities their households participated in. The results, cited by the U.S. Bureau of the Census (1983a), indicate the extent of the participation, in part, as follows: Watching television, 81 percent, listening to music, 64 percent; taking pleasure trips in cars, 44 percent; going to the movies, 42 percent; vegetable gardening, also 42 percent; watching professional sports on TV, 39 percent; taking vacation trips in the U.S., 34 percent; exercising for physical fitness, 31 percent; also fishing, 31 percent; using the workshop for home repairs, 29 percent; bicycling, 22 percent; bowling, 20 percent; jogging, 19 percent; playing tennis and golf, each 12 percent; and skiing, 10 percent. The same Census Bureau source provides additional information about the social and economic characteristics of participants in selected types of recreational activities, but it does not distinguish between activities engaged in alone and those engaged in by all members of the family.

FAMILY ECONOMICS

Family income

Because of the changing value of the dollar, comparisons of family income over time are improved by the use of "constant dollars." Moreover, the income information presented here for a given year was collected in March of the following year. Thus, the median income in 1982 reported by families in 1983 was $23,400 (U.S. Bureau of the Census, 1984d). Nearly a decade earlier, in 1973 the median family income in constant 1982 dollars had been 11 percent higher, at a peak of $26,000. Therefore, the 1982 level was intermediate between the 1973 and 1960 levels; for 1960 the comparable figure was $18,300 (23 percent below the 1973 peak).

Because of variations in the average number of persons per household from one demographic group to another, a refined measure that I consider preferable in making comparisons among these groups is the average (mean) income per household member. Accordingly, in 1982 the average income per household member in the United States was $8,900, but it ranged from $9,600 in the West to $8,450 in the South. Since about three-fourths of the household population live in married-couple households, the average for these households, $9,000, was only a little higher than the overall average. But the range of average incomes among persons in other types of households was very large, varying from $14,100 for persons in households maintained by divorced men to $7,700 for persons in households maintained by widowed women.

Personal expenditures

In order to provide a glimpse of the way Americans spend their money, the following information is presented, once again, from that valuable source, the *Statistical Abstract of the United States: 1984* (U.S. Bureau of the Census, 1983a). In 1982, $180 billion were expended on *private* health services and supplies. This figure, not adjusted for inflation, is all of 816 percent higher than the corresponding figure in 1960. Moreover, *public* health expenditures in 1982 were $129 billion, representing an increase of more than 1,000 percent since 1960.

Among the many personal *consumption* expenditures, a few deserve special mention. Not surprisingly, more money was spent in 1982 on housing ($173 billion) than on any other consumer item. Other expenditures include household operations ($63 billion), furniture ($60 billion), automobiles ($57 billion), and transportation ($32 billion). Of these items, the greatest increase since 1960 in constant dollars was housing, up 168 percent; automobiles

44

were up 135 percent, and transportation was up 86 percent. In regard to housing, a little over one-third of all housing units are rented. Over the 11 years from 1970 to 1981, the median rent more than doubled (from $108 to $270); meantime, the median value of owned homes more than tripled (from $17,000 to $55,000).

Although the field of expenditures is not one of my specialties, it appears from the foregoing facts and figures that expenditures have been increasing faster than income. One explanatory factor is that consumer credit outstanding tripled between 1970 and 1982 (from $143 billion to $431 billion). However, because of inflation and tax increases, the ratio of credit to disposable personal income remained fairly steady at close to 20 percent.

Dependency ratios

Because of the ups and downs in the birth rate and the continually declining death rate, the ratio of young children and elderly persons to the population in the main ages for employment have been in the process of change. This "dependency ratio" is an approximation to the relationship between the nonworking and the working population. In 1970, the number of young children was at a peak because of the many survivors of the baby boom, and accordingly there were 61 children under 18 for every 100 persons 18 to 64 years old (U.S. Bureau of the Census, 1983b). Also, in 1970, there were 17 persons 65 and over for every 100 persons 18 to 64. Taken together, there were 61 plus 17, or 78, persons of so-called dependency ages for every 100 of working age in 1970.

But as the birth rate fell sharply and is expected to remain low, while the death rate has declined moderately, the young dependency ratio has gone down all the way from 61 in 1970 to 44 by 1982 and is likely to go on down to 41 by the year 2000; meanwhile, the elderly dependency ratio has gone up only from 17 to 19 between 1970 and 1982 and is expected to reach 21 by 2000. The combination of the two types of dependency ratios has therefore resulted in an overall decline from 78 young and old persons per 100 of working age in 1970 to 63 in 1982, with the prospect that it will still be at about the same level, namely, 62, by the year 2000. It is obvious that the primary reason for the trend of the dependency ratio has been past changes in the birth rate and the prospect for a relatively stable birth rate in the years to come. As a consequence, the American population has evidently been moving away from a relatively child-centered population to more of a relatively adult-centered population.

Outlook for the elderly

More people these days are living into old age, and their economic circumstances have been improving substantially. For one thing, people can now expect to live 20 years longer than their grandparents did. Back in 1920 the expectation of life at birth was only 54 years for the average American (U.S. Bureau of the Census, 1983a). During succeeding twenty year periods, the lengthening life expectancy has increased at a slowing pace. It went up by nine years to 63 by 1940 and by seven more years to 70 by 1960. Now, during the last two decades or so it has risen 4.5 years to 74.5 by 1982. Looking far ahead, projections indicate that the average life may be extended yet another five years to 79.8 years by the middle of the next century, 2050 (U.S. Bureau of the Census, 1983b).

There is evidence that people are not only living longer but are also enjoying a greater measure of independence and of economic well being. For example, among persons 65 years old and over, those who were maintaining their own household or were living with a marital partner increased from 80 percent in 1960 to 92 percent in 1983 (Glick, 1984b). Another useful indicator that can be cited is income per family member. Thus, for householders 65 years old and over, the average income per family member went up from about $4,600 to about $7,600, or by about 65 percent, between 1975 and 1982 as compared with an increase of only about 50 percent for all other family members (U.S. Bureau of the Census, 1984d). With luck, these indications of the improving state of the elderly will continue.

CONCLUSION

One of the consequences of the delay in marriage and the decline in childbearing during recent years has been the concentration of marital and childbearing events into a shorter period of time (Tsui, 1984). These developments, along with the increase in divorce and the lengthening of life, have resulted in more "child-free" and "spouse-free" years for adults below middle age as well

46

as more years in the "empty-nest" period in middle age and old age. Moreover, the more extensive use of effective means of family limitation has aided in the process of having many fewer unwanted children brought into the world, most of whom would have faced a gloomy future.

Persons born during the low-birth-rate decades of the 1930s and 1970s have been referred to as the lucky cohorts. Those persons have found, or will find, conditions relatively favorable to upward mobility in keeping with the traditional American way, whereas those born during the baby boom are finding it difficult to establish families with a confident outlook for the future. Even in the best of times, many individual families drift into poverty and rise above it again. Therefore, the average situations that must be presented in a brief chapter like the present one deal largely with central tendencies around which there is much dispersion.

In conclusion, let me return to my opening observation, namely, that recent social changes have produced many noteworthy modifications of the conventional family norms, but yet the similarities with past family norms are still very great and are likely to remain that way.

Notes

Carlson, Elwood, "Divorce Rate Fluctuation as a Cohort Phenomenon," *Population Studies*, 33:523-533, 1979.

Glick, Paul C., *American Families*, New York: John Wiley & Sons, 1957.

_____, "Social Change and the American Family," *The Social Welfare Forum, 1977*, pp. 43-62, 1978.

_____, "Marriage, Divorce, and Living Arrangements: Prospective Changes," *Journal of Family Issues*, 5:7-26, 1984a.

_____, "American Household Structure in Transition," *Family Planning Perspectives*, 16:205-211, 1984b.

Glick, Paul C., and Arthur J. Norton, "Marrying, Divorcing, and Living Together in the U.S. Today," *Population Bulletin*, 32, No. 5:1-41, 1979.

Glick, Paul C., and Graham B. Spanier, "Married and Unmarried Cohabitation in the United States," *Journal of Marriage and the Family*, 42:19-30, 1980.

Henshaw, Stanley K., Jacqueline Darroch Forrest, and Ellen Blaine, "Abortion Services in the United States, 1981 and 1982," *Family Planning Perspectives*, 16:119-127, 1984.

Tsui, Amy Ong, "Zero, One or Two Births: 1975 and 1980," paper presented at the annual meeting of the Population Association of America, 1984.

U.S. Bureau of the Census, "Household and Family Characteristics: March 1970," *Current Population Reports*, Series P-20, No. 218, 1971.

_____, "Marital Status and Living Arrangements: March 1975," *Current Population Reports*, Series P-20, No. 287, 1975.

_____, "Number, Timing, and Duration of Marriages and Divorces in the United States: June 1975," *Current Population Reports,* Series P-20, No. 297, 1976.

_____, "Population Profile of the United States: 1979," *Current Population Reports,* Series P-20, No. 350, 1980.

_____, "Household and Family Characteristics: March 1983," *Current Population Reports,* Series P-20, No. 388, 1984a.

_____, "Marital Status and Living Arrangements: March 1983," *Current Population Reports,* Series P-20, No. 389, 1984b.

_____, "Households, Families, Marital Status, and Living Arrangements: March 1984 (Advance Report)," *Current Population Reports,* Series P-20, No. 391, 1984c.

_____, "Money Income of Households, Families, and Persons in the United States: 1982," *Current Population Reports,* Series P-60, No. 142, 1984d.

_____, *Statistical Abstract of the United States: 1984,* 1983a.

_____, "Population Profile of the United States: 1982," *Current Population Reports,* Series P-23, No. 130, 1983b.

U.S. National Center for Health Statistics, "Final Marriage Statistics, 1970," *Monthly Vital Statistics Report,* Vol. 23, No. 2, Supplement 1, 1974a.

_____, "Final Divorce Statistics, 1970," *Monthly Vital Statistics Report,* Vol. 23, No. 2, Supplement 2, 1974b.

_____, "Advance Report of Final Divorce Statistics, 1981," *Monthly Vital Statistics Report,* Vol. 32, No. 9, Supplement 2, 1984a.

_____, "Advance Report of Final Marriage Statistics, 1981," *Monthly Vital Statistics Report,* Vol. 32 No. 11, Supplement, 1984b.

_____, *"Advance Report of Final Natality Statistics, 1982,"* *Monthly Vital Statistics Report,* Vol. 33, No. 6, Supplement, 1984c.

_____, "Births, Marriages, Divorce, and Deaths for October 1984," *Monthly Vital Statistics Report,* Vol. 33, No. 10, 1984d.

Chapter 3

The Family Life-Cycle

Beth J. Soldo, Ph.D

THE FAMILY LIFE-CYCLE AS A CONCEPT

The concept of "family life-cycle" expresses sociologically what we each perceive as members of our own families: the family as a unit has an intrinsic life and life course all its own. Central to the family life-cycle concept is the idea that families pass through largely predictable and age-related stages. Most of the existing typologies of the family life course define discrete stages around the primary task of the family unit at different times in its existence; for example, the child-bearing stage, the child-rearing stage, or the "empty-nest"stage.

In the previous chapter Dr. Paul Glick presents an impressive array of socio-demographic information about the family. His data have four important implications for our understanding of the family life cycle. *First*, the age-relatedness of key family life-cycle stages is changing. Women are marrying later, postponing child-bearing and thereby delaying, to later in their own life course, the age at which the last child leaves home. Couples are surviving together longer and spouses, usually women, are losing their partners at a later age. The duration of the widowed stage also is lengthening. *Second*, there is considerably more variability in the ages at which individuals experience key family life-cycle transitions. The child-bearing stage, for example, used to roughly correspond to the early to mid-twenties of both husband and wife. Today, the age of the wife at entry into this stage spans nearly a twenty-year range, from late adolescence to the mid-thirties. Increasing numbers of first births are occurring to women at the extremes of this age range. And, herein lies one part of the new reality of contemporary families — stages of the family life-cycles are no longer clearly defined by age. For individuals, this means reaching across decades of chronological age to find families sharing the same experiences. For policy and planning, this change implies that family assistance programs, including both educational and service programs, can no longer be easily targeted at specific or narrow age ranges.

Dr. Glick's data also clearly demonstrate the *third* feature of the changing life cycle: specific family life-cycle stages are no longer associated with specific normative structures. Families in the child-rearing stage, for example, include both single-parent households as well as traditional, intact marital households. From this follows the *fourth* and last significant change in the family life cycle. Increasing numbers of families are passing through more life-cycle stages than ever before. These additional transitions usually involve the recombining of fragmented family units after divorce, widowhood or the loss of independence of older family members. Single-parent families often initiate new families. This may occur as often as two or three times during just the "growing up" years of the children. Older parents and adult children come together again under the same roof not only to accomodate the care needs of the older parents but oftentimes to respond to the financial or child-rearing needs of the younger family unit.

In sum, the contemporary family life course is much less predictable in terms of the number of transitions encountered, the age of family members at these transitions and even the structure of the family at specific stages. As a result, norms, expectations and behaviors appropriate to each family life-cycle stage are less clearly defined. But, as Dr. Glick also emphasized, evidence of dramatic change in significant aspects of family life cannot be allowed to overshadow insights into the core stability of the family as a social institution. In spite of all the changes in the regularity of its life-cycle, the family continues, in most instances, to fulfill its two basic missions — the introduction, nurturing and socialization of new members into society and the emotional and physical care of its members at all stages of their development. Repeated studies testify to the adaptability, flexibility, and even success of the modern family in all its various forms. Parent-child contact, support and involvement continues to be the norm, not the exception, in families splintered by divorce or extended over four generations.

The new reality of the family life-cycle poses any number of challenges to the Church both as a spiritual and social institution. Traditionally, the Church and the family have been united as partners, sharing common standards of what is "good" and moral behavior for family members at different ages and at different stages in the family life course. The Church, through the community of the parish, has sustained families, both spiritually and physically, in times of difficulty. At issue today is how the Church can continue to maintain its important links with the family even as actions she condemns, such as divorce and contraceptive use, are increasing in prevalence. This is perhaps the most obvious implication for the Church of changes in the family life-cycle. But this concern is part of a much broader issue — how can and should the Church, with her diminished clerical capacity, relate to the family across its less predictable, more varied life course?

The following discussion focuses on one aspect of this challenge: the Church and later stages of the family life cycle. Note that my concern is not specifically with the Church and its aged members, *per se*. Rather my concern is with how the effects of aging rebound across generations, linking young and old families, as well as the Church, in the struggle to integrate the very different needs and resources of these units at markedly different stages in their life cycles.

Framing the issue in this way broadens the traditional understanding of the family life-cycle. Rather than focus on discrete family units of origin, I am juxtaposing the life course of the family of origin with that of the families of procreation to which it gives life. This broader understanding allows for a more accurate render-

51

ing of the tensions and tasks confronting modern families in the age of aging, that is, the multiple family life-cycle perspective acknowledges the persistence of family ties across households and across generations. These connections describe a web of obligations and duties that is often overlooked in more traditional family life-cycle approaches. The multi-family life-cycle perspective also encourages viewing the transformation of individual families with a longer time horizon. Families at early stages in their life-cycle today are the older families of tomorrow. How these young families relate to their parents' families will shape the social and moral environment in which these younger families themselves will age.

THE CHURCH, THE FAMILY AND AGING

Just as other social institutions are aging, so too is the family, The aging of the family can be measured in terms of the number of related, coincident families of different generations. During this century alone the relative number of three-generation families has increased from 10 to 47 percent. The proportion of older persons embedded within four-generation families reached 40 percent in 1968 and is undoubtedly higher today (Brody, 1985). Although we lack firm estimates, this conclusion is justified by the considerable increases in old-age life expectancy during the period 1968 to 1980. Today women at age 65 can, on average, expect to live an additional 18 years; for those who survive to age 85, life expectancy is six years. Nearly one-half of all females born in 1980 can expect to celebrate their 85th birthdays. And the proliferation of the four-generation family is likely to continue since the age group "85 and over" is the fastest growing segment of our population (Manton and Soldo, 1985).

Another way to appreciate the aging of the family is to examine the probability of having surviving parents at various ages. Recent estimates indicate that the chances of a woman in her late fifties having a surviving parent at any given time are four out of ten: for those in their early sixties, the odds drop to one in five. But projections of family structure indicate that these odds will increase over time. When the "baby-boom," (children born immediately after World War II), reach 65 (starting in 2015) as many as sixty percent of them will have at least one surviving parent (Wolf, 1983). Those surviving parents will then be 85 years of age or older — the age of high risk for chronic disability.

This "aging" of the family implies that increasingly there will be not *one but two* related old-age family units. At a minimum, the life-cycle typology must be revised to reflect this change. But this is not mere picture-straightening in the world of academic theories. Rather, there are important differences among old-age families in terms of their needs and priorities. As with other, earlier stages in the family life-cycle, however, the stages of older families only loosely correlate with chronological age.

FAMILY LIFE-CYCLE STAGES AND OLD AGE

In order to understand the family life-cycle stages of old age it is necessary to pause for a minute to consider the nature of human aging. The process of human aging begins the moment one is born. Physiological change is the natural concomitant of the passage of time. But aging does not imply a linear, downhill course in functional, physical or mental capacity. In the absence of specific pathology, for example, cardiac function declines negligibly with age while renal function shows much more marked deterioration simply as a function of aging (Manton and Soldo, 1985). To a large extent the rate of aging of individuals is determined by the extent to which specific pathologies are superimposed on the normal aging process. Thus, there are considerable differences among individuals of the same age in the accumulation of what we think of as age-related changes.

But our concern is not with the aging of individuals but rather with the aging of families. Thus it is necessary to distinguish between the family life-cycle stages of "old-age independence" and "old-age dependency." Unlike earlier life-cycle stages, however, the stages of old-age independence and dependency often repeat. By way of simple illustration of this point consider only the aging of an intact husband and wife family. At the time of retirement, or entry into the "empty-nest" stage, both husband and wife are likely to be fully functional. Each may experience some of the chronic diseases common to old age such as arthritis or hypertension, but not to the extent that their ability to sustain themselves in an independent household is compromised. But males typically

53

age faster than females in the sense that their risks for chronic disease and chronic disability are greater at any age. This relatively independent husband-wife family unit is likely to confront a stage of dependency when meeting the husband's chronic care needs dominate the focus of family life. Upon his death, the now widowed single-person family unit may again experience a period of independence. This in turn is likely to be followed by a second stage of old-age family dependence as this widow herself ages.

Earlier I emphasized that my concern was with the multi-generational family life course. From the perspective of the younger child-rearing family the scenario of alternating independence-dependence-independence of older family units may play out numerous times as both parents and the grandparents of *both* the husband and wife age. Furthermore, the younger family may confront periods of overlapping dependency of different older family units *and* sequential stages of old age dependency as the care needs of grandparents are replaced with those of parents (Brody, 1985). Thus, the impact of aging family units is unlikely to be confined to a specific time, age or stage in the younger family's life-cycle. Moreover the time frame during which this younger family deals with the dependency of its older members may span some 20 years.

THE EFFECT OF MULTI-GENERATIONAL AGING ON THE FAMILY

At this point in our discussion it is reasonable to address the basic question: what is the effect of multigenerational aging on the family and its life course? Obviously the effect is minimal if younger families, because of the pressing needs of their own life cycle stage, disassociate from the dependencies of older family units. But this is *not* the case. In spite of the myth of family abandonment of the elderly, research is documenting time and time again the extensive involvement of younger families with older relatives (Brody, 1978; Shanas, 1979). Often times this involvement is a two-way street with the older generation providing financial assistance and child care services at one point in time and younger families providing care services appropriate to their parents' or grand-

54

parents' dependencies at a later point in time. Keeping this pattern of mutual exchange in mind, however, let us now focus specifically on the ways in which the care needs of the elder family units impinge on the life cycle of younger families.

It is important to note the three aspects of aging that differentiate old-age dependencies from those experienced earlier in the life-cycle. *First,* the care needs of the elderly are, for the most part, chronic, i.e., medical or service interventions seldom restore the older person to full functional capacity. Thus, the care needs of the elderly are distinctively long-term. *Second,* the care needs of the elderly are mainly for personal care and assistance, i.e., long-term care needs include assistance with fairly discrete tasks, such as grocery shopping, and also the more basic activities of daily living, such as eating, bathing and dressing. After age 85, nearly half of all community residents require such assistance on a regular basis (Manton and Soldo, 1985). *Third,* chronic disability of old-age is degenerative. Until death intervenes, care requirements accumulate and worsen. In sharp contrast to the dependencies of children, the dependencies of old age offer little promise of abating. The parents' investment in child-rearing is compensated for by the psychological gratification of contributing to a new, autonomous life. No such psychological rewards convey with involvement in parent-care. The vista is one of increasing needs, increasing loss of independence and eventual loss of a loved one.

The distinctive care needs of the elderly do not mesh easily with the existing, acute-care orientation of either the medical care system or the current reimbursement system of the U.S. The family, with its life course tradition of flexibility, care and affective support, however, is ideally suited to meeting the care needs of the elderly. And the family does meet these care needs. Over 90 percent of all disabled elderly in the community rely in whole or in part on their families for chronic caregiving, although the family is neither compelled or compensated for undertaking this task (Soldo, forthcoming). Rather it appears that families are motivated to provide what is often exhausting, unrelenting care out of love, obligation and a sense of reciprocity.

Although younger families typically *want* to provide care to their parents, and undertake the effort voluntarily, caregiving superimposes an array of tasks and strains on whatever life-cycle stage with which it coincides. Although there are very real costs associated with caregiving, e.g., the purchase of special foods or equipment not covered by health insurance schemes, research indicates that the major problems of caregiving are emotional stress and strain, and loss of privacy, leisure time and autonomy for the caregiving units (Cantor, 1983). These problems are often juxtaposed with child-rearing, job-related demands, or adjustment to retirement. Our data also indicate that reconciling the demands of their own family life-cycle stage with the old-age dependency stage of older family units falls to women — as spouses, daughters, daughter-in-laws, or even granddaughters (Brody, 1981). The improvement in women's status may have succeeded in lowering some social and economic barriers, but societal expectations still almost inevitably ascribe caregiving — whether to an ill child or a disabled parent — to the women of multiple generations. However, other family members of the caregiving family also may be affected. Parents and children may need to renegotiate the division of household tasks; husband and wives must adjust their expectations of their relationships. Sibling tensions and rivalries often resurface as well, as multiple families of adult children try to accommodate the care needs of their parents.

THE CHURCH AND AGING FAMILIES

In conclusion it is appropriate to consider the implications of an extended and aging family life course for pastoral duties. Here, I believe, the Church has a well-defined opportunity to partially fill the void left by current public policies in assisting multiple generations of aging families. By this void I mean specifically the dearth of publicly-financed services directed towards the well-being of both carereceiving and caregiving families. Neither Medicare nor Medicaid currently reimburse for either personal care services, such as those provided by a home-health aide, or caregiver-support services, such as geriatric day care or respite care. It is accurate to describe the current U.S. situation as decidely biased towards the nursing home as a solution to the chronic care needs of the elderly. In spite of this policy bias, the nursing home is the *last,* not the first, resort of aging families. The success of the family in preventing or delaying nursing home admissions is suggested by the statistic that there are two functionally limited elderly in the community for every one in the nursing home.

Current discussion of family policy speaks in terms of providing "incentives" for family care involvement, of concerns for the substitution of publicly financed services for family provided services. Two assumptions define the tone of this debate: *one,* the government should *not* compensate the family for what it *should* do and, *two,* families need to be induced to provide care. The Church, however, can draw on its humanistic tradition, to more appropriately frame the question in terms of what can be done to *support,* not induce, family caregiving (Brody, 1985).

The local parish is obviously well-structured to organizing for this task. Already many local churches have in place programs such as Meals-on-Wheels designated to sustain older persons in the community. But the notion of family caregiving dictates concern for the special needs of the family, in its entirety, for assistance, respite, and emotional support. Attention to the family life course also implies that such programs be marked by flexibility to respond to different constellations of needs of caregiving families at differing stages in their own family life cycle.

In conclusion, it also is important to note that aging families are not unique to the United States or even to the developed countries of the world. Indeed the challenge may be most formidable in the developing regions. While three, rather than four generation families are the norm in such areas, rapidly developing societies often trap their elderly in a vacuum of social support. Policies are put in place that encourage the rural-to-urban migration of the young. Oftentimes the elderly stay behind in the rural homestead, stranded without the family support they've counted on for meeting their emotional, physical, and economic needs. Few of the developing countries have the breadth of resources to accomplish their economic objectives, including the education of the young, while at the same time establishing old-age support programs. In such areas the challenge is more complex, requiring local Church leaders to initiate outreach programs that mimic the flexibility and emotional support characteristics of the family.

The Church has always demonstrated and organized around the principle of respect for human life. The changing nature of the laity and their needs now dictate that this concern be extended, and aggressively so, across the *entire* life course of both individuals and families.

Bibliography

Brody, E.M. 1978. The aging of the family. *The Annals of the American Academy of Political and Social Science,* 438, 13-27.

_____ 1981. "Women in the middle" and family help to older people. *The Gerontologist,* 21, 471-480.

_____.1985. Parent care as a normative family stress. *The Gerontologist,* 25, 19-29.

Cantor, M.H. 1983. Strain among caregivers: A study of experience in the United States. *The Gerontologist,* 23, 597-604.

Manton, K.G. and B.J. Soldo. 1985, in press. Dynamics of health changes in the extreme elderly: New perspectives and evidence. *Milbank Memorial Fund Quarterly/Health and Society.*

Shanas, E. 1979. Social myth as hypothesis: The case of family relations of old people. *The Gerontologist,* 19, 3-9.

Soldo, B.J. Forthcoming. In-home services for the dependent elderly: Determinants of current use and implications for future demand. *Research on Aging.*

Wolf, D.A. 1983. Kinship and the living arrangements of older Americans. Final Report, The Urban Institute, Washington, DC.

Chapter 4

New Approaches To Understanding The Family

The Reverend Steven L. Preister, M.S.W.

I. SUMMARY

This paper makes five basic points, with further explication of each:

1. Today, we are coming to a new (or more correctly) renewed understanding of the importance of families in society and in the Church, partly because of some societal developments, partly because of some ecclesial developments.

2. We are facing new challenges in the Church in regard to family life. These challenges do not require us to initiate many more new programs and ministries for families (though some are needed), but rather, to examine *how* we minister and the *impact*

of these ministries on families.

3. We need to broaden our definition of the term "family" in two ways:

- Our social definition needs to be broad enough to include the diversity of families present in society and the Church today, but narrow enough to preserve the true meaning of the word.

- Our ecclesial definition needs to be one which will foster the family's belief in its own mission; too often today, our Christian families do not have this sense of mission, and consequently, feel more "sin-full" than "mission-full."

4. The fundamental challenge society faces today in regard to family life is (put negatively) to stop institutions from replacing families, and (put positively) to strengthen a partnership between families and institutions to support families in fulfilling their own mission and functions. This is equally as important a challenge for the Church as it is for society.

5. Another fundamental challenge for both society and the Church is to understand how present services and ministries impact on families.

In summary, this chapter focuses on how we can provide for our current ministries in the Church in a more family-oriented way.

II. BACKGROUND

To even the casual observer, there is a growing emphasis today both in society and in the Church on the family and its importance. Let me state in the beginning that societies which are primarily agriculture-based have never lost that emphasis. But western industrialized nations have, over the last three centuries, increasingly de-emphasized the family in preference for an emphasis on the individual. However, we are beginning to see a change today. Why?

One major reason is that today we are at the beginning of a paradigm shift in western society. A societal paradigm is some major theory — eventually defined as truth — which is used by a culture to provide an explanation for phenomena and behavior. Western civilization, since the end of the Middle Ages, adopted a scientific paradigm based on reductionism. (For example, if you want to understand a star fish, you dissect it to its smallest parts.) This scientific paradigm, an emphasis on monads or parts, led us first into the period of industrialism, with all the benefits and problems of an industrial society. Today it is leading us into post-industrialism, sometimes called the technological period, the information and service society or, significantly, the systems age.

The previous paradigm is breaking down: it is no longer adequate to explain the complexity of biological and social life as we know it today. Instead, it is being replaced by a new paradigm, first formulated as "general systems theory." Systems thinking does not deny the importance of the individual "parts" of a system. But it stresses that it is the relationship of the parts and how they work together in a system — whether a biological system or a social system — which is most important today.

Systems thinking is emerging around us in many fields. It is the basis of the emphasis today on environmental and human ecology. General systems theory which first arose out of biology and affected the birth of cybernetics is affecting every major field. It is also affecting the Church. Systems thinking appears in different places and in different ways in the Church. One way, I believe, is the growing emphasis on the family in both the ecclesial and social societies.

For example, in 1978, the Bishops of the U.S. promulgated the Plan of Pastoral Action for Family Ministry. It called for ministries to, with and for families across the entire lifecycle. Since that time, there has been a major growth in family-related ministries in the Church in the U.S. It is an important development.

One process mandated by the Pastoral Plan was a listening process: dioceses were encouraged to set up some sort of apparatus to listen to married couples and families themselves, so that we had a better sense of family's strengths, needs and problems. The Commission on Marriage and Family Life, established by the Bishops to promote the implementation of the Pastoral Plan, was to oversee this listening process. Interestingly, the Commission concludes from this listening that a different kind of growth in family ministry is needed today, that a further, important adjustment needs to be made in the Church, because we have heard something that the whole Church must hear and to which it must respond:

First, families need the support and affirmation of all the ministries of the Church, not just one designated ministry, however valuable and necessary that one may be. We cannot segregate family life and family ministry into a separate ministry or designate this ministry to just one department of the Church.

Second, our ministries in the U.S. are oriented toward a radical individualism that permeates our culture. Our ministries, therefore, do not respond to families as a unit in an appropriate way.

This is the result, I believe, of the overemphasis on the individual in industrialized western culture. The Commission believes that we do not need many more new, compartmentalized programs and ministries in the Church. Something else is needed to support Christian family life.

Consequently, the Commission has drafted a paper entitled, "The Necessity of a Family Perspective in the Ministries of the Church." As a consultant to the Commission, I assisted in drafting the paper. I am presenting part of that paper here because it represents, in a concrete way, the application of a new understanding of the family in the Church: the family as a system in the larger systems of the Church and society.

The Commission believes the next step in ministry in the United States requires us to develop a family perspective in all the ministries of the Church at every level, to counter this pervasive radical individualism and to offer families the support of all ministries. This is exactly what John Paul II calls us to do in *Familiaris Consortio,[1]* his recent apostolic exhortation on the family, when he states that no plan of pastoral action at any level of the Church must ever be undertaken without first understanding its potential impact on families (Paragraph 70). This is also the implicit message of the Pastoral Plan. It is the logical next step in the Plan — not necessarily anticipated, but essential.

III. INTRODUCTION

The fundamental premise of the Commission Paper is that our families are central to each of us becoming and remaining a Christian and becoming a full person in the society of humankind. We are realizing that it is in the best interest of the Church and society to ensure that families are helped to fulfill their responsibilities:

- For an individual to come to emotional, spiritual, intellectual, social and sexual maturity, the primary community of a family is needed (see appendix 2).

- There is an intrinsic connection between families and society, since they are the most effective means of humanizing and personalizing society (*Familiaris Consortio,* Paragraph 42, ff.).

- The family is the first and vital cell of all societies, social and ecclesial. The very core of the Church is linked to the well-being of the family, and the future of the Church passes through the family (*Familiaris Consortio,* Paragraphs 3, 75).

This realization has led us to a renewed emphasis on the family in the Catholic community, as evident in the following developments:

- **The Plan of Pastoral Action for Family Ministry:**[2]

In the Catholic Church in the U.S., the Bishops' Plan of Pastoral Action for Family Ministry (1978) called for the growth of ministries to, for and with families at all levels of the Church. This growth has been seen in the seven areas of ministry called for in the Pastoral Plan: ministry with singles, pre-marrieds, married couples, parents, developing families (i.e., assistance throughout the entire family life cycle), hurting families (i.e., support for families in crises), and individuals, couples and families in positions of leadership (i.e., support for individuals engaged in family ministries and development of leadership skills).

- **The 1980 Synod and Familiaris Consortio:**

John Paul II convened a Synod of Bishops in 1980 to examine the role of the Christian family in the modern world.[3] The Pope and bishops shared a vision of how basic the family is to living the gospel today. John Paul has addressed this perspective numerous times in his papal audiences. In *Familiaris Consortio* (1981), based on the recommendations of the Synod, he emphasizes the mission of the family (Paragraph 17) and the ways the family's well-being affects the whole Church (Paragraph 3). He brought us to a new understanding of family ministry and emphasizes that pastoral care for the family should be treated as a real priority in the Church (Paragraph 65).

- **The Charter of the Rights of the Family:**

The Vatican has recently proposed a Charter of the Rights of the Family (1983)[4] (recommended by the 1980 Synod of Bishops), which spells out the rights, needs and responsibilities of families in the context of societies and governments. Unlike past documents, it no longer presents only the rights of the individual within the family and society, but presents the family as a corporate reality with its own rights and responsibilities. It identifies principles for assessing social policies as they affect families. It encourages families and associations of families to become involved in the political process in order to protect the rights of families.

- **The Code of Canon Law:**

In the revised Code of Canon Law (1984),[5] two fundamental structures are posed as basic to the local Church — with a third implied — each with its own rights and responsibilities: the organization of the local Church into diocese, parishes and groups; and the leadership of the local Church: the bishop, clergy and other designated ministers.

Reading between the lines of the Code, and looking at how the Code views families, another structure in the Church is implied, another structure parallel to the Church of the Parish: parents and families. Parents and families are not designated solely as recipients of the Church's ministry, nor simply as responsible for making sure their members participate in the life of the Church, as too frequently has been the case in the past. Rather, their role is fundamental: the family is an agent of ministry, the Little Church or — in the words of *Familiaris Consortio* — the Domestic Church, the Church of the Home (Paragraph 49), with the role of Christian formation and service parallel to the role of the Church of the Parish, and in partnership with it. The realization of this mission and these tasks of the family is in itself a ministry of the Church (*Familiaris Consortio*, Paragraphs 38, 39, 53).

Efforts to implement these pastoral challenges in the whole Church on behalf of families, assisted by the designated family life office, have started to show results on the parish, diocesan and national levels. We should be proud as a Church of these efforts. What we have accomplished, by and large, is a growth in family-related programs. But this is not enough.

A different and parallel kind of growth is needed today. This different kind of growth needed today is really evident in the documents and events reviewed above, because these documents do not call for new programs and ministries for families, but instead, call us to make a change in our perspective. They are evidence that we are becoming increasingly aware that all ministries of the Church, even in their ministry to individuals, touch the very fiber and life of the family. There are some ministries in the Church that are explicit family ministries, but all others are implicitly so, since they impact families. Thus it is crucial that the entire Church, including those ministries to individuals, incorporate a family perspective.

IV. A FAMILY PERSPECTIVE IN SOCIETY AND IN THE CHURCH

There are five perspectives for viewing social reality: the perspective of the individual, the family, the small group, the organized social institution, (such as the Church or a neighborhood organization), and society as a whole. It is important to be aware of all these perspectives to guide our ministries. If one is neglected or forgotten, the balance of the whole system will be affected.

The purpose of the Commission Paper is to clarify and strengthen one of these perspectives, the family perspective, for the benefit of all ministries in the Church and to call all ministries to review how they impact families.

Defining Family

Before defining a family perspective, we need first to clarify how the word "family" is used in the Commission Paper, both social and ecclesial definitions. Any working definition of the family and its place in the Church must include both. The social definition provided is neutral and descriptive in its nature; it is a definition necessary for assessing the impact of the Church's ministries on a variety of families and family situations. The ecclesial definition states the family's identity, tasks and mission from a perspective of Christian faith; it is a definition necessary for assessing the adequacy of Church ministries in supporting the family's identity, tasks and mission. We need to weave these two definitions together for our understanding of families before we begin to develop ministries for them.

1. Social Definition

A social definition of the word "family" must be broad enough to include the variety of families and family situations in our society, as well as exclusive enough to maintain its real meaning:

- A family is defined as two or more persons related by blood, marriage or adoption.[6]

- Families come in many forms, configurations and structures. Some family members live together in the same household, others live apart in multiple households. Thus the word "family" is not restricted to those relatives living together in one household: family ties can be equally important where members live in different households from each other.

- This definition includes families spanning and developing across the life cycle: families in formation, married persons, parent(s) and children, childless couples, middle-aged couples, families with elderly dependents, aging families, etc. Thus we are not only referring to families as married couples living with their dependent children, but are using the term "family" in a more comprehensive way.

- This definition includes families that are hurting which have special needs and problems, whether these needs are chronic (e.g. chronic poverty), critical (i.e., a crisis or emergency such as a death in the family or the sudden illness of a family member) or developmental (e.g., problems with an adolescent in trouble in the community).

- This definition includes some aspects of the lives of so-called "single" persons, since they too have families and are involved in the lives and needs of their family members. It does not, however, include all the aspects of the lives of singles, which are not addressed in this Statement, but which are obviously important.

- This definition is a descriptive, value neutral one, not a normative one. But it recognizes that families can be the source of much tension, pain and anger as well as comfort, support and love.

- This definition does not include other more symbolic uses of the word "family" which are drawn by analogy from family life, such as the need all persons have for intimacy, support and community, or metaphors such as the parish as a family.

2. Ecclesial Definition

An ecclesial definition of family life identifies the identity, tasks and mission from the perspective of the Christian faith, most recently articulated by John Paul II in *Familiaris Consortio.* John Paul defines the family as an intimate community of life and love whose mission is to "guard, reveal and communicate this love" (Paragraph 17). Its four tasks in realizing its identity and mission are to:

1) Form a community of persons in mutual self-giving.

2) Serve life in its transmission and sharing of values.

3) Participate in the development of society by becoming a school of social life, a household of hospitality, a protagonist of a family politic.

4) Serve in the life and mission of the Church by becoming a believing and evangelizing household in dialogue with God and at the service of humanity.

Thus the family, in this definition, is not a passive agent in these tasks, but an active one in accomplishing them. The imperative to families to "become what you are" (Paragraph 17) is the hallmark of this mission.

Defining A Family Perspective In Society And In The Church

Thus a family perspective, based on the social and ecclesial definition of the family, is a wholistic one. It does not eliminate the need for the other perspectives, but it is a deliberate focus on the primary community to which most people belong: his or her family.

• It recognizes that an individual lives in the context of a series of relationships, not in isolation.

• Among the most important of these relationships are family relationships.

• Relationships evolve and change, and any change in a family or family member affects the life and vitality of the family and each of its individual members.

We believe this perspective is urgently needed today both in society and in the Church. It is needed not because, as some assert, our society is anti-family; rather, because our society is pro-individual and pro-institutional, a result of the earlier paradigm.

1. A Family Perspective in Society

In the height of industrialism and post-industrialism, we have witnessed the tendency of institutions, which were originally created to support families, to replace them in the provision of functions such as education, health care, recreation, religious education, etc. Modern institutions tend to validate the family functions of intimacy and mutual support, but to subtly suggest that they, the institutions, can perform the other functions better than families can. Thus family members were and still are sometimes viewed as a hindrance to the healing of a sick person (e.g., limited visiting hours, exclusion of children from hospitals, exclusion of family members in birthing and dying, etc.).

But in fact the family is a stronger agent of educational success than the school; it is the primary health care provider; it is a stronger teacher of religious values than the institutional Church. Institutions can empower or disempower families. They can also be renewed so that their role is one of partnershp with and support of families.

Practically, what does a family perspective mean in society? It means, for example, that:

- A hospitalized person heals more quickly when the family is involved in his or her care and treatment, rather than when only the hospital staff works with the individual.

- A supportive family life improves a child's capacity for learning; parent involvement is especially important in helping a child do well in school.

- When human services are provided to adolescents and young adults of an immigrating/migrating family, it is important to realize that they frequently promote cultural assimilation. Yet such assimilation may cause turmoil, conflict and value clashes within the extended ethnic family.

• Those who attempt to assist a troubled individual (e.g., an alcoholic or depressed person) are much less likely to succeed if they do not at some level also work with that individual's immediate family. This is especially true of an individual in a troubled marriage.

2. A Family Perspective in the Church

A family perspective in the Church is one which recognizes that Church ministries, though often designed for or targeted on individuals, affect families throughout their entire life cycle. The purpose of utilizing a family perspective in the Church is to help sensitize ministers so we shape our ministry in light of its impact on families. A family perspective recognizes the impact of ministry with individuals on his or her family, and the impact of his or her family on the ministry to the individual.

Ministry with individuals affects families for better or for worse, whether working with youth, a dying person, a pregnant teenager, a sick elderly person; in the celebration of the sacrament of Reconciliation with a middle-aged person; or in the preparation of a youth for the sacrament of Confirmation. We need to understand that all these ministries, directed primarily to the individual will: (a) affect the family as a whole and the other family members; and (b) will be affected by the individual's family, thereby influencing the benefits from these ministries that the individual receives.

a. How Church Ministries Affect Families

The Church, like other social institutions, has sometimes participated in the trend to replace families in the provision of family functions. For example, religious education had been viewed primarily as the job of professionals in the Church, and not that of the parents, except to expect them to sometimes reinforce the efforts made by the professionals. But in our Church renewal, we attempt to empower families and support them in fulfilling their own functions, rather than replace them. Thus today, the emerging practice in the Church is more commonly one of helping parents participate in the religious education of their children.

Incorporating a family perspective means first that we need to sensitize ourselves to how our ministries impact on families. These are some examples how the Church has impacted on families:

• The religious education of children presents a prevalent example of negative unintended impact. As a result of practices discussed above, religion and religious values did not always take their proper place in the home. However, today, as a result of some changes, parents are more often being prepared to educate their children in the religious faith, moral values, and sacramental preparation. This is an excellent example of a partnership between the Church of the Home and the Church of the Parish. A true partnership between Church and Home makes consideration of the parents, their culture, background and general situation a major concern in structuring a religious education program which will encourage their participation. Research supports such an approach. A recent study of 200,000 religiously educated children indicated that the most significant variable in determining the religious and social behavior of children was not their religious education, but whether they discussed religious and moral matters with their parents.[7] The combination of religious education and home discussion is very potent.

• Historically, fundamental theology demonstrated its negative impact on families. In the Catholic community, following the Reformation and the Council of Trent, the parish intentionally was made the normative model for religious participation in order to eliminate certain abuses, as opposed to religious participation through religious and community associations and family groups. To accomplish this, issues of faith, salvation, the sacraments and sin increasingly were emphasized as the domain of the individual. Unintentionally, the subsequent theology did not emphasize enough the role of the family and its importance in the development and maintenance of faith, nor the familial and social consequences of sin.[8]

• Many parish activities are traditionally and properly segregated by sex, age and status. But this practice may at times have a negative effect on building family relationships. It could alienate generations from one another and promote society's tendency toward age segregation. It could isolate singles from the life of the parish. It could discourage networks of families forming in the parish unless parish leaders consciously think about the family impact and try to prevent negative effects. Even when the nature or purpose of parish activities necessarily segregate them by age, sex or status, a family dimension can be maintained. Senior citizen activities can include a grandparents' day or program which brings together extended families. Parents and family groupings can be encouraged as integral to awards or recognition ceremonies for sports or recreation programs.

• Another example shows that even the most well-intentioned parish practices of lay participation and scheduling need to be consciously examined. The most generous and religiously active families may often be at the greatest risk: the mother may be called upon to read at the 9:00 liturgy, while the father assists at the evening liturgy and the daughter at the noon liturgy. An unintended result can be the prevention of the family from celebrating together as a unit, assisting together at one liturgy, and having a family day together on the weekend.

How ministries affect families becomes critical today as American culture continues in its diversity. we need to ask ourselves whether our parishes and ministries are making the necessary adjustments to support families today in all their diversity, as families are affected by seven social and demographic trends.

• *Aging of America:* with the lengthening of life, the four generation family is now the norm.

• *Feminization of Poverty:* families with female heads now have a poverty rate six times that of two-parent families. Many women work full-time outside the home but are still poor because of low wages and discrimination in employment opportunity (First Draft, Pastoral Letter on Catholic Social Teaching and the U.S. Economy, National Conference of Catholic Bishops).

• *Economic Distribution:* the top five percent of American families own almost 43 percent of the net wealth in the nation. The top one percent of families hold almost 20 percent of the net wealth. At the other end of the scale, the bottom 50 percent of American families hold only four percent of the net wealth of the nation (*ibid.*).

• *Mobility:* 50 percent of all Americans changed residence between 1975 and 1980.

• *Later Marriages, Fewer Children and More Divorces Are Producing More Single-Parent and Blended Family Households:* nearly one-half of all children in the U.S. will live with one parent before they finish high school. By 1990, the combined total of single-parent and blended households will be larger than the total of never-divorced two-parent families.

• *Working Parents:* 60 percent of all women with children are now employed outside the home; thus in the vast majority of families, both parents or the only parent are employed.

• *Minority Families:* Hispanics now comprise 25 percent of the Catholic Church in the U.S. Blacks are increasingly using Catholic parish and the private schools. Recent immigrations of Catholic Asians to the U.S. are continuing.

b. How the Family Affects Ministries to the Individual

An individual plays various roles in his or her family. As particular ministries and services of the Church seek to help an individual, he or she learns new attitudes, values, behaviors and skills. This causes changes in how he or she relates to the family as a whole and to individual family members. The family must adjust to the changes in the individual, and this may introduce conflict and tension within the family as it adjusts to the changed individual.

Typically, the family will greet change in one of its members with one or a series of responses which include:

- Conscious or unconscious pressure to resume former roles, attitudes, values and bahaviors.

- Expulsion of the individual from the family.

- A struggle to live with the changes and tensions the changes create.

- Change within the family unit and in other family members numbers themselves in response to the changed individual.

Ministers need to become more aware that these dynamics are present as they work with individuals. There is present today in the Church an emphasis on a number of ministries and educational programs which can trigger these family dynamics, such as:

- The *Rite of Christian Initiation of Adults,* which takes a person through the conversion process.

- Intensive *weekend experiences* for youth, married couples, the separated and divorced, which seek to change or deepen attitudes, values, behaviors and skills.

- The *restoration of the permanent diaconate* and subsequent training of married men as deacons, which creates a new role and relationship for them in the Church and with their families.

- The *rise of prayer and scripture groups* for individuals, which help them to confront how they are leading a Christian life.

- *Parish renewal processes,* which focus on how individuals lead a Christian life in the context of the parish community.

A family perspective helps us understand how these ministries and programs for individuals affect his or her family life, and how his or her family life affects the reception of these ministries by the individual. It builds into ministries an awareness of the interaction of the individual and his or her family. It seeks to bridge potential conflict and provide support to both the individual and the family to cope with the changes that have been initiated by the Church ministries.

V. CONCLUSION

As both a social and ecclesial community, the Church needs to continue to renew itself in its role with families. A family perspective calls the whole Church to support and not replace the primary community to which individuals to whom it is ministering belong, even though they may not constitute a single household, because these communities profoundly affect the development and healing of individuals, and the Church and society as a whole. For the Church's leadership, a family perspective ensures awareness of:

- The importance for the individual, the community, the Church and society that families accomplish their mission.

- The importance of the Church's role in supplementing and supporting the family in the fulfillment of its mission, since no other institution or group can replace the family.

- The importance of the ways families can be helped or hindered in fulfilling their mission by each institution of society, including the Church.

- The importance of sensitivity to the impact of the family on the individual receiving ministry, and the impact of a changed individual on his or her family.

Because of this commitment of the bishops of the U.S. and the whole Church to marriage and family life, the Church is now more aware, in the words of Vatican II's Decree on the Laity,[9] of the family "as the first and vital cell of society." Thus we have begun, through the implementation of the Pastoral Plan, to promote a family perspective in our Church. But it remains for us to address this urgent task more systematically.

I do not focus in this chapter on the ways the Commission on Marriage and Family Life recommends to more systematically incorporate this family perspective in the Church's ministries. I seek to present new approaches for understanding the family in the Church. But I recommend the Commission paper for your reading and meditation so you can think about how we can begin to address this formidable but important task.

The Bishops of the United States who wish to get a copy of the Commission Paper may do so by contacting the Family Life Office of their Diocese. The Bishops of Canada, Mexico and Central America may obtain a copy by writing:

Rev. Thomas Lynch, Representative for Family Life
Executive Secretary, Commission on
   Marriage and Family Life
The National Conference of Catholic Bishops
1312 Massachusetts Avenue, N.W.
Washington, D.C. 20005
U.S.A.

Notes

1. U.S. Catholic Conference. *Familiaris Consortio: The Papal Exhortation on the Family.* Washington, D.C., 1981.

2. U.S. Catholic Conference. *The Plan of Pastoral Action for Family Ministry: A Vision and a Strategy.* Washington, D.C., 1978.

3. U.S. Catholic Conference. *The Role of the Christian Family in the Modern World: The 1980 Synod of Bishops.* Washington, D.C., 1980.

4. U.S. Catholic Conference. *A Charter of the Rights of the Family.* Washington, D.C., 1983.

5. *The (Revised) Code of Canon Law.* Vatican City, 1983.

6. This definition of the term family is one developed and used by The Family Impact Seminar, various publications, 1977-1985. Washington, D.C.: The Catholic University of America, The Family Impact Seminar, The National Center for Family Studies.

7. National Catholic Educational Association. *That They May Know You.* Washington, D.C., 1982.

8. *American Catholic Family.* "Family and Parish: Historical Tension?" Washington, D.C.: The Catholic University of America, The National Center for Family Studies, Vol. I, No. 2, pp. 1, 10-11, September, 1982.

9. Abbot, Walter M., ed. *The Documents of Vatican II.* "The Decree on the Laity." New York: Association Press, 1966.

Chapter 5

Pastoral Concerns Regarding The Family Today

PART I — DISCUSSION WITH MONSIGNOR CAFFARRA

Question: A tension exists between what you are saying to us this morning and what Dr. McCready was saying to us last night. Dr. McCready was suggesting that we as Bishops must pay much more attention to the human experience of our people, and from their experience get some sense about how we should pastor our flocks. Your orientation this morning appeared to us to take a more deductive approach, namely, the design which God has for the family and how we as pastors should then deal with our own flocks accordingly. Thus there seems to be a tension between induction and deduction in our attempts to pastor our families. We felt that perhaps you tended to neglect the human exprience, and that perhaps Dr. McCready last night tended to neglect the theological principles. How would you bring these two together?

Monsignor Caffarra: I think that this is a most important question. For me, the separation, so to speak, of ethical and theological reflection on the truth of man from discussions which go on in sociology and psychology is all for nothing. Such a separation makes no sense and serves no purpose. It comes from thinking about the truth about man as if that truth were some idea abstracted or separated out from the human person himself or herself. The truth about man is mistakenly treated as something outside of man. But the truth of man is nothing else but the human person himself or herself. The truth about the human being *is* the human being himself or herself. When we speak about the "the truth of man", we are not speaking of some kind of divine blueprint in the mind of God showing how the human person *might* be structured and built. To the contrary, when we speak of the "truth of man" we are speaking of man himself, as he *really is.*

The Church does not teach us an ideal about man and the family, but the *truth* about man and the family — the way man and the family are *de facto* made. In some of this teaching of the Church we have real ethical criteria and guidance regarding society, culture, etc.

Also another reflection: Is there a relation between the study of a culture in sociology on the one hand, and the "truth of man" on the other? Yes, I think so. Not only is there such a relation, but for us as pastors it is an important relation. For we must judge any culture or society as to whether they are in accordance with the truth and goodness which is the human person.

When I talked about the "essentially human experience" I was referring to something very, very simple. It means precisely what anybody experiences in himself when he asks about: a) What is the meaning of existence? b) What is good and what is bad? (that is, an ethical experience) c) Why do I exist? d) Where do I come from? To ask such questions is to have the "essentially human experience." If psychology does not understand that these are most important human questions, I don't know how such a psychology can be of any possible use. For every human person — not merely the intellectual who has studied Plato or theology, but any and every human person who is simply *alive as a human person* asks: What is the meaning of human experience? If such questions did not have to or could not be answered, the mission of the Church would be absolutely useless, because there is no meaning to Jesus' having preached his Gospel. If the human person does not have his own truth, he or she does not need to be saved by a Redeemer. There is nothing to save.

Sociology and psychiatry center on important facts, but the facts which they study are only on the surface The questions they ask are only about numbers. But the "essentially human experience" is not one of being simply a number.

Question: Regarding the identity and definition of a family, you said that the husband-wife community becomes a family community only through the act of procreation. But is not the husband-wife community already a family community, whether or not God grants children to that community?

Monsignor Caffarra: I think that it is safe to say that, in every culture, when we speak of a family community, we mean husband and wife and child. The husband-wife community is not yet a family community, but only a conjugal community. If in a neighborhood newly-weds with no children move into a house, people say: "A new couple has moved into that house." They are not inclined to say: "A new family has moved in." Moreover, if a couple with children move into a house, people are not inclined to say: "A couple has moved in," but "A family has moved in." And so for purposes of clarity I prefer to keep this natural distinction.

But I think also a very important point is involved in this question. For the husband-wife community exists intrinsically in order to become a family community — for procreation, for children. Conjugal love expressed in the physical act designed specifically to express it is, in its own profound nature, a cooperation with and openness to the creative act of God. So though I prefer to distinguish the husband-wife community from the family community, the distinction does not mean a separation.

Question: In the framework of the human family, the human person is born and in a certain sense the truth is born. We had a concern about the human person who is created by God, but from a union which is not a marriage. God has given the gift of the human person to this parent, but is not this human person part of a family?

Monsignor Caffarra: The tragic fact that a human person is born outside a husband-wife community shows simply that human beings can dissent from God's design — that is, dissent from what they *are*. For the human person can dissent from God's design for and in himself or herself. Only the husband-wife community is the place in which the human person may be begotten in a way faithful to our humanity. For only this community has the sanctity for the great act of God, the creation of a human person. That sanctity is centered in the lifelong love which the conjugal act is meant to express. But the human person can dissent from that design of God's.

Question: We speak about "the truth about man" from God's point of view, and we draw our knowledge of this truth from revelation and faith. For instance, it is by faith that we teach the dignity of the human person, because the person has a spirit imbued by God and that is what makes the human person unique. We know that because of our faith. It is part of revelation.

Our people, however, sometimes have a difficulty with the conclusions which we have drawn from the principles which we have established from our interpretation of revelation and of human nature. For instance, you spoke about God's knowing and willing a person into existence. Our people have a difficult time undersanding that, because a new human existence can happen through incest, rape, and unwanted teenage pregnancy. Does God will a new human life into existence through incest, rape, or unwanted teenage pregnancy? You can interpret that in terms of "It's God's will," of course, — and I heard also your answer before that it is God's human instruments who foul up the process. But that doesn't always satisfy our people, because there seems to be some kind of contradiction here. They say: your theological conclusions don't seem to jibe with our experience of what we see and understand and feel. I wonder, then, whether this is not the reason for some of the social data we have on our people and their problems and difficulties with the Church's teachings. Perhaps it is simply not all that clear to them that we are interpreting God's plan rightly, because our interpretation seems to them contradictory.

Monsignor Caffarra: The Church has two great problems in theology. One is the contradiction between the theological conclusions we draw and life itself. This contradiction is precisely the sign of dissent between God and man, and demonstrates not that the Doctrine of the Faith is untrue regarding man, but that man can dissent from God's design. And so in these situations the problem is not to measure the truth of God by the ability of the human person. It is rather to save, redeem, and liberate the human person from these terrible situations in which the human person does not consent to God's design.

But the question is more difficult than that. For the Church has a twofold challenge: a) to penetrate into the meaning and obtain a more profound knowledge of God's design for marriage and the family; b) to be a teacher, here and now, of human persons. *These* human persons, then, and *these* truths. Sociology and psychology can help the pastors of the Church. By their research, we pastors can know the situation of these persons better and so plan our pastoral action. This challenge can be resolved precisely through a strong witness both to God and to the "truth about man". For this truth is not — I repeat — something up in the clouds, but it *is* the human person himself. The human person *is* "the truth of man." We Catholics and pastors can speak to the heart of the human person. At times, is the human person unable to hear us because of the profound nature of the "truth about man?" Of course!

Question: We had some difficulty, as everyone else did, with last night's talk about the sociological approach, our people's experience, and how we as pastors should deal with that experience. That approach does not seem to show regard for the Word of God and the design of God which must be preached. But, then, as we preach it, we give the impression that we are judging those that have an experience opposed to what the Word of God proclaims. Still, as one of the bishops remarked, the Word of God itself judges and, in judging, saves.

We were wondering about something else, too. Sociology deals with the majority experience. But what about the *anawim,* those who seem to be associated, all the way through salvation history, with the Word of God and the design of God? The charismatic communities — are they not the *anawim?* In one bishop's Word of God community, there has been not a single divorce in ten years. The Mormons and Mennonites are renowed for their family life stability. What about the couples who are concerned about Natural Family Planning, and what great things it has done for them and their family life? All these are remnant groups in the Scriptural sense of the term. But often they do not find support from bishops and priests. Is this not a world-wide problem that we must face as pastors?

Monsignor Caffarra: I am entirely in agreement. ''Perfettamente d'accordo.''

Question: Regarding the contrast between Dr. McCready and Monsignor Caffarra, perhaps their presentations are complementary rather than contradictory if we don't look to the sociologist to determine what is the ''truth about man'' and what it means to be true to one's self as a human person, but rather to tell us how truth is transmitted. I think also that what hasn't been brought out — in terms of what Dr. Glick said — is that there has been a tremendous upheaval in values in my short life-span, basically in the lifetime of many of us. It is this upheaval that makes possible a wide acceptance of divorce, premarital sex, etc. It seems that people's outlook was changed, not apodictically but in an *a priori* way, — more in the way Dr. McCready was talking about it last night, namely, by floating ideas through stories and experiences. People's attitudes change by what they see on TV and read in books, by what they see people doing a block away, rather than by argumentation. You cannot really argue logically, for example, for premarital sex.

Perhaps it is possible for us to put together a more comprehensive teaching if we combine Scripture, theology, the Magisterium and experience. That's the way Jesus taught: he told stories; he wept over Jerusalem. We need it all as a package. Our responsibility is to stress more the traditional values of family and parenthood, so that they are seen, not only by Catholic families but by all, as valid options in society. On television you don't see more than 2 or 3 families in situations which are really normal. You don't see young men or women who are fighting to preserve the virtue of chastity. To make that believable, people need to see it reflected in real situations about real life.

Questions: Should we expend our energies on preserving the nuclear families or on healing the broken ones?

Monsignor Caffarra: Both. Defend and prevent the disintegration of families which are still healthy, and reconstitute destroyed families which have been ravaged or destroyed. On the first point, the family must be defended more than ever today against contraception and abortion. These kill the family community, as I said. This community is constituted by the meeting between God's creative love and the couple's procreational love, and thus contraception and abortion destroy this meeting of love and destroy the family community.

PART II — DISCUSSION WITH DOCTOR GLICK

Question: Dr. Glick, in many cases divorces are not sought until well after the marriage has broken up, so that the number of divorces in a particular year may not have the same indications or same implications. Are there any statistics on the break-up of marriages, so that you might determine in a particular year what the effect of the present way of life is?

Dr. Glick: Well, there are separations that don't result in divorce. A small fraction of them, but maybe as many as 20%, become reconciled so that these couples do not have divorces. People who live together without being married and then split up also do not contribute to divorce statistics. Maybe the divorce level would be even higher if these people had married and then split up after marrying. So the numbers that we cite are limited in their scope.

Question: We have some questions that we would propose to Dr. Glick to comment on any item if he would. Recent trends seem almost universally contrary to what the Church would consider healthy. Are there any trends that the Church would consider positive or hopeful? Secondly, do Catholics or the Catholic family generally follow the changing trends of a nation or a culture with regard to say abortion, or divorce, or contraception, or weekly Mass attendance? And thirdly, what are the major forces in a society that really shape the changing cultural and social trend? And how would you rate the impact of the Church in that framework?

Dr. Glick: Indications on the positive side are a little hard to find, but the fact that people are getting married at an older age should mean that they are more mature at the time of marriage and that should make for more marital stability. On the other hand, the same people perhaps may have more experience these days than others with marriage-like behavior before they get married and there is a question as to what effect that might have on their ultimate degree of marital stability.

The major force that seems to impact on marriage, it seems to me, is the increase in education which tends to reduce the average student's attachment to traditional ways of thinking. The impact of the Church on the young Americans may be less than it used to be. This means that young people are more responsible on their own for what they do, and many of them make errors.

There are statistics on the changing adherence of Catholics to what are regarded as ordinary Catholic attitudes on family practices. There tends to be a convergence towards the same level as non-Catholics on matters like contraception, abortion and sterilization, but in each case the Catholics still have a more traditional point of view expressed in their behavior. It's just a matter that there's less difference now than there used to be. I don't see any recent statistics that show an increasing divergence as compared with the non-Catholics.

Question: The gap between what the Church believes and teaches and actual family practices given by the sociologists is a tremendous cause of pastoral concern for us. Part of the problem depends upon how one views the Church. The ecclesiology, for example, of the Church as being a sort of a club with the bishops as part of the bureaucracy seems to weaken Church authority. It seems that a lot of our people are flocking to fundamentalist Churches which are in fact very absolutist and authoritarian. Can Dr. Glick give us an insight as to whether people from fundamentalist Churches that are very absolutist and authoritarian have greater stability in their marriages?

Dr. Glick: Largely through my efforts the Census Bureau asked a question on religion in 1957. We had hoped to update that information in 1977, which would have been 20 years later, to see the changes that have taken place, but the people who made the decision decided that it was too controversial and that they would not go further in that direction. So the Census Bureau just doesn't ask questions about religion.

From the earlier study there was a definite indication that people with religions that were more fundamentalist were more strict about marriage stability and they had larger families. I should not personally be surprised if that same pattern tends to persist. But remember we have communication media now that reach everybody. This tends to diminish the ability of people with a certain point of view to pass that type of view to their own offspring or to the members of their organizations, so perhaps the fundamentalists are tending to be somewhat less identifiable than they used to be. All religions are tending to come closer together.

Question: Invited to this workshop are Bishops from the northern part of North America, meaning Canada, and also Central

America and the Caribbean. Does Dr. Glick have anything to offer them by way of data on the family in their respective countries?

Dr. Glick: Some time ago, I heard one Canadian expert express a rather apt answer to the question about Canadians. He said, give us about 10 years and we'll have the same patterns that you have in the United States. There has been a parallel change but with somewhat of a time lag. Our own statistics about Hispanics in the United States show that they have much more family solidarity, lower divorce rates, higher fertility rates and the like. Although I'm not a student of the Central American countries themselves, there is this kind of information about those who have moved to the United States. In the Caribbean, there are, of course, have large numbers of people who have children outside marriage. So there's a wide range from the Caribbean through the United States up into Canada.

PART III — DISCUSSION WITH DOCTOR SOLDO AND FATHER PREISTER

Question: We would like to know what percentage of elderly people are in nursing homes, and what percentage of older people live below the poverty line? Has any research been done concerning the treatment of older people who remain in their homes?

Dr. Soldo: At any point in time about 5% of all elderly are in a nursing home. However, it makes a lot more sense for planning both in the parish as well as on a national level to talk in terms of what are your lifetime odds of being in a nursing home? Here it's much higher, although we have quibbles among ourselves in gerontology as to who has the best way of estimating these lifetime probabilities. Nonetheless most of us can agree that at birth probably each individual has about 1 in 2 chance of spending some time in a nursing home. At age 65 this increases to about 3 out of 4 chances of spending some time in a nursing home. Now that may seem to be quite discrepant with the tone of what I said above. But, it's very compatible. The typical sequence or pattern is for an older person needing assistance to be cared for in the community by their family. But no family has unlimited emotional, psychological or financial resources. At some point in time, they're likely to literally "burn out." At that point often the nursing home admission is precipitated. My concern is how to provide the necessary kinds of services and support and Church involvement to forestall that burn-out period.

Secondly, the latest statistics indicate that about 15% of all the elderly in the U.S. are in poverty. However, poverty rates are much higher among the very old, (85 and older), much higher among black elderly, and much higher among women. The overall statistic basically reflects the higher retirement incomes of typically younger white males (60-69), many of whom are still working or drawing on a time-limited pension.

Thirdly, regarding the treatment of older people in their own home, there has been considerable research to estimate what are the unmet needs of the elderly both in the community as well as in the nursing home. What we find is that the more the family's involved, the fewer the unmet needs. Also, the more extensive the needs, the more likely there are to be unmet needs. This would include a situation where an older person had intensive care needs, for example, because of incontinence. In that situation, perhaps all the family can do is to meet the basic, physical needs and hence neglect the emotional or the affective needs for the intimacy that characterizes the parent/child bond. There is considerable research about both environmental and service supports to sustain the older person in the home.

Question: How can we as Bishops be advocates for the elderly out on the parish level and in their relationship to government aid or government housing?

Dr. Soldo: One approach is to infuse all aspects of parish ministry with concern for family. I would even include in this introducing concerns of the family into the ministry of the laity. The reduced clerical capacity of the parish presents an interesting opportunity to reinvolve the laity in the life of the parish. Often you have talents within the local parish that can be mobilized, whether it's simply the availability of someone to parent-sit one afternoon a week and give that care-giver predictable time off, or the availability of a retired nurse who can educate a care-giver dealing with a catheter situation. I firmly believe that the parish is the ideal unit for this because only they know the local differences and variations.

Question: We would like Fr. Preister to be more specific. You mentioned that there's not a need for new programs but how can we bring to bear our efforts right now on family life to make it better? What can we do more to improve family life?

Fr. Preister: I don't mean that there's no need for no new programs. Obviously, there are areas that we need to address that we don't presently address. But I think the larger concern that we have is how can we be doing more to support family life in a diocese or in a parish? From my point of view, one of the essential things that we need to do is to make sure we do not convey the attitutde that the pastoral care of families or programs for families emanate only from Catholic Charities or from the Family Life Office. For example, the Religious Education Office is a family ministry and the Office of Evangelization is a family ministry. Each of those Offices, both on a diocesan level and on a parish level, should look at what they do and how they do it from the perspective of the family. They should put on the "family lens". When we're planning the sex education program for the Catholic schools, we should look at how we could involve parents in the design of that program and how we can involve them when the program is actually in effect. If the children are learning at both at home and in school, it will be a potent combination.

The important thing is not to segregate care for families to one office or one ministry, but to help all the ministries look at the family. Some dioceses have done this in different ways. Some are advocating, for example, conducting a family impact study, where each department uses a process called family impact assessment to look to how they do their ministry and to look for unintended consequences on families. Other dioceses, for example, have established a family commission, where every ministry of the diocese meets together to look at their ministries to families from the perspective of what they do and how it impacts on families. So there are different vehicles for doing it, but the important thing is that this is a responsibility for the whole Church, not just the Family Life Director.

Question: Is it possible that we can agree on a definition of the family?

Fr. Preister: The White House Conference on Families that was held in 1978 got a lot of bad press, although there were some very useful things that came out of it. One of the things that was not useful was their attempt to define family. They got into such a battle that there was a question whether the Conference would continue.

The United States is the only industrialized Western nation that does not have an explicit family policy. Why is it, for example, that the French, or the Swedish, or the British, should have an explicit family policy and the United States does not?

The reason, from my point of view, is because we are so diverse. We come from many, many ethnic traditions. To the Chinese, the word family includes one's ancestors. To the WASP, the family is a husband and wife and two children. To the Italian, the family is collateral and includes aunts and uncles and non-relatives who are given the titles of aunts and uncles. Each of us inside of us know qualitatively what the word family means because we have experienced family. But it is very difficult to find a definition that everybody in the Untied States will be willing to accept.

But what we can accept is that when people are related by blood, marriage, or adoption, whether they live in the same house or not, there is a bond there that is worth preserving and fostering. And that unit has a mission in Christian theology and Christian faith. I don't want to get hung up on the definition because I think our own personal experience is so potent that it gets in the way of coming to a consensus in such a pluralistic country as ours. But I don't want to define the word family so broadly that we use it analogously, meaning that a friendship is a family, or that a parish is a family.

Question: Just a comment on that last statement. As I recall the big debate at the Washington Conference, it was over the attempt to include homosexuals living together under the title of family. I am sure that we disagree with that approach.

I have a question though, which may be related to the theme of pervasive individualism. The preference seems to be growing for diocesan priests to live by themselves in a rectory or elsewhere, with some strongly insisting on that. Is there any study of that phenomenon? How would you see it as affecting their approach to the issue of individualism versus family?

Fr. Preister: I'm not sure I would take it simply on face value as a sign of this excessive individualism we have in our country. If you look at, for example, the life cycle of an adult today in the United States, most American adults will live alone for a portion of their adulthood, so in that context maybe it's not abnormal or maybe it's not a sign of kind of a rugged individualism among the clergy. I would think, though, that clergy, like all others, have need for affiliation and support, whether they live alone or whether they live in groups.

Question: I have two questions. The first is the whole question of long term consistent commitment? Will that be there to take care of the elderly? Sometimes we wonder if there's enough long term commitment to make a marriage today. Will it be there to look after the older people later on and how do you teach that or how do you try to bring that about?

Secondly, turning it around from the other end, is there any way of teaching people to know how to be old? Can you practice to be old while you are young? Can the Church teach people as they're growing older how to handle the advancing of age?

Dr. Soldo: You are asking whether or not within the present young generation, the young adults in their 20's are going to be able to sustain long-range commitments whether to spouses or to parents? My understanding of what data we do have speaks to this very clearly in the affirmative. However, when you talk about family and relationships, you've got to be careful to make some distinctions between form and function. Yes, the sense of obligation is there. But, whether or not their obligation will be exercised in this same way as by previous generations, we can't say. We may see new approaches. Young college students in their courses on aging discuss how they as a group can plan for and deal with their older parents. You see increasing opportunities for geriatric education in the under-graduate student body. Any number of us regularly teach such courses and they are oversubscribed. There's a curiosity among our young to understand what aging is. One of the things we've accomplished in the last ten years is to role back the taboo about talking about aging and about death. We are laying a firm foundation for commitment and concern to continue across succeeding generations.

What can the Church do? Can you teach people to be old and age gracefully? Some of the principles that I'm going to suggest may seem mere common sense. Many of our research efforts to understand what human aging is all about come to the following two conclusions.

1) Aging is not disease, you do not necessarily "treat" aging. There is a new emphasis on learning just how to distinguish between what's pathological and what's normal in aging. Is it normal for an old person to be depressed? If you say yes, you're not going to treat the depression aggressively, and if you don't aggressively treat, you're going to potentially doom the older person to additional years of depression.

2) We have learned that for every vital medical system, we must apply the principle: "use it or lose it." This involves exercise, and keeping cognitively alert, involved, and active. We must present opportunities for the elderly and, especially the young old, to sustain the intensity of their involvement they have as workers. The United States is different from the rest of the world in lots of ways, and one of the ways that we are different is that retirement in this country is abrupt. You wake up a worker one morning and the next morning you're not a worker. Many of the European countries, for example, have programs that gradually allow for transition out of the labor force. On that morning you wake up as a non-worker, how do you structure your time? That's an opportunity for

the parish, I think, to become involved again.

Fr. Preister: I see no reduction in people's willingness to commit themselves to each other, but for people to make that commitment, say to our parents or to the elderly, there's also got to be an issue of the support that's needed. The traditional caretakers of dependents in our society have been women. But 60% of all women with children are employed outside the home today. Now, if a woman chooses to have children, she faces two situations: 1) she has employment and 2) she has the care of the young dependent. But with the lengthening of life, she's going to face the care of her elderly parents as well. By and large, that commitment is there, but it will burn out fast with no support.

We do not support it well in this country. First, in terms of policy there is not financial remuneration for home care if a family wants to take care of their elderly. Reimbursement will pay for a nursing home but will not pay family members. Secondly, by and large, the research is pretty clear that there's no support for the women from other family members. Husbands, by and large, have not made the adjustment that for women employed outside the home they now have two jobs, not just one. They have their employment plus they have the care of the dependents. So if you expect the family to maintain that commitment to an aging parent, you have to look at some better ways of supporting the family to help them maintain it.

With regard to research, there was some done out at the University of Maryland asking young children, pre-school children, what is their conception of old people? By and large, they conceived of old people as monsters, because they have never met one. Now, for myself whose grandma is one of the most important people in my life, that's a very sad thing to hear. We have age-segregated our society: Our parishes can be places where young children and old people can be together for mutual benefit. That's teaching aging.

Dr. Soldo: I just want to mention two additional points. One is that in considering the role of women and their dual and sometimes triple burden, it's important to understand that the vast majority of women work out of economic need, not out of some desire to buy themselves expensive clothes. The second point, in my opinion, is that families don't need financial reimbursement for care giving, they're not looking for that. They're not looking for tax breaks even. What they're looking for are services supportive of them, which is somewhat different than services that meet the needs of the older impaired person him or herself. And it's important that you come away with an understanding of those distinctions.

Question: We have a problem, a practical problem: the Church must be careful not to take family members out of the home every night of the week. How do you prudently involve members of the family and at times the entire family in Church life and not burden that individual family?

Fr. Preister: I had a member of a family say to me once it would help to hear from the pulpit that it's okay if you all sit down and decide what you can be involved in and what you can't be involved in. I think just telling families that that's an issue and you know it's an issue is a helpful thing to do. We're not the only ones facing this problem, you know. The Mormons have a family home night, and I understand they had to just renew that policy because it was not being followed. We all deal with this, everybody's very busy.

Question: The dilemma, Dr. Soldo, of the single parent increases in our country. If this trend continues, how then would you project the assistance coming from a single parent towards an aged mother or father? What is the projection or the data on hand pertaining to single parents now helping their elderly parent and what would you project in the next ten years, since we're able to project at least for 5 to 10 years right now?

Dr. Soldo: The data that I'm familiar with suggests that those single parents, again typically mothers, are somehow managing to juggle their own work schedules, the care needs of their parents, and attention to their child. Our data on this point is somewhat difficult to interpret though, because if households combine, if grandma moves in with the adult daughter and her child, there are any number of benefits that accrue to that single parent. There is an adult to talk to when you come home at night. There are services available, for example, babysitting.

93

There also will be available what economists call "economies of scale." When the two adults, the one widowed and now the other divorced, combine households and income, they stave off some of the financial implications of single parenting. So we have some very rough cut data to suggest that, for whatever reasons, the aged parent's single daughters are responding to many of the same of care needs as married daughters.

But this raises another interesting issue: the relationship of children coming from splintered families to grandparents and great-grandparents. In the near future many adult children will have not only surviving parents but also stepparents. These individuals might have obligations to 6 or 8 older adults. How do we choose among them? Is obligation based only on biology? Is it the parent or parent figure with whom a child lives most of their young life? We're just beginning to ask these questions. This is an issue that public policy as well as the Church will be confronting in the next 10 to 15 years.

Question: You said that aging is a fact of life and that aging begins at birth. Taking into consideration the position of the Church on life, is it not more accurate to say that aging begins at conception?

Dr. Soldo: To be internally consistent in our argument, you would certainly need to make that adjustment.

Question: We are wondering whether or not the Church must, in its outlook and in its acceptance, be prepared to care for the family situation which we do not perhaps canonically recognize as a marriage? Take the case of the divorced man with another woman and children and his former wife with another husband and children. Should we be concerned about such things as, for example, facilitating visiting rights between the children of one and the other where perhaps the children feel very uncomfortable going to see their father now because there is a stepmother there who does not recognize them or does not accept them too well?

Fr. Preister: Well, you raised a very, very crucial area, divorce is so pervasive in our society that there's not one of us here, at least from the United States, whose families have not been touched by divorce. We follow the saying of Jesus that marriage is permanent, and we can't change that saying. I do not want to advocate for change in the divorce laws of the Church. I think, for example, that even on a societal level there's so much that encourages people to split when they encounter difficulty, that we need institutions that say "try to work in out". But with that given in mind, I think we've also got to deal with the realities of families that have experienced divorce.

First of all, on the level of the children, one of the largest emotional issues that children have to face to successfully weather the divorce that parents are going through, is to come to understand and experience and believe that while the adults may be divorcing as partners, they are not divorcing their children. If they don't experience that, the divorce can be very, very developmentally tramatic. One of the major difficulties we have is that the divorce process in this country is such an adversarial process that it encourages the altercation that already exists through the break of the relationship. What we can be doing in the Church is to really be working more when couples inevitably have to divorce to encourage, for example, mediation, so that both parents can participate in the parenting of the children, so there is visitation. We must help the parents cooperate as parents, even if they are not going to continue to be married partners.

The other area which is crucial is the area of marriage preparation. Eighty percent of all men and women in the United States who divorce will remarry. Men usually marry within 2 years, women usually within 4 years. Now generally there are children involved. Second marriages are now failing at a faster rate than first marriages. Now whether or not that first marriage has gone through an annulment and whether or not they are seeking the sacramental marriage, if we hope those children will be raised as Christians, is there something we can do in a pastoral sense to help prepare these people for marriage? The research is pretty clear that marriage preparation will help them avoid some of the problems and pitfalls. But if we lump people who are remarrying into the first marriage preparation programs, that's not going to help them. They've got unique issues. If we have a marriage preparation program for people who are remarrying, is it for only those people who have gone through annulment? Is there some sort of pastoral practice that we could evolve to help the others without condoning divorce? I don't know how to do that, but I know the kids are there, and if those families are cut off, the kids will be cut off too.

PART II:
INSTITUTIONS
AND THE FAMILY

OVERVIEW
OF PART II

Part II of this volume explores the way modern families relate with the Church and society (Chapter 6), public policy and the law (Chapter 7), education (Chapter 8), and the health care community (Chapter 9). The final chapter offers dialogue between the four chapter authors and the Bishops who attended the Workshop.

Father Ashley's penetrating analysis in Chapter 6 points out that the personalist approach to marriage and the family used by Pope John Paul II should not be identified with the individualist and superficial approach which some humanist experts identify as "personalism." Father Ashley calls for a clear recognition of the difference between a (secular) humanist and a Christian understanding of marriage and family.

Professor Destro in Chapter 7 first explores the problem of defining the family and then outlines several models of family-state relations that have emerged in the legislative and judicial arena. He voices his ultimate concern that we find a "trend toward respect for the family as a unit only when it serves the specific policy purposes of the legislative or judicial decision-maker."

In Chapter 8, Dr. D'Avignon writes both as a mother and as an educational psychologist. She voices considerable concern that Post-Vatican II trends in catechetics have neglected the doctrinal content of religious education in favor of an approach which might be called "naturalism." She describes this in the sections on "Secularization of Values" and the "Loss of the Sacred."

Dr. Pellegrino chooses the theme of stewardship for his discussion of family health in Chapter 9. He emphasizes that health care "in" the family and among its individual members needs to be linked with health care "of" the family as a unit. Healthy families, he suggests, will have healthy members.

Chapter 10 presents the pastoral concerns raised with the four chapter authors. In all cases the family is seen in interaction with the institutions in which it participates.

Chapter 6

The Family in Church and Society

The Reverend Benedict M. Ashley, O.P., Ph.D.

When Was the Sexual Revolution?

The brilliant historian of the family, Edward Shorter, has argued that the so-called "Sexual Revolution" of the 1960's was only the completion of a more fundamental sexual revolution that took place over two hundred years earlier in about 1750. At that time, he writes:[1]

There was an enormous rise in illegitimacy and pre-marital pregnancy in the years of the French and Industrial revolutions. Late in the eighteenth century, the number of out-of-wedlock pregnancies began to skyrocket in virtually every community we know about, often reaching three or four times the previous level. In case after case, from interior Massachusetts to the Alpine uplands of Oberbayern, the number of infants conceived before marriage increased markedly. Indeed this is one of the central phenomena of modern demographic history.

Between 1850-1940 this trend was partially reversed but in the 1960's resumed. Shorter believes it will continue and marks an irreversible change in the structure of the family.

Whatever the value of Shorter's predictions, his identification of this historic trend up to the present seems certain. What are the causes of this trend? Shorter himself suggests many causes of an economic and psychological order, but says little of a dominant influence which, from a theological viewpoint, is the most significant. The date 1750 coincides with the full emergence of an ideology which is usually called the Enlightenment, but which I have elsewhere[2] argued is really a new rival of the Christian religion comparable to Islam, which has never adopted a name for itself, but which is most appropriately called "Humanism."

Humanism is a world-view and value-system, originating in the European intelligentsia's disillusionment with Christianity as a result of the religious wars between Catholics and Protestants and within the Protestant camp, which placed its faith and hope in the power of scientific human reason and creativity independent of God. Too often it is identified with "modernism" or "secularization" as if these were simply developments within the Christian tradition, when in fact Humanism is a complete system of life which today serves a large part of the world's population as its "religion", as does Marxism, both in direct competition with the traditional world religions. Hence it should not be surprising that the rise of Humanism in Europe and America was quickly felt in a new attitude to sexuality and the family very different than that of the Christian Church, since all religions are concerned with the sources of life and the meaning of death.

The Christian View of Sexuality and the Family

In his Apostolic Exhortation *Familiaris Consortio*[3] John Paul II has synthesized in a remarkable way all the teaching of previous

102

magisterial documents on sexuality and the family by showing that, according to God's own revelation, He has designed the family to fulfill five closely inter-related functions in the service of true human happiness.[4]

1) *Out of love* God created us in his own image *for love.* As God's love is creative, so our love also must be co-creative — fertile. Although it can be either biologically fertile as in sexual love, or only spiritually fertile as in celibate love, in both cases it must be co-creative, because love is essentially the gift of self — of the totality of the person. Thus the fundamental purpose of sexuality and of the family is *self-giving, life-giving* love after the image of God revealed to us in its plenitude in Jesus Christ wed to his Church, fruitful for the salvation of all humankind.

2) From this fertile, self-giving love flows the second function of the family which is the forming of the *basic community of human persons,* whose heart is a man and a woman permanently and exclusively committed to each other, and which completes itself in children and in the linkage of one generation to another. The unity of this community is not merely functional or external, but is a personal union whose purpose is the enhancement of the life of each member and the right of all, including that of the woman, the children, the elderly.

3) This community of persons united in self-giving love does not exist merely for its own brief time, but in the *service of life,* that is, in the preservation and expansion of the human community in space and time, by the generosity to beget children and to educate them to maturity. This education of children is more than a biological fertility since it is a spiritual motherhood and fatherhood that extends beyond the family to many forms of life-giving and affirming in which the dedicated celibate also shares, since it is a building of the Reign of God.

4) Out of this loving service of life through self-giving comes the *development of organized human society* of which the family is the life-cell. The family forms in each of the members of that society the values by which it lives a common life and the respect for the rights of each without which that society becomes oppressive and self-destructive. Therefore families must maintain their rights in the face of oppressive national states and international forces.

5) The Christian family has been called by God to a special role in the *life and mission of the Church* through which the true message of God's love is communicated to the world. It is through the family that this faith is handed on and can be spread through word and example to others, and it is in the family that the worship of God through prayer goes on daily in an especially effective way. Thus it is first of all in the family that God's great commandment of love is realized at the very heart of Christian living.

The Paradox

The beauty of John Paul's vision is beyond question and its firm foundation in Scripture and Tradition can be demonstrated, although I will not attempt that here. If, however, we compare this Christian model of the family with its actual historical realizations, a striking paradox appears. In the frequent New Testament exhortations to family harmony[5] we can detect a good deal of actual conflict. According to some feminist authors,[6] what was going on was a gradual compromising of Gospel ideals of equal respect for persons to conform to the oppressively patriarchal structure of the pagan Greco-Roman family. In the patristic period patriarchalism, they say, won out. In the Middle Ages the evidence shows that the Christian ideal was further distorted by the tribal customs inherited from barbarism and the extended family interests fostered by feudalism.[7] Finally, as Shorter shows in the work I have already quoted,[8] the "traditional family" as it predominated in Europe and colonial America between 1500 and 1750 was something quite different than the Christian model of John Paul II.

As Shorter describes it, this "traditional family", although it did conform to the Christian model in its *permanency* and its *exclusivity* (at least on the part of the woman) was not at all based on "love" as in the Christian model but on *economic* motives. The couple did not marry because they loved each other, nor was there much more than physical intimacy within marriage. Although reproduction was an important function of traditional marriage, it does not mean that there was much affection of parents for their children, nor even that the parents played a great role in their upbringing. In upper-class families mothers turned their children over to wet-nurses and early sent them away to school; while in peasant families mothers were too hard-working to give their children much attention, infant mortality was very high, and children left home to work at adolescence. Even in Puritan families where there was a very serious attempt to carry out New Testament teachings and a considerable love-mystique prevailed, there was also a very heavy-handed patriarchalism and great severity toward children.

The first sexual revolution, which as I have indicated was fostered by the new value-system of Humanism, was what first made popular our present view that marriage ought to be based on romantic love, that it should be not for the sake of economic or dynastic reasons but from the intimate affection between the couple and for the loving care and prolonged education of the children. But as Shorter also shows,[9] this new idea that sex is for human happiness and loving intimacy, also produced an astonishing increase in extramarital sex and illegitimacy, and eventually contraception, abortion, and divorce. If the purpose of marriage is love, then when love dies and marriage ties become a source of misery, divorce and re-marriage seem the only answer. Moreover, if a couple has children with a view to lavishing love on them and taking a personal part in their prolonged education, then they are likely to insist that they control the number of their children, or exclude them altogether if they cannot care for them under ideal conditions. Thus what underlay the first sexual revolution was Humanism's insistence on the freedom of the individual to control his or her own life in the "pursuit of happiness."

Thus we are faced with a paradox. If Shorter's historical account is essentially correct, then Pope John Paul II's model of Christian marriage seems to be an unrealistic attempt to combine two value systems (neither one of which is really Christian)[10] which in historical reality have stood in sharp opposition. On the one hand the Pope bases his model on a defense of the "traditional family" which was permanent, exclusive, reproduction-oriented, and socially enforced, yet on the other hand he attempts to base this on a characteristically modern, Humanist notion of freely-chosen, intimate, communicative, personalist love between the partners which overflows in a caring, loving, educative attitude

105

toward the children. If Shorter is right, it was just this emphasis on personalistic love which has inevitably led to the break-up of the traditional family and in the future will make it impossible ever to return to that kind of institution again!

Individual, Person and Community

This paradox, although confusing and confounding, can be very illuminating, if we resolve the ambiguity of the terms in which it is stated. The first of these ambiguities is in the term "person." Vatican II and Paul VI insisted on a personalistic anthropology and, as is well known, John Paul II has devoted a great deal of philosophical and theological reflection to clarifying the notion of "the dignity of the person."[11] It is ambiguous because it is used in different ways in a Christian context than in a Humanist one. Generally speaking Humanists mean by "person" the *individual* as an autonomous subject striving for his or own goals against competition with others and restriction by society. As the abortion controversy has made painfully clear, Humanists are wary of any *ontological* definition of the person and insist on a purely functional one.[12] Only those beings are truly persons who can assert their own interests.

In Christian usage, on the other hand, the term "human person" indicates an ontological relatedness of a being, endowed with a spiritual intelligence and free will, to God and neighbor whom it is created to know and love in a temporal and eternal community. It possesses this human nature in its essential relatedness from the first moment of existence long before it can exercise it fully and will arrive at this full exercise only through life in an earthly and a divine, eternal community. To realize one's personhood, therefore, is not to fight free of community restrictions in order to seek one's private happiness, but is to learn to cooperate freely and intelligently in the pursuit of the common good.

The basic structure of the family, consequently, is not a human invention, although it is a task of human invention to adapt it to different historical circumstances and cultural styles. What the Pope has attempted in *Familiaris Consortio* is to define that basic structure, intrinsic to the human person as created in God's image, in its essential relatedness.

106

Love and "Love"

The term "love" in the Pope's usage also has a different meaning from the notion of "romantic love" which in the first sexual revolution of the eighteenth century came to be regarded as the essence of true marriage. Shorter himself maintains that in the second sexual revolution of the 1960's this "romantic love" began to be superseded by a frank emphasis on sensual pleasure as the true meaning of human sexuality[13] — a fact which raises the question whether "romantic love" was merely a mask for hedonism from the beginning. In both revolutions, however, there has been much stress on the notion that unless human sexual union leads to a personal intimacy, a deep level of communication, and what is often called a "responsible relationship" it is not fully satisfying, although it may be good entertainment.

The Pope, however, means by "love", even when he is speaking of sexual love, the Christian *agape* which is self-giving even to the point of sacrifice, that is, the acceptance of suffering and the immolation of one's own autonomous freedom for the sake of another. Such love, of which the Father's sending of his own Son to die for us, and of the Son's acceptance of servanthood and the Cross in order to do the Father's will is the exemplar, must be the source of all Christian action and therefore even of married life in all its earthy domesticity and bodily expression. That is indeed a lofty ideal, but in the humble power of the Incarnation the Pope is confident that it can become a reality even in the lives of poor and simple Christians, because it has been realized countless times in the history of the Christian community. It may be true, as Shorter maintains, that in the "traditional family" in the period 1500 to 1750 the predominant pattern of life was harshly patriarchal and without affection or intimacy or adequate child care, yet the Gospel leaven was still at work and many Christian families achieved something much better than this statistical model.[14]

Child Care

The description given by Shorter of the high infant mortality, the failure of many mothers to nurse their own children, the low level of education, the early age of working, and the harsh methods of discipline prevalent in the traditional family is indeed shocking. We can only be grateful to the sexual revolution for introducing (as perhaps it did) a much greater concern for the rights of the child; although it would seem, as Shorter admits[15] that much of this amelioration is due simply to the rise in the standard of living in developed countries which has made it possible for parents to give their children the kind of care which before they could not, not because of a lack of love but from the harsh lack of means.

Nevertheless there is an ambiguity in the notion of "child care." For John Paul II the parent is not only the source of a child's physical life, nourishment, clothing, shelter, entertainment, and education for self-support, but of the child's *spiritual* life. It is the transmission of the Christian faith and the example of conscientious Christian living which is the highest gift of true love from parent to child. In the modern family it is this gift which may be the last to be thought of. Genuine concern for the transmission of the faith provides an entirely different measure of loving child care than if the adequacy of that care is measured primarily by raising her or him to be a success and a credit to the parents. It also means vicarious suffering and intercessory prayer for the prodigal; as well as for the child's stewardship of talents and for a generous reponse to God's vocation.

More and more we see today under the influence of the Humanist view of life that the child is viewed not so much as an infinitely precious person in its own right, but as a means to satisfy the parents' own needs. When the child is not needed, it is aborted. When the parents are sterile, then a child is obtained by some form of artificial reproduction. The God-designed relation between the love-act of the partners and the completion of this expression of love and the child as its ultimate fruit is being eroded. Even in the traditional family at its worst when the child was thought of as another "hand" for farm work, or as the heir to maintain the family property, the depersonalization of the child was never so complete.

Fatherhood and Motherhood

The traditional family sharply distinguished the male and female roles, and although it gave the woman real power over her own domestic domain, it subordinated her and the children to stern patriarchal control.[16] The individualism of the modern family, on the other hand, has also resulted in greater equality and less rigid definition of family roles. This has been strongly supported by the economic autonomy of married women who have jobs which has freed them from total dependence on their husbands. Hence in the modern family there is no subordination to the father and the roles of man and wife are becoming increasingly interchangeable.

John Paul II also rejects patriarchalism in the sense of essential inequality between man and woman and in the sense of "the oppressive presence of the father, especially where there still prevails the phenomenon of 'machismo,' or a wrong superiority of male perogatives which humiliates women and inhibits the development of healthy family relationships." But nevertheless the Pope does not reject the Pauline doctrine that "the head of every man is Christ; the head of the woman is her husband; and the head of Christ is the Father" (I Cor. 11:3), since he says:[17]

> In revealing and in reliving on earth the very fatherhood of God (Eph. 3:15), a man is called upon to ensure the harmonious and united development of all the members of the family: he will perform this task by exercising generous responsibility for the life conceived under the heart of the mother, by a more solicitous commitment to education, a task he shares with his wife, by work which is never a cause of division in the family but promotes its unity and stability, and by means of the witness he gives of an adult Christian life which effectively introduces the children into the living experience of Christ and the Church.

In other words the Pope does not pass over in silence the fact that the man has by the very nature of his masculine body and his specific biological relation to the reproduction and raising of the child a different role in the family than does his wife, a role which the Scriptures do not hesitate to compare to the relation of the head to the body, but he does not identify this "headship" with oppressive domination but with a Christ-like servanthood. The father is "head" of the family and like God the Father in the sense that he "is called upon to ensure the harmonious and united development of all the members of the family."[18]

The woman as mother of the family also has a specific role which, far from making her the inferior of her husband, constitutes her as his complementary equal. One has only to read John Paul II's conferences, *Original Unity of Man and Woman: Catechesis on the Book of Genesis*[19] to see how profoundly the Pope, making use of current exegesis, phenomenological philosophy, and Jungian psychology, has reflected on the dignity of woman in the divine scheme of things. His own great personal devotion to the Mother of God, the New Eve manifest in all his writings and preaching, has made him acutely sensitive to the mystery of femininity. In *Familiaris Consortio* he says:[20]

> There is no doubt that the equal dignity and responsibility of men and women fully justifies women's access to public functions. On the other hand the true advancement of women requires that clear recognition be given to the value of their maternal and family role, by comparison with all other public roles and all other professions. Furthermore, these roles and professions should be harmoniously combined, if we wish the evolution of society and culture to be truly and fully human.

Thus the Pope affirms the rights of women equally with men to occupational and political choice, but insists that this includes the right of women to choose to devote themselves full time to the work of motherhood which has equal dignity to other forms of work. For this reason the Pope supports the "family wage" and also the recognition of mothers for their domestic labors.[21]

The Christian model of the family, therefore, should not be identified with the patriarchalism of the traditional family anymore than with the spurious, amorphous androgeneity of the modern family. In the Christian family the roles are clearly but not rigidly distinguished because they are defined by a mutual dialogue of man and woman in which each discovers his and her true masculine and feminine self through self-giving communication.

Resolution of the Paradox

We have seen that the Christian model of the family presented in *Familiaris Consortio* which expresses both the mind of the Synod of Bishops and Pope John Paul II's personal vision must not be confused with the so-called "traditional family" of the past, nor is it a compromise with the "modern family" of the Humanism that dominates western society today. Instead it is a clear and forceful statement of the intentions of the Creator as He has revealed them to us through Scripture and Tradition as the Church has come to understand this revelation through a long history of attempts to realize this teaching practically in the changing circumstances of human culture. These attempts have never perfectly succeeded, but the Church has learned from its failures as well as from its successes, so that its understanding as well as its convictions have deepened. In an imperfect world, Christian families are imperfect, but the Christian family is no mere ideal. It can and is being realized in its *essentials.* Even in broken families it is possible for Christians to remain or become faithful to these essentials with the support of the Christian community.

The fact that today this Christian vision of the family meets such resistance from a world largely committed to the very different vision of Humanism, should not confuse or weaken our faith, but should awaken us to the need to take our Gospel lamp out from under the measure and put it on a lampstand so that "it will give light to all in the house."

Notes
1. Edward Shorter, *The Making of the Modern Family* (New York: Basic Books/Harper Torchbooks, 1977).
2. *Theologies of the Body: Humanist and Christian* (Boston: Pope John Center, 1985).

3. *The Role of the Christian Family in the Modern World* (Boston: St. Paul Editions, 1980).

4. *Ibid.,* Part III.

5. For example: Col. 3:18-21; Eph. 5:22-33; Titus 2:1-8, I Pt. 3:1-7.

6. For example, Elizabeth Schussler Fiorenza, *In Memory of Her:A Theological Reconstruction of Christian Origins* (New York: Crossroads, 1983).

7. George Duby, *Medieval Marriage: Two Models from Twelfth Century France,* trans. by Elborg Forster (Baltimore: John Hopkins University Press, 1975).

8. Note 1 above.

9. Shorter, Chapter 3, pp. 79-119.

10. The "traditional family" was not Christian because it was based primarily on economic rather than personalist motives; and the "modern family" was not Christian because it is based on individualism rather than personalism.

11. See for example his work *The Acting Person,* trans. by Andrzes Potocki, *Analecta Husserliana,* vol. x (Dordrecht: D.Reidel, 1979).

12. *Humanist Manifesto II, The New Humanist* 33 (Jan./Feb.), 1973, pp. 4-9.

13. Shorter, pp. 109-119.

14. See R.W. Chambers, *Thomas More* (Westminister, MD: Newman, 1935) pp. 92-96, 108-9, 175-90 for an account of the two marriages of a saint. These were not ideal but they exemplify the essentials of Christian marriage with its very real but not insurmountable problems.

15. Shorter, Chapter 5, pp. 169-204.

16. *Ibid.,* pp. 65-78.

17. *Familiaris Consortio* (note 3 above), n.25

18. *Ibid.*

19. Boston: St. Paul Editions, 1981.

20. *Familiaris Consortio* (note 3 above), n.23.

21. Cf. *Charter of the Rights of the Family,* Oct. 22, 1983, article 10 in *Pope Speaks* 29 (1) 1984: 78-86, p. 84 and *Laborem Exercens, On Human Work* (Boston: St. Paul Editions, 1981) n. 19; and *Familiaris Consortio* (note 3 above) nn. 23, 77, 81.

Chapter 7

The Family and Public Policy

Robert A. Destro, J.D.

INTRODUCTION

What is a family? Should the law recognize it as a functional unit, or as merely as an aggregate of autonomous individuals? When, if ever, is the distinction meaningful? Why is the concept of "family" important? When, if ever, should government intervene in its affairs? How should government deal with families and their problems?

These are but a few of the many questions which arise when the law attempts to deal with "family" issues. With the advent of government programs intended to facilitate and support family

113

life,[1] and the ever-expanding judicial recognition of "privacy" rights for family members,[2] the courts have become increasingly involved with diverse value questions involving marriage and divorce,[3] the rights of parents and children,[4] the rights of grandparents,[5] sexuality,[6] education and moral training,[7] family health questions,[8] and intra-family dispute resolution.[9] The purpose of this short introduction to what is both a complex and immensely interesting area of the law is to identify some of the cross-currents and directions in contemporary state and federal family policy, with particular emphasis on their relationship to the statutory and constitutional law of family rights. It is intended to lay the foundation for the oral presentation of which it is a part. The oral presentation will argue that it is essential for those who claim to be concerned about the health and status of the family to establish clearly, at the outset, precisely what their vision of "the family" is. Without a clear impression of the ultimate goal, useful discussion of policy options leading toward attainment of the goal is difficult, if not useless. This introduction, therefore, will begin with a working definition of what most people — and most policy formulations — consider to be "the family" unit; it will suggest several possible conceptual frameworks for analysis of decisions dealing with what might be called "structural" family law issues; and it will introduce some of the statutory and judicial developments in several areas of particular concern to parents, religious institutions, policy-makers and scholars.

I. "FAMILY" — REFLECTIONS ON THE CONCEPT AND ITS DEFINITION

A. Defining the term "family"

Perhaps the most difficult task which besets the observer of contemporary American family policy is to define the term "family" without immediately plunging into a host of related, yet distinct, controversies. But without a working definition, meaningful discussion of the many complex legal and social issues involved in even the most straightforward family law problem is virtually impossible. Thus, for purposes of this chapter, a "family" will be defined as a group of individuals who are related by blood, marriage or adoption living together as a unit which contains at least one natural or adoptive parent and children. This definition, while somewhat restrictive in terms of the possibilities for more "expansive" definitions of family "membership", is not unlike the more traditional sociological definitions of Burgess, Locke and Murdock[10] which focus on what most observers call the "nuclear" family. More importantly, it is also the "family" with which the vast body of American law concerns itself.[11]

By defining the term "family" in a broad, yet traditional, manner one obviously excludes other voluntary associations of individuals which function, either in practice or by design, in much the same manner as traditional families, but which are not commonly perceived as fitting into that category. Examples of such groupings would be married or unmarried, childless, cohabiting heterosexual couples, cohabiting homosexual couples and communal living groups.[12] A discussion of the special issues raised in each of these cases is beyond the scope of this chapter, but it is important to note that they are excluded here for a very specific reason: semantic clarity. Current sociological literature does not contain a clear definition of the term "family", and the definitions which are found often implicitly, rather than explicitly, reflect the philosophical biases of the writer with respect to the related, yet distinct, issues which are raised in the notes and which will be discussed in the oral presentation.[13] The historian Alan C. Carlson discussed this problem in his article, "The Family: A Problem of Definition"[14]:

> Semantic clarity progressively deteriorated . . . as the discipline embraced the heretofore unknown notion of a "pluralism of family forms." An important benchmark of such change was the Forum 14 Report of the 1970 White House Conference on Children, which celebrated a "pluralistic society of varying family forms and a multiplicity of cultures." Defining family as "a group of individuals in interaction," the Report described optional forms, ranging from nuclear families to "single parent," "communal", "group marriage," and "homosexual" varieties. Decrying American society's excessive

conformity, the Report's authors welcomed the contemporary movement "to destroy the cultural myth of a 'right' or 'best' way to behave, believe, work, or play." As family professionals, they viewed the family principally as "a vital, yet often unrecognized partner of bureaucratic service organizations having health, welfare, and rehabilitative objectives." Secure in such a controlling partnership, their primary recommendations focused on recognizing and fostering "the right of individuals to live in any family form they feel will increase their options for self-fulfillment."[15]

The significance of such semantic confusion for the development of law and public policy should not be underestimated.[16] Law is influenced by the other social sciences, and they often play an important role in defining legal relationships. Some of the most important constitutional decisions governing basic social and legal policy rest explicitly on somewhat controversial non-legal conceptual approaches to the issues which were presented for decision,[17] and the current constitutional law of family rights is not without its examples of reliance on such material. A fixed definition of the term "family" is therefore crucial if the participants in the discussion are to fully understand one another.

B. The Significance of Affinity

Once having provided a working definition of the term "family" for purposes of this discussion, it is also important to appreciate the significance of affinity to the analysis. Although Murdock has pointed out that the nuclear family includes the four most fundamental functions of human social life: the sexual, the economic, the reproductive, and the educational,[18] it goes without saying that the force which ties these functions together and which enables families to interact as a unit is emotional. The significance of this observation is twofold: first, it helps to define the character of the social grouping under study; and second, it limits the ability of the law to affect fundamental changes in family structure without also revising large areas of related legal theory to reflect the changes thought to be desirable.[19] The law, in short, both defines

116

and is limited by the "family". "Family law," therefore, has the power to affect some degree of fundamental change in that which the "family" is and does.[20] In a representative democracy, such power is significant, not only for the individuals affected by it, but for the society as a whole. Thus, it only stands to reason that governmental "family policy" should be scrutinized — as a whole — from this perspective.

The law draws its customary deference to familial ties from simple observation of human relationships: from the basic emotional ritualism which develops in the interactions of a mother with her infant child,[21] to the highly complex expectancies which develop among spouses, parents and children, and siblings. As a result, American law[22] defines the family relationship as one which is deserving of the same level of protection as an express constitutional right,[23] and it has generally sought to insulate that relationship from outside influences which are not intended to deal with a specific threat to the health or welfare of the family or its members.[24] It is only when the law seeks to foster policies which are at odds with familial choices that actual attempts to regulate intra-family relationships are imposed.[25] Whether such regulation is appropriate or legitimate in a given context depends, of course, on the policy involved and the interests affected. Whether such policies will work as planned without unintended negative consequences, even if otherwise appropriate, is another matter entirely.[26]

In his 1969 essay, "Human Interaction and the Law," Professor Lon Fuller pointed out that the qualities of enacted law which "lend to it a special capacity to put in order men's interactions within the larger impersonal society" are "the very qualities . . . that make it an inept instrument for regulating intimate relations" within the family.[27] Professor Caplow explains:

> The family depends for its continuance, either abstractly as an institution or concretely as an individual family, on the maintenance of certain sentiments, obligations, and reciprocities that are neither automatic nor self-generating. The reasons why husband and wife cleave together, why children honor their parents, and why brothers do not take pay from each other are not derived

from the state or its secular culture. There are moral sentiments underlying the interactions that constitute the family: otherwise, there would be no family. Self-interest alone will not account for them, and the legal order cannot enforce them.[28]

Since the family is not a creature of the law, and its relationships and obligations are neither created by nor generally enforced through legal means, it is critical that the student of family law policy distinguish between the law's recognition of what is (its descriptive function), and its attempts to define what should be (its normative function). Of equal importance is the frank recognition that the ability of the law to enforce a policy which is intended to effect a non-destructive change in the fragile fabric of intra-familial relationships is often dependent upon the understanding and creative ability of the policy-maker, who must adapt traditional formulations of legal rights and duties to the reality of family life.

II. CONCEPTUAL MODELS OF FAMILY/ GOVERNMENT RELATIONS

An examination of the law of family relations would be incomplete without some discussion of the various conceptual approaches to family law issues found in the literature and the cases. Although judicial respect for the integrity of the family unit is often cited as a rationale for decision in cases which have grave implications for individual families,[29] an understanding of the conceptual approach employed to decide the case or resolve the issue is a far better key to the sincerity of the concern than the words of the opinion. The conceptual models suggested below are intended to illustrate several possible ways to view the state/family relationships which appear in the cases. Each contains three basic elements: parents, children and the state as *parens patriae,* and each model is, to some degree, involved in the decision of nearly every family law issue. The listing below is not meant to be exhaustive; it merely reflects some of this writer's observations on the subject.

118

A. The Linear Model

The first of these conceptual models is linear. It posits that either the state or the parents are the primary source of family rights and obligations. In this, and all subsequent models, responsibility for the morals component of family life is equated with the parental role. It should be apparent that an absolutist application of either form of this model would result in the extremes of intervention or isolation. In graphic form, the variations on the model would appear as follows:

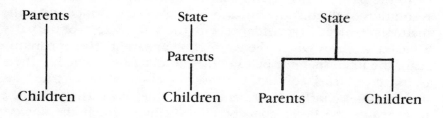

B. The Balance Model

The second of these conceptual approaches is best described as a "balance" wherein the state mediates disputes by weighing intra-family interests in accordance with the weight assigned by current public policy. Although the state would, in the ideal situation, play the role of an entirely neutral arbiter, such a role is, in fact, a practical impossibility; for it is the state which assigns the weights to the respective interests and the state which determines the legitimacy of the type of intervention described by this model in the situations in which it applies.[30]

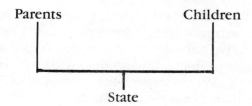

C. The Interests Model

The third approach can best be described as one which examines "interests" in much the same manner as the late Professor Branerd Currie's "interests analysis" approach to difficult issues of public policy arising in the area of Conflict of Laws.[31] A problem involving important family interests is examined to determine whose interests are involved, whether they are in conflict, and, if so, whether their apparent conflict can be resolved without damage to either the interests of the respective parties to the dispute, or to the basic family relationships which will be affected by the resolution of the dispute. In cases of "false" (i.e. no) conflict, the matter is resolved in accordance with the best interests of the party affected. In cases where the conflict is "apparent" (i.e. apparently real), the interests must be examined to determine whether there is, in fact, a "true" conflict. In those rare cases where a "true" (i.e. unavoidable) conflict is presented, the rule of decision must be taken from the basic conceptual principles which the society employs to resolve issues of fundamental social importance. (e.g., constitutional or moral principles concerning "right" or "just" relations among the state, parents and children). This approach can best be illustrated through the use of the following diagram:

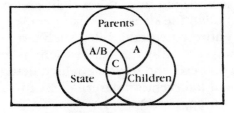

A = Family Unit Interests
(Parents & Children)

B = State Interests

C = Shared Interests

While there may be other conceptual approaches to family/state relations, it should be apparent that the three chosen here for illustrative purposes are not mutually exclusive. They may be applied alone or in conjunction in a wide variety of situations. It should also become apparent upon examination that the distinctions between them is a given case can often be more apparent than real. They are mentioned, therefore, only as a convenient way of organizing an introduction of the rather distressing tendency of recent case law to utilize an almost purely result-oriented approach to the decision of extremely difficult intra-familial problems.

III. IDENTIFYING THE ISSUES

The unique role in our society of the family, the institution by which "we inculcate and pass down many of our most cherished values, moral and cultural," requires that constitutional principles be applied with sensitivity and flexibility to the special needs of parents and children.[32]

The foregoing statement of principle has been reaffirmed by the Supreme Court as a guide for judicial decision-making on many occasions,[33] but the sensitivity and clarity of analysis required to do justice to the sometimes clashing interests involved in cases which involve potential intra-family or state/family disputes is often lacking when the rationale supporting recent judicial decisions is examined.[34] The reasons for this lack of sensitivity for the interests of the family are easy enough to discern, but they are tremendously difficult to work with, for both political[35] and policy reasons.[36] For precisely such reasons, it is rare indeed when either a court or other policy maker will set forth the underlying philosophical or political assumptions upon which the decision rests.[37]

The common law imposed a duty on parents to care for, protect and guide their children and allowed delegation of that duty to others, but such delegation was not operative to grant prerogatives coextensive with those of the parents.[38] Recent developments in family policy, however, rest on a perception of the family very different than that of the common law and most current statutory law. It holds that parents exercise only powers delegated to them by the state, and that the governmental recognition of parental prerogatives is limited by currently accepted constitutional limitations on the power of the states to interfere with individual liberty.[39] It is within this shifting conceptual framework that much of the current debate over "family", "parents'" and "children's" rights occurs. Because parents continue to fulfill the role of guardians of their childrens' health, welfare, safety and morals; and because the law continues to presume that children lack the

121

capacity to choose their own style and philosophy of self-governance,[40] parents continue to be recognized as being responsible for nurturing and developing their children's capacity to function indpendently and make reasoned life choices. It is only when those choices involve controversial parental value judgments which are not in accordance with judicial or professional opinion that the difficulties described in the notes begins. Unfortunately, the rhetoric employed by most parties to the various controversies tends to focus on "rights" and "status", rather than interests and capacity. Some writers have even gone so far as to portray the possible range of status choices for children as limited to either total libration or serfdom,[41] and the result has been, quite predictably, confusion and the development of a fair amount of bad law and questionable legal reasoning.

Because an approach which emphasizes only rights and status leaves very little room for compromise, the unfortunate result appears to be a trend toward respect for the family as a unit only when it serves the specific policy purposes of the legislative or judicial decision-maker. Given the importance of the substantive constitutional rights of the family members involved in such cases, it should be clear that governmental tinkering with family structures in pursuit of policy which is either ill-defined or lacking a base of broad public support is a serious matter indeed.

As a result, development of a sensitivity for the needs of the family as the unit of society which performs the basic tasks of nurturing, educating, and socializing children should be one of the major goals of this conference and should rank high on the list of future topics for pastoral guidance on the part of the Church as a whole. But before such guidance is attempted, every attempt to attain a clear understanding of the influences of traditional and emerging sociological, philosophical, psychological, and legal theory on those interests should be undertaken. The reasons for this suggestion should be obvious to anyone with a desire to influence the course of public policy development in a manner which is consistent with the long-term protection of the family, and of Church itself; for it goes without saying that the Church could not survive in its present form without the assistance it receives from dedicated parents who pass the faith on to their children by both word and deed.

Because the processes of American law are both incremental and dynamic, it is absolutely essential that the participants in the process have a clear understanding of the degree to which their own goals and philosophy are reflected or rejected in recent developments in the law. If the current result-oriented trends which prompt this writer's concern are to be reversed, the approach taken by proponents of family integrity must be both forthright and uncompromising; for if issues of constitutional and moral principle are seldom perceived as negotiable, one can be certain that issues of family integrity will never be when the issue is joined directly.

Among the questions which should concern this conference are: the ongoing debate over the rights of the child as an individual *sui juris* within the family; the relationship of constitutional and statutory emancipation to the rights and duties of parents; and the meaning and potential uses (and abuses) of a broad concept such as "the best interests of the child". Because public policy discussion concerning family issues often proceeds on the assumption that someone's "rights" or "best interests" should be "protected" by (or from) government intervention, and that it is improper for anyone to "impose" any sort of rigid philosophical structure on discussions which have moral dimensions,[42] the proper analytical perspective is one which seeks to identify what — and whose — interests are being served by existing or proposed public policy formulations. Thus, it is critical for the student of family policy to scrutinize both the practical and the theoretical implications of government intervention in family affairs, especially that which involves fundamental decisions concerning the welfare of children and the preservation of the family structure. Although all government intervention in family life is a serious matter and warrants careful scrutiny, much of it is clearly beneficial and intended to preserve the family as a functioning unit.[43] But other forms of intervention, such as emancipation by recognition of constitutional or legal rights enforceable against the parents,[44] or by governmental action on behalf of a minor child which is said to be in the "best interests" of that child when there has been no prior showing of parental neglect or unfitness,[45] are not designed to preserve the functional integrity of the family unit, but rather to further other interests which may or may not be beneficial to either the family itself, or to the individuals in whose name the intervention proceeds.

This chapter will serve as a brief introduction to some of the legal and public policy arguments over family and child-centered rights to make important, life-influencing decisions concerning education, life-style, health care and moral training of children. It is hoped that, given the importance of the subject matter, the readers of this book will consider carefully their own role in the future development of public policy on this important topic.

Notes

1. *See, e.g.*, 40 U.S.C. section 484b (transfer of surplus real property to low income families and others); 42 U.S.C. ss 300z(b), 606 (family-based sex education programs, aid to families with dependent chldren); 43 U.S.C. section 433(a) (preferences for needy families in newly-opened irrigation projects). For an overview of some of the programs, suggestions for programs and the rationale for government interaction with and support of family life see *The Report "Listening to American Families"* (White House Conference on Families, October, 1980).

2. *See, e.g., Akron v. Akron Center for Reproductive Health*, — U.S. —,103 S.Ct. 2481, 76 L.Ed.2d 687, 701 n.10, 708-710 nn.29-31, 728-729 & n. 12 (1983) (majority opinion per Powell, J. and dissent per O'Connor, J.) (parental/judicial notice/consent for abortion); *Planned Parenthood of Kansas City, Missouri v. Ashcroft*, — U.S. —, 103 S.Ct. 2517, 76 L.Ed.2d 733, 744-745 & nn. 16-21) (same); *Planned Parenthood of Central Missouri v. Danforth*, 428 U.S. 52 (1976).

3. *See* generally, B. C. Hafen, *The Constitutional Status of Marriage, Kinship, and Sexual Privacy — Balancing the Individual and Social Interests*, 81 Mich.L.Rev. 463 (1983).

4. *See, e.g.*, Cal. Civil Code, ss4600,4600.5. (West) (joint custody after divorce). *Carey v. Population Services International*, 431 U.S. 678 (1977); *In re Snyder*, 85 Wash. 2d. 182, 532 P.2d 278 (1975).

5. *See, e.g.*, 25 U.S.C. s1914 (placement of American Indian children); Ark. Stat. Ann. section 34-1211.1 (Supp. 1977) (visitation); Cal. Civ. Code ss 197.5, 4601 (West supp. 1978) (same); Mich Comp. Laws Ann. 722.27a (Cum. supp. 1977-78) (same). *A.B.M., Natural Mother v. M.H. & A.H., Prospective Adoptive Parents*, 651 P.2d 1170 (Alaska, 1982) (statutory preference); *Smith v. Smith*, 270 Cal.App. 2d 605, 75 Cal. Rptr. 900 (1969) (adoption); *People, in the Interest of P.D., formerly M.A.D., a child, V. M.G.*, 41 Colo. App. 109, 580 P.2d 836 (1978) (custody, support, right to terminate); *In the Interest of Summers Children v. Wulftenstein*, 571 P.2d 1319 (1977) (applying rule that grandparents have "some dormant or inchoate right or interest in the custody and welfare" of their grandchldren). *See generally*, Grandparents' Visitation Rights: Hearings on S. Con. Res. 40 Before the Senate Subcommittee on Separation of Powers, "The Legal Rights of Grandparents in Domestic Relations Cases Involving Issues Other Than Visitation Rights" and "The Legal Rights of Grandparents in Domestic Relations Cases" (statements of R.A. Destro and L.S. Mullenix) (collecting cases and other sources).

6. *See, e.g., D.H. v. J.H.*, 418 N.E.2d 286, 290-293 (Ind. App. 1981); *Schuster v. Schuster*, 90 Wash.2d 626, 585 P.2d 130, 134 (1978) (en banc) (Rosellini and Hamilton, J.J. and Wright, C.J., dissenting).

7. *See, e.g., Board of Education v. Pico,* 457 U.S. 853 (1982) (community control of public school library materials); *Doe v. Irwin,* 428 F.Supp. 1198 (W.D. Mich., 1977), *vacated and remanded,* 559 F.2d 1219 (6th Cir. 1977), *aff'd on remand,* 441 F.Supp. 1247 (W.D. Mich., 1977), *rev'd,* 615 F.2d 1162 (6th Cir. 1978) (parental notice prior to involvement of children in publicly-funded educational program involving discussion and evaluation of issues involving sexual morality); *Kendrick v. Heckler,* Civ. No. 83-3175 (D. D.C.) (pending) (constitutionality of Adolescent Family Life Program).

8. *See, e.g., United States v. University Hospital,* — F.2d. —, No. 83-6343 (2d Cir. filed Feb. 23, 1984) (Baby Jane Doe).

9. *See, e.g., In re Snyder,* 85 Wash. 2d. 182, 532 P.2d 278 (1975).

10. *See* E.W. Burgess and H.J. Locke, *The Family: From Institution to Companionship* (New York: American Book Co. 1945) at 510-511; G.P. Murdock, *Social Structure* (New York: Free Press). *See also* A.C. Carlson, *"The Family: A Problem of Definition,"* 6 Human Life Rev. 41 (Fall 1980) (collecting these and other sources) [hereafter cited as Carlson].

11. *See, e.g.,* 5 U.S.C. s 8701(d); 18 U.S.C. s 1116; 25 U.S.C. s1903 (extended family member);, 26 U.S.C. 613(a). *Moore v. City of East Cleveland,* 432 U.S. 494 (1977) (extended "nuclear" family); *May v. Anderson,* 345 U.S. 528 (1953); *Lehman v. Lycoming County Children's Services Agency,* — F.2d —, 49 U.S.L.W. 2642 (3d Cir. 1981) (child custody). See also sources cited at note 5 *supra.*

12. *See, e.g., Re Adult Anonymous II,* 88 A.D.2d 30, 452 N.Y.S.2d 198 (1st Dep. 1982) (homosexual adoption).

13. *See* sources cited in Carlson, *supra,* note 10. *See also,* J. Hitchcock, *Family is What Family Does,* 4 Human Life Rev. 52 (Fall, 1980).

14. Carlson, *supra,* note 10.

15. *Id.,* at 47.

16. In *Re Adult Anonymous II,* 88 A.D.2d 30, 452 N.Y.S.2d 198 (1st Dep. 1982), the Appellate Division of the New York Supreme Court made the following comments regarding the existence of homosexual "families". Although the issue was whether or not a man could adopt his homosexual lover, the case is significant for what it says concerning both the definition of the term "family" for legal purposes as well as the mechanisms by which such definitions develop. The court stated:

> Homosexual relations in private are now constitutionally protected. *People v. Onofore,* 51 N.Y.2d 476, 434 N.Y.S.2d 947, 415 N.E.2d 936, under the right to privacy. In any event the parties do not seek the adoption in order to cultivate their sexual relationship. They wish to formalize themselves as a family unit, for the purposes of publicly acknowledging their emotional bond and more pragmatically to unify their rights. . . .
>
> The "nuclear family" arrangement is no longer the only model of family life in America. The realities of present day urban life allow many types of non-traditional families. The statutes involved do not permit this court to deny a petition for adoption on the basis of this court's view of what is the nature of a family. In any event, the best description of a family is a continuing relationship of love and care, and an assumption of responsibility for some other person. Certainly that is present in the instant case." 452 N.Y.S.2d at 201.

The analytical method employed in the court's opinion is immediately apparent upon examination. First, the court finds that the case involves the right to privacy, in that New York's highest court, the Court of Appeals, has decided that consensual homosexual activity in private is constitutionally protected; second, it extrapolates from the existence of the privacy right to the position that the admitted existence of such activity within an adoptive parent/child relationship should not be considered by the court — or, by implication, the state — in the determination of whether the adoption is in the "best interests" of the adoptive child; and third, the court recites the "pragmatic" reasons for its decision to permit the adoption (the pair feared eviction by their landlord on the grounds that they were not related). Once past this point, having relegated the issue to one of private concern and recognizing the private utility of its proposed decision, the court then reaches the point where it must come to grips with the fact that a homosexual living arrangement, even if supported by an adoption decree, is not the type of "family" relationship which the law generally recognizes.

In order to rationalize the change in the traditional law of family relations it has just made in the name of "privacy", the court undertakes to discuss the nature of the family relationship itself and to justify its position on the grounds that times have changed. The court states that "nuclear family *arrangement* (emphasis mine) is no longer the only model of family life in America", and that the courts are free to recognize whatever "non-traditional [family] forms" they choose. The fact that the New York Legislature had never considered the issue of homosexual adoption, and that most states reject adoption for sexual purposes on public policy grounds, is simply ignored.

Although the court has now changed the public policy of New York concerning "the family" in a manner which is totally at odds with traditional notions of family life, it appears to state that to do otherwise would impose its view of the "proper" family form on society. See note 42 *infra*. In reality, however, the court has just done so anyway; for once all the justifications, legal or otherwise, for the decision have been stated, the court's own view of the "proper" family form is stated very clearly. Its definition of a "family" for public policy purposes is contained in the following statement: "the best description of a family is a continuing relationship of love and care, and an assumption of responsibility for some other person."

While one may choose to agree or disagree with either the definition of "family" chosen or the result in the case (i.e. the legality of the adoption at issue), neither of those points is relevant to the point made above. The real issue from a policy perspective is that courts, under the rubric of defending the right to privacy, are busily writing their own views of what is, or is not, a "family" into the law of the land. Past experience has shown that legislative attempts to make the law reflect a more traditional view of family life will meet with both political and judicial opposition, see sources cited at notes 2, 19, and 42.

Since the entire process is incremental, such decisions have a long-term effect on the development of two important branches of legal principle. First, they legitimate the process by which courts become institutions with the power to define fundamental social concepts such as "family". In a representative democracy, this is a "power" or procedural question of great importance, especially when the court is not subject to the controls inherent in the electoral process. (*e.g.*, life-tenured federal judges, and state judges appointed for long terms without electoral supervision) Second, an important legal term, "family", is robbed of its fixed meaning.

For purposes of present law and future policy development, the lack of a fixed meaning for such an important term as "family" violates the cardinal principle that the law must be certain, and capable of being clearly understood by those who must implement or obey it. On a more practical level, the lack of a clear definition of "family" already makes it virtually impossible to devise strategies for encouraging nuclear or extended "family" life along the lines of the traditional model. Examination of The *Report "Listening to American Families"* (White House Conference on Families, October, 1980), cited at note 1 *supra*, discloses some of the difficulties which arise when no fixed definition of the term can be agreed upon.

17. *See, e.g., Roe v. Wade,* 410 U.S. 113 (1973); *Doe v. Bolton,* 410 U.S. 179 (1973); *Brown v. Board of Education,* 347 U.S. 483, . . .n. 11 (1954).

18. Murdock, *supra* note 3 at 9-10, *also quoted in* Carlson, *supra* note 10 at 43.

19. *Compare, e.g.,* 42 U.S.C. 300a *et seq.* (Public Health Services Act, Title X) (contraception and teenage pregnancy) and *Planned Parenthood Federation of America, Inc. v. Schweiker,* 559 F. Supp. 658 (D.D.C. 1983), *aff'd sub nom. Planned Parenthood of America, Inc. v. Heckler,* 712 F.2d 650, 660 (D.C. Cir. 1983) (confidentiality requirements as applied to parents) *with* 42 U.S.C. 300z, *et seq,* 300z(a) (10)(A), 300z-5(a)(22) (Public Health Service Act, Title XX) (Adolescent Family Life Program) (requiring parental involvement and consent) and *Kendrick v. Heckler,* Civ. No. 83-3175 (D. D.C.) (pending) (constitutionality of

Adolescent Family Life Program). *See also Akron v. Akron Center for Reproductive Health*, — U.S. —, 103 S.Ct. 2481, 76 L.Ed.2d 687, 701 n.10, 708-710 nn.29-31, 728-729 & n. 12 (1983) (majority opinion per Powell, Jr. and dissent per O'Connor, J.) (abortions may be performed on immature minors without parental notice or consent upon the order of a court notwithstanding provisions of Ohio Juvenile Court statutes and rules requiring that parents be notified of any proceeding involving the interests of their children); *Baird v. Bellotti*, 450 F.Supp. 997, 1001 (D. Mass. 1978) *aff'd sub nom. Bellotti v. Baird* (II), 443 U.S. 622 (1979) (parents with strong religious views opposed to abortion should not be informed of the fact that their minor daughter is to have an abortion performed upon her because their reaction might not be in her best interests).

20. The degree to which government policy affects the family is a matter of some debate, but the fact that there is some effect is not seriously disputed. Examination of particular policies will generally indicate the assumptions concerning family life and relationships upon which the policies are based. In *Re Rose Child Dependency Case*, 161 Pa. Super. 204, 208, 54 A.2d 297 (1947), for example, the court discussed the policy behind involuntary deprivation of child custody for neglect and stated:

> It is a serious matter for the long arm of the state to reach into a home and snatch a child from its mother. It is a power which a government dedicated to freedom for the individual should exercise with extreme care, and only where the evidence clearly establishes its necessity . . . Under our system of government children are not the property of the state to be reared only where and under such conditons as officials deem best. . .

> The power of the juvenile court is not to adjudicate what is for the best interests of a child, but to adjudicate whether or not the child is neglected.

In re Rinker, 117 A.2d 780 (Pa. Super. 1955). *Accord Petition of Kauch*, 358 Mass. 327, 264 N.E.2d 371 (1970).

21. *See* E. Erikson, "Ontogeny of Ritualization" in Lowenstein, *Psychoanalysis — A General Psychology — Essays in Honor of Heinz Hartman* (1966) at 603, in L.L. Fuller, *Human Interaction and the Law*, 14 American J. of Jurisprudence 1 (1969).

22. References to "American law" in general should be understood as references to the laws of the several states unless otherwise indicated. The states have primary responsibility for the protection and preservation of family interests, *compare, e.g.,* U.S. Const. Amends. I, IX, X *with e.g.,* Ohio Rev. Code, Title 31, and it is only in recent years that the federal government's policies have begun to supplement, see, e.g., Ohio Rev. Code ch. 3115 (reciprocal child support), and, in some cases, intrude upon, *see, e.g., Planned Parenthood Federation of America, Inc. v. Schweiker*, 559 F. supp. 658 (D.D.C. 1983), *aff'd sub nom. Planned Parenthood of America, Inc. v. Heckler*, 712 F.2d 650, 660 (D.C. Cir. 1983) (confidentiality requirements of Title X as applied to parents of minor children receiving government funded contraceptive services and related sex-education programs), this traditional state function.

23. *See, e.g., Smith v. Organization of Foster Families*, 431 U.S. 816 (1977); *May v. Anderson*, 345 U.S. 528 (1953); *Benn v. Timmons*, 345 So.2d 388, 389 (Fla. App. 1977) ("a natural, Godgiven right"); *New Hampshire v. Robert H.*, 118 N.H. 713, 393 A.2d 1387 (1978).

24. *See, e.g., Moore v. City of East Cleveland*, 431 U.S. 494 (1977) (attempt by city to ban extended family living groups); *Wisconsin v. Yoder*, 406 U.S. 205 (1972) (education). *Cf., Quilloin v. Wolcott*, 434 U.S. 245 (1977) (adoption).

25. *See, e.g., Prince v. Massachusetts*, 321 U.S. 158 (1944) (child labor). *See generally, Thomas, Child Abuse and Neglect Part I: Historical Overview, Legal Matrix, and Social Perspectives*, 50 N.C.L.Rev. 293 (1972); *Note, State Instrusion into Family Affairs: Justifications and Limitations*, 26 Stan. L. Rev. 1383 (1974).

26. Compare, for example, the divergent views of the federal government's attempts to limit the growing number of teenage pregnancies. The family planning provisions of Title X of the Public Health Service Act, 42 U.S.C. § 300a, et. seq. emphasize the provision of information on contraception and abortion to teenagers. The underlying assumption seems to be that government policies have little, if any, practical positive or negative effect on the rate of adolescent sexual activity, and that the best way to minimize unwanted teenage pregnancies is to maximize their access to birth control and abortion information and services. *See Planned Parenthood of America, Inc. v. Heckler, supra* note 18, 666 & n.13 (D.C. Cir. 1983). The provisions of Title XX, on the other hand, appear to proceed from the opposite assumption: that government should assist in the development of programs for teenagers which will dissuade them from early sexual activity and abortion, and that it is possible for government to encourage such activity if it restricts its efforts to the provision of birth control devices and information, and referral for abortion in an alledgedly "value neutral" setting. See Senate Report No. 97-161, 97th Congress, 1st Sess., July 21, 1981 at 4-9. *See also* Memorandum of Points and Authorities in Support of Defendant-Intervenors' Motion for Summary Judgment and in Opposition to Plaintiffs' Motion for Summary Judgment, *Kendrick v. Heckler, supra* note 7.

27. L.L. Fuller, *supra* note 20 at 34.

28. Caplow, *The Loco Parent: Federal Policy and Family Life,* 1976 B.Y.U.L. Rev. 709, 712.

29. *See, e.g., Bellotti* v. Baird (II), 443 U.S. 622 (1979) (plurality opinion, per Powell, J.).

30. *See, e.g., Planned Parenthood of Central Missouri v. Danforth,* 428 U.S. 52, 71 (1976) ("balancing" of relative spousal interests in the case where the wife/mother desires an abortion, but the husband/father refuses consent). In *Danforth,* the Supreme Court resolved the controversy in favor of the mother because, in its view, "[t]the obvious fact is that when the wife and the husband disagree on this decision, the view of only one of the two marriage partners can prevail. Inasmuch as it is the woman who physically bears the child and who is the more directly and immediately affected by the pregnancy, as between the two, the balance weights in her favor." This is precisely the sort of "balancing" which is inappropriate for a federal court which purports to be deciding a case on constitutional grounds. The law governing the relationship of spouses *inter se* is governed by state law, see sources cited at note 22 *supra,* not federal constitutional law, and the implication that the state may not legislate in the area to protect the rights of the husband is questionable. The Court's approach to the issue is best described by the "linear model" in the text above, for it assumes that the rights of the husband/father to the child are derived by grant from the state, and that to protect his rights to the child is, inevitably, to deprive the woman of hers).

31. *See generally,* Crampton Currie & Kay, *Conflict of Laws:* Cases-Comments Questions (West 3d ed. 1982?); H.H. Kay, *The Use of Comparative Impairment to Resolve True Conflicts: An Evaluation of the California Experience,* 68, Calif. L. Rev. 577 (1980).

32. *Wisconsin v. Yoder, supra,* at 233.

33. *See, e.g., Parham, v. J.R.* and *J.L.,* 442 U.S. 584 (1979); *Wisconsin v. Yoder, supra; Pierce v. Society of Sisters,* 268 U.S. s510 (1925).

34. *See, e.g., H.L. v. Matheson,* 450 U.S. 398 (1981); *Bellotti v. Baird* (II), 443 U.S. 622 (1979); *Bellotti v. Baird* (I), 428 U.S. 132 (1976); *Planned Parenthood of Central Missouri v. Danforth,* 428 U.S. 52 (1976); *In the Matter of Phillip B., a minor,* 92 Cal. App.3d 796, 156 Cal. Rptr. 48 (1979), *cert. den. sub. nom. Bothman v. Warren B.,* 445 U.S. 949 (1980).

35. Recent debates over the fitness of homosexuals to serve as custodial parents, and the ongoing debate over the access rights of adopted children and natural parents to adoption records are but two examples of the political sensitivity of these issues.

36. The first amendment questions inherent in the debate over the degree to which the government may involve itself in the moral development of children are some of the most common examples of difficult policy questions. See sources cited at notes 7, 18, and 35 supra.

128

37. *Compare, e.g. Akron v. Akron Center for Reproductive Health,* — U.S. —, 103 S. Ct. 2481, 76 L. Ed.2d 687, 710 n. 31 ad text accompanying note (1983) (indicating the Supreme Court's unwillingness to trust Ohio's juvenile courts to follow its instructions in abortion cases involving immature minors) *with, e.g., Baird v. Bellotti,* 450 F. Supp. 997, 1001 (D. Mass. 1978) *aff'd sub nom. Bellotti v. Baird* (II), 443 U.S. 622 (1979).

38. Blackstone, *Commentaries on the Law of England,* *446-459 (Lewis ed. 1902).

39. *See Planned Parenthood of Central Missouri v. Danforth,* 428 U.S. 52 (1976). In legal terms, the concept is known as the "state action" rule. *See generally* Lockhart, Kamisar & Choper, *The American Constitution* (5th ed. West 1981) at 1044-1989.

40. Recognition of this lack of capacity can be found in statutes or constitutional provisions which limit or deny to minors the right to marry, *see, e.g.,* Mich. Comp. Laws Ann. 551.03; vote, *see, e.g.* U.S. Const. Amend, XXVI; contract, *see, e.g.,* Mich. Comp. Laws Ann. 750.137; or purchase liquor, *see, e.g.,* Mich. Comp. Laws Ann. 750.141.

41. *Compare, e.g.,* J. Holt, *Escape from Childhood* (1974) and P. Wald, *Making Sense Out of the Rights of Youth,* 4 Human Rights 13 (1974), with K. Kemmonton, *All Our Children* (Carnegie Council on Children, 1977) and R. Mnooken, "Children's Rights: Legal and Ethical Dilemmas," *The Transcript,* Summer, 1978 (Boalt Hall School of Law, University of California, Berkeley).

42. The most obvious of these issues is abortion, but it is by no means the only one. Interestingly, this argument can be used both to defend current policy formulations, *see, e.g.,* M.M. Cuomo, "Religious Belif and Public Morality: A Catholic Governor's Perspective" delivered to the Department of Theology, University of Notre Dame, South Bend, Indiana, September 13, 1984 (arguing that the Catholic view on abortion ought not to be "imposed" on society to replace the Supreme Court's view [which was also "imposed" on society] in the absence of a clear consensus in the political sphere), and to argue that the political sphere has no right to make any rules at all in areas deemed to be matters of "private" concern or choice, including such basic issues as the religious education and moral development of minor children. *See, generally,* Knudsen, *The Education of the Amish Child,* 62 Calif. L. Rev. 1506 (19794); *Note, Adjudication What Yoder Left Unresolved: Religious Rights for Minor Children After Danforth and Carey,* 1226 U. Pa. L. Rev. 1135 (1978). See also sources cited at notes 7, 9, 11, and 15 and accompanying text.

43. *See e.g.,* sources cited at note 3 *supra.*

44. *See, e.g., Akron v., Akron Center for Reproductive Health, supra; Planned Parenthood of Central Missouri v. Danforth, supra; In re Snyder, supra.*

45. *See., e.g., Bellotti v. Baird* (II), 443 U.S. 622 (1979); *United States v. University Hospital,* — F.2d —, No. 83-6343 (2d Cir. filed Feb. 23, 1984) (Baby Jane Doe); *In the Matter of Phillip B., a minor,* 92 Cal. App.3d 796, 156 Cal. Rptr. 48 (1979), *cert. den. sub. nom. Bothman v. Warren B.,* 445 U.S. 949 (1980). *Compare, Linn v. Linn,* 205 Neb. 218, 286 N.W.2d 765 (1980) ("best interests" standard is unconstitutionally vague without description of prohibited parental conduct); *Gonzalez v. Texas Dept. of Human Resources,* 581 S.W.2d 522 (Ct. Civ. App. 1979), *cert. den.* 445 904 (1980).

Chapter 8

Parents As Primary Educators

Janice Plunkett D'Avignon, Ph.D.

INTRODUCTION

This chapter was not an easy one to write. In the initial stages, the language was too technical, the ideas seemed unrelated, and the whole issue touching on the struggles of modern parents somehow seemed so removed from what I was writing. After praying, thinking and rethinking, it suddenly came to me. The problem was that I was trying to write a paper relying on my expertise in psychology, when the real perspective on this topic comes from my experience as a Catholic wife and mother.

Now certainly my educational and professional experiences have *in*formed my view, but they have not formed it. For the definition of my role as a parent comes out of a very old tradition. One based on the idea of parents being people with authority — an authority described by Abraham Heschel in his writings as one rooted in the responsibility to fulfill a sacred trust.[1] And most often it is this idea that accounts for my actions in the role of a parent as a primary educator of my children.

Let me give you an example of what I mean. Sometimes when I am involved in a conflict with one of my children, I find myself thinking: "Oh yes, he's displaying egocentric thought characteristics of early formal operational thinking." Or, "this is an example of the individuation/separation process of early identity formation." But before these thoughts are even formulated in my mind, I find my mouth saying something like this: "Get that look off your face and just do what I tell you because I am your mother, and I'm telling you to do it."

Listen to those words. "I am your mother." They are time-worn words for sure, but they carry a very deep meaning. They touch in us, even as adults, a sense of something different, something special, something sacred. It is something not easily defined but so readily understood. It is an authority rooted in the sacred. As Kirk Kilpatrick points out in his article entitled "Why the Secular Needs the Sacred,"[2] it is the kind of authority that represents the position *from* which one argues, and not the positon *for* which one argues. And yet today, so many of us, (bishops, priests and parents), find ourselves increasingly being put into the position of justifying our authority when we attempt to act on it out of responsibility to the sacred truth that defines it.

What has happened here? What is it that works to undermine this authority? As a parent involved in the real struggle of maintaining my position as one of the two primary educators of my children (my husband is the other one), I see this problem springing out of attitudinal changes directly related to our experiences with living in what I call "the age of experts."

Increasingly in the public sector (particularly in the schools), in the Church and in the family, the advice of experts is sought and then accepted as if it were carved in stone. And this despite the fact that the experts often don't agree among themselves. What happens is that a particular line of thinking gains popularity and becomes the "sine qua non" of living a normal, healthy life. And today, unfortunately for all of us, it is this line of thinking that has taken hold and created very subtle (and sometimes not so subtle) attitudinal changes that affect our lives. For the family, there are three areas in particular in which we can really see the changes of attitude being brought to us by "the age of experts." The first is the change in perception of both the roles of parents and children. The second is reflected in the modern trend to psychologize and secularize values. And the third is evident in our loss of the sense of the sacred as it has been traditionally reflected in family lifestyles, practices and rituals.

Let's now turn and look at the first of these attitudinal changes: the new perception of parents' and children's roles in the family.

NEW PERCEPTIONS OF ROLES
OF PARENTS AND CHILDREN

Today's parents are assumed to have little or no expertise on knowing how to bring up their children. As Kenneth Keniston points out in his book, *All Our Children,* instead of being asked about their children, parents are more often than not, told about their children.[3] This happens in doctors' offices, in schools and in parishes. The emphasis today is on teaching parents to acquire an understanding of their children, even though, in most cases, nobody understands a child better than his/her parents. But parental wisdom and understanding, once very respected, are not what is being sought. The new understanding is far more psychological than that. It emphasizes the parents' role as a facilitator and equal partner in the development of the child. Marie Winn tells us in her book, *Children Without Childhood,* that today's parents are asked to act more like therapists to their children than like mothers and fathers.[4] This view encourages parents to identify underlying motivations for behaviors rather than to teach appropriate behaviors. It urges parents to be completely accepting of all behaviors and to help their children to become completely accepting of their own thoughts, actions and feelings.

132

Let me add an example here. When I was in the process of writing my doctoral thesis, I often drove my children to C.C.D. class and spent that hour waiting for them in the resource room of the school in which their classes were held. It was a quiet room with big library tables and chairs. For me, it was a good opportunity to read and take notes to add to the voluminous pile of notes I often carted around with me out of fear of losing them. One day while I was there a little girl, about the age of seven, we'll call her Suzie, came over to where I was sitting and started coloring on my notes. You can imagine my horror! I grabbed her arm and said, in my best psychologist voice, "No, no Suzie. These are my papers. Go over to your seat and color on your own papers." At this point, her mother called her, I released her arm and fully expected her to return to her seat. But she didn't. Instead she started coloring on my notes again. I again stopped her by grabbing her arm. This time her mother came over and much to my amazement made no attempt to control her child's behavior. Instead, in a voice far more psychologist-like than mine, she said, "Now Suzie, why are you doing this to this lady? Are you upset that she wasn't paying attention to you?" Suzie's response was simply, "I want to color on *these* papers." "I understand that, Suzie," her mother replied, "but I can't help you in that. Are you feeling hostile right now?" Well, I don't know how Suzie was feeling, but I was feeling pretty hostile. I gathered up my papers with my free hand, and then released my grip on Suzie's arm and moved to a safer spot in the room. As I left them, Suzie's mother was still attempting to get to the root of Suzie's hostility.

After getting over some very uncharitable thoughts, it occurred to me that I had witnessed the result of this new approach to childrearing: the parent as a therapist. And the question before me was, why would any parent what to do this? I realized that it was not really a matter of wanting to behave in this manner, but more a matter of wanting to do the right thing by her child. And for this woman, the advice of experts was what she had to rely on. What I'm sure she didn't see was how much this advice was undermining her authority and compromising her responsibility as a parent. Instead, she showed herself to be "in touch" with current expert opinions.

You see, today, to play the role of a traditional parent is to be "out of touch." And here, we can draw another parallel between relationships that exist among clergy and those that exist among varying types of parents. For the words, "out of touch" have only recently been applied to parents, but have a long history of application to clergy. Yet today we find among our clergy and religious educators many who have escaped that label and who, like so many parents, have been seduced by "the age of experts." They rely on popular experts to guide them. They are "in touch" with the latest findings of Masters and Johnson; they are "in touch" with the popular use of expressive language; and they are "in touch" with the most recent view aired on the Phil Donahue Show. But the result is that they are more "out of touch" than ever. For they have lost touch with all that is sacred and binding in the exercise of authority. And their authority itself becomes questionable. And when this authority is seen as questionable, attitudinal changes result.

For parents, a subtle attitudinal change takes place. As parents become more like equal partners with their children, authority gets shared between them. And, as a number of writers like Kirk Kilpatrick, David Elkind, and others have noted, perceptions of children as children begin to change.[5] One has only to look at today's children to see this. They more closely resemble miniature adults than they do children. They wear adult-like clothes, they talk in an adult-like fashion, they are included in adult conversations, and they have access to very adult issues. They are no longer distinctive as children.

Marie Winn points out that at one time, distinctions between adults and children were more obvious.[6] Certain subjects of conversation and events of adult life were kept hidden from children. It was not that things like divorce, infidelity, drug addiction and homosexuality didn't occur. They did, but they were not considered suitable material for children. But today, all material is considered suitable for children. We see this showing up in themes of popular T.V. shows, movies, songs and even in books designed for children. Let me give you two examples here. One day, a couple of summers ago, I was sitting on my front porch when a group of young children about ten years old walked by, singing a song. It was a song from the movie, "Grease." The words I heard were "Look at me, I'm Sandra Dee, stinking of virginity." I remember thinking, "My God, I hope so!"

As a second example of this phenomenon, I refer you to the popular books being read by children in approximately the 9, 10, and 11 year old age group. The heroes and heroines of these books are no longer characters who overcome some incredible obstacle in order to help others. Instead, they are children who overcome terrible sociological evils (drug addiction, cruel and abusive parents, prostitution) and they manage to find help for themselves. Today's heroes and heroines do not go blissfully off into the sunset to live happily ever. Instead, they find their happy ending at the rehabilitation center where they can learn to cope with their very adult-like problems.

Psychologically, the result of this attitudinal change so prevalent in our society, places children at great risk. For they are not equipped mentally or emotionally to be able to deal with the complexities of today's society. Culturally, they are also at risk. The child who looks, talks and acts like an adult, tends to get treated as if he/she were an adult and consequently runs the risk of losing some of the protections adults in our society once felt compelled to extend to children. They become expected to venture beyond their capabilities and assume responsibilities once reserved for adults. We can best see this happening as we move to our second point and examine the ways the experts tell us we should teach moral values to our children.

SECULARIZATION OF VALUES

The modern trend centers on helping children acquire the skills to become good decision-makers. Psychologists like Sidney Simon urge parents to teach children to think for themselves, to help them to clarify their values, and to encourage them to choose those values that the children themselves feel most comfortable with. Now this places parents in a very difficult position. They are being told that they must formally educate their children in the process of choosing values, and yet, at the same time, be careful not to impose their own values on the child. Did I say this is a difficult position? It is an impossible one! First of all, parents don't formally teach values as such. Rather, children learn family values when they live them. Someone once said to me, "Kids don't learn values, they catch them." There's a great deal of truth to that statement. From the tiniest toddler to even the most rebellious adolescent, the values that guide parents are obvious to the child. And, as studies have shown, they are the values most likely to be incorporated into the lifestyle of the child when he or she becomes an adult.[7] But what happens when the parents begin to doubt their own values? Where then do children "catch values?"

In a society that undermines parental authority by changing the perception of the parents' role in the formation of their children, doubt about one's own values is not unusual. And when children are increasingly encouraged in both schools and religious education programs to think for themselves about value choices, this lack of confidence in traditional values is easily heightened in the parent.

Let me give you another example here. One day my daughter (who was about ten years old at the time), and I got into an argument about the use of foul language on the part of one of her playmates. My daughter was incensed because I had sent the child home telling her she could come back when she thought she could behave better. The argument my daughter gave me went something like this: "You have no right to force your values on me or my friends. We can think for ourselves. We have our own values and we learned that in our religion class!" Now, thank God, I had the advantage of knowing the theory behind her idea of "forcing values," and could dismiss this particular piece of advice from the experts. But for many, this idea of "thinking for ourselves and choosing our own values," carrying all of the weight of expert opinion as it does, can be very intimidating. It sows the seeds of doubt in the parents' own ability to teach the child.

Now please don't get me wrong here. Of course children should learn to think for themselves. After all, critical thinking is the most important component of intelligent thought. The point is that before one can learn to think critically, one has to have something about which to think. It must be something solid to grapple with, to understand, weigh and evaluate. And it is here where our psychologized secular values fall down. For the value system they comprise is based on the attitude of "anything goes." If it feels right for me, it is right. And this system makes the act of choosing more important than the actual choices being made. By fostering such a system in schools, in religious education programs, and in the home, we once again undermine all that is important in the traditional structure of the family.

And that brings us to our third point: What is it that is so important to the traditional family structure?

LOSS OF THE SACRED

This question brings us back to the point at which we began: it is the sense of the sacred. Family values are rooted not in trendy secular/psychological thought, but in something very profound and very mysterious. They are rooted in the essential goodness of some actions as opposed to others and the necessity to adhere to a way of life that reflects something very deep and something very sacred. I know I am not being clear here, but these things do not lend themselves well to rational discussion. For they go beyond reason and they define, in a wordless fashion, the very essence of our existence.

I think we can best see the sort of thing I'm talking about in the expression of love within families. It is not the kind of love currently valued by the secular society in which we live. Rather, as Stanley Hauerwas points out in *Vision and Virtue*, it is the kind of love that is constant.[8] It involves commitment and fidelity. It is not always sentimental and romantic, although it can be. And neither is it always easy. It can require great sacrifice and sometimes great acts of self-denial. It is truly a sacred thing.

And yet today, this kind of love is being undermined and/or trivialized by the popular emphasis on love of self. Children and adults alike are being told of the importance of "being number one," of "being your own best friend." And, as Kilpatrick notes in his book entitled *Identity and Intimacy,* the result is that friendships and love relationships are being treated like paper products — use them and throw them away.[9]

137

Paul Vitz and Kirk Kilpatrick tell us that when the self becomes the center of all things, it requires all things to adjust to it rather than the self adjusting itself to anything outside of it.[10,11] And, I submit, along with this comes a loss of reverence for all things that cannot be adjusted to the immediate requirements of the self.

I think the prevalent attitude in so many sex education courses is a reflection of this. Instead of teaching children about the sacredness and exclusivity of marital sex, the emphasis shifts to the importance of teaching children to adjust to and be comfortable with their own sexuality. We can see examples of this attitude in some of the popular texts used in religious education programs. On the one hand, children are told that sex is to be reserved for marriage which is a sacrament and, on the other hand, they are then given explicit information on "what young women should know about young men in lovemaking" and on "what young men should know about young women in lovemaking."[12] And the main point of the lesson, even though, as Elkind points out, is not always the one intended, is that "You are a sexual being and you can learn how to express your sexuality freely."[13] This kind of message keeps sex in the purely physical realm and leaves little room for the notion of sex as the very sacred, exclusive and joyful expression of love between husband and wife.

But then profound experiences are themselves reduced to this new attitude of adjusting all experiences to fit into a fashionable relevance based on personal comfort and understanding. With this criterion we reduce all things to a conscious level and, as Kilpatrick argues in his book *Psychological Seduction,* we become very self-conscious, and we lose our ability to abandon ourselves to all that lies beyond our consciousness.[14] We lose our freedom to forget ourselves: to really laugh or really cry. We lose our freedom to share with others in profound joy and profound grief. And we lose our ability to participate in the sacred realm which is, as defined by Otto and Eliade in their books on this subject, the very thing that characterizes us as religious people.[15,16]

At one time, traditional family practices and rituals added a special shared dimension to family life. We all have stories we could tell. Stories like: "Remember the time Uncle Ed ran the family cookout and dropped the hamburgers into the sand and then went ahead and cooked them anyway, sand and all!'' It's the kind of story that gets told and retold at family gatherings. It's a shared memory — something funny and special to all the family members. It makes *this* family distinctive, different from *that* family. And, it's the kind of memory that reflects the sacredness of that distinction.

Something as simple as shared family dinners has the same effect. It's a time for families to pray together and really share in one another's lives. Celebrations of family birthdays, of holydays and holidays do much the same thing. Not only are they fun, but they provide us with memories that give us a sense of something special, something distinctive and something sacred about us as a family.

But today, there seems to be little time for family gatherings or even for family dinners. We can grab a fast bite to eat at McDonald's. It can be fun, but it's fast fun. It doesn't have the same element of joy about it, and it doesn't usually provide us with the stuff that memories are made of. It's not likely to put us in touch with our sense of the sacred.

Again we can see another parallel here between Church and family life. For in the Church, just as in families, it's our rituals that remind us of sacred things and sacred times. Special liturgies and services traditionally celebrated by the Church for centuries are key to maintaining our sense of the sacred, our sense of the mysterious. Without them we sacrifice reverence to a fashionable relevance, and we cling to trendy teachings of experts, treating them as if they were eternal. And, we end up treating all that is eternal as if it were very transient.

SUGGESTIONS

I have outlined the problems I see facing today's parents as they struggle to both understand and fulfill their responsibilities as primary educators of their children. More than ever before, parents need the help and support of the Catholic Church. Let me offer specific suggestions on how the Church can help in each of the three areas I've discussed: the role of parents; the secularization of values; and the loss of the sacred.

First, support us in the definition of our roles as parents. This can be done by:

1) Encouraging homilies that focus on the sacred trust that exists in the parent/child relationship. While I know it is important for families to worship together, occasional separate liturgies for adults and children, with homilies geared appropriately, would go a long way in giving us the kind of reinforcement we need in defining our roles.

2) Consulting with parents first when members of the clergy do call in outside experts. Identify the needs of the parents and choose the experts carefully. When the session is over, allow the parents to talk among themselves about the value of the advice. Guide them in making their assessments based on the teachings of our Faith, and take their evaluations seriously. These evaluations could serve as a tool for choosing trusted experts to participate in a diocesan speakers' bureau for parish-run programs.

Secondly, help us to combat the secularization of values. This can be done by:

1) Encouraging and supporting the teaching of traditional values. This, too, can be done in homilies. It can be done in family retreats or through parish newsletters.

2) Choosing very carefully the directors of religious education programs. Also, just once in a while, screen a textbook or two, the ones being used in the dioceses. If it's a book designed for younger children, check it for doctrinal content. Does it really present the tenets of the Catholic faith? If it's a book designed for older children (pre-adolescents and adolescents), look for indications that the morality being presented reflects a truly Catholic morality. Or, is it more in keeping with the "you decide" approach?

Thirdly, help us to maintain our sense of the sacred by:

1) Encouraging family rituals. In my parish, St. John the Baptist, in Quincy, Massachusetts, on Holy Thursday the priests distribute small loaves of blessed bread and prayer sheets that describe a rather simple service to be used before the family meal. It's a lovely service that involves the lighting of candles and scriptural readings for each member of the family. It provides my family with an additional practice to keep us in touch with the sacred realm of things.

2) Celebrating holy days and feast days with parish services that involve a special liturgy, processions, and a social event for the whole family. Again, I can give you an example from my parish. The Feast of St. Anthony is marked by all of the above. The social event is a fiesta of food, music and games geared for young and old alike. It's a wonderful time, enjoyed by us both as a biological family and as members of a parish family.

Other suggestions that would help to strengthen our sense of being Catholic families might include:

1) Sponsoring missionary-work days within the parishes. Design a program that would give whole families a chance to give up a day in service of others — the poor, the elderly, the sick, the homeless.

2) Sponsoring missionary-work weeks for whole families to participate in. Organize trips to poorer areas of the country in which special skills of each family member would be utilized in some needed area of work (e.g., restoring a Church; helping people to adjust to a new culture; etc.).

3) Actively supporting public demonstrations centered on specifically Christian issues (pro-life, needs of the hungry and homeless).

These last suggestions would strengthen both our ties to each other and our ties to the whole Catholic community.

I suggest all of these things as concrete ways in which the Church can help us. But, above all, we must pray. Pray that families will be strengthened and through that strength will come to an even deeper appreciation and support for the Catholic Church and all it represents, for the success of the Church's mission on earth is inextricably bound to the strength of the families she is called to serve.

Notes

1. Heschel, A.J., *The Insecurity of Freedom: Essays on Human Existence.* New York: Schocken Books, 1972.

2. Kilpatrick, W.K. "Why the Secular Needs the Sacred." *The Human Life Review,* Winter, 1984.

3. Keniston, K. *All Our Children.* New York: Harcourt Brace Jovanovich, 1977.

4. Winn, M. *Children Without Childhood.* New York: Pantheon Books, 1983.

5. For related discussions of parent/child roles and relationships see: Elkind, D. *The Hurried Child.* Reading, Massachusetts: Addison-Wesley Publishing, 1981; Howard, T. *Hallowed Be This House.* Wheaton, Illinois: Shaw Publishers, 1979; Kilpatrick, W.K. *Psychological Seduction: The Failure of Modern Psychology.* Nashville: Thomas Nelson, 1983; Postman, N. *The Disappearance of Childhood.* New York: Delacorte, 1982.

6. Winn, M., *Ibid.*

7. For a summary of studies on comparisons between parents' and adolescents' attitudes see: Hopkins, J.R. *Adolescence: the Transitional Years.* New York: Academic Press, 1983, pp. 213-223.

8. Hauerwas, S. *Vision and Virtue.* Indiana: University of Notre Dame Press, 1981.

9. Kilpatrick, W.K. *Identity and Intimacy.* New York: Dell Publishers, 1975.

10. Vitz, P. *Psychology as Religion: the Cult of Self-Worship.* Michigan: Eerdmans, 1977.

11. Kilpatrick, W.K. *Psychological Seduction: the Failure of Modern Psychology.* Nashville: Thomas Nelson, 1983.

12. Discussed in: D'Avignon, J. and W.K. Kilpatrick. "On Serving, Two Masters." *Catholicism in Crisis.* August, 1984.

13. Elkind, D., *Ibid.*

14. Kilpatrick, W.K., *Ibid.*

15. Otto, R. *The Idea of the Holy.* New York: Oxford Press, 1980. (Originally published, 1923).

16. Eliade, M. *The Sacred and the Profane.* New York: Harcourt Brace Jovanovich, 1959.

Chapter 9

Family Stewardship
of Health

Edmund D. Pellegrino, M.D.

I. INTRODUCTION

There are at least two senses in which we may understand the Christian concept of stewardship. The first has its origins in *Genesis* and takes all things as creations of God given to man to cultivate, care for, and use for temporal and spiritual good. The second sense has its origins in the New Testament parable which treats of holding other people's goods in trust to be managed in their interests. In both cases, the steward must answer to the Master for the way he manages what the Master entrusts to him.

Stewardship for health encompasses both these senses. Our bodies and health are gifts God entrusts to us to be maintained and

143

protected. We are also responsible for the health of other persons entrusted to us — the members of our family. Health professionals have an even more explicit stewardship for the health of those whose trust they invite, and who, in consequence, entrust themselves to physicians, nurses, dentists, or pharmacists.

The moral grounding of the family's stewardship for health is both natural and supernatural. It is natural since human nature receives its nurture and fulfillment in a healthy family. It is spiritual since the family is a Christian community whose members are joined in a common pilgrimage towards salvation and eternal life.

In this essay, I will examine both senses of stewardship as they apply to 1) the stewardship of the family for its own health as a family 2) the stewardship of the family for the health of each of its individual members, and 3) the stewardship of the Church as an extended Christian family for the health of its members. I have related elsewhere the specific stewardship of Christian health professionals and will not discuss that topic in this chapter.[1]

II. HEALTH "OF" AND "IN" THE FAMILY

The term "family" must today be interpreted realistically. It includes the classical "nuclear" and extended families, but also a variety of less formal "arrangements" among persons who live closely together for mutual benefit. These arrangements may exist in addition to, or sometimes in opposition to, the "natural" family. They have significance for our discussion because they, too, are social organisms that can produce health and illness, and which, by that fact, impose obligations of stewardship.

To accept the realities of the many living arrangements that characterize our society is not to give a moral benediction to all of them. However, for the Church to ignore them would be to fail in its charitable concern for all, and to ignore these obligations of stewardship that bind all who live in "household" communities.

The human family can be, and often is, the single most influential factor in human health and illness. When it is well-functioning, it promotes the well-being of each of its members, and when they are ill, becomes a healing instrument. When it is malfunctioning, the family becomes the fertile seedbed for sickness and a powerful obstacle to the healing of its members.

144

A healthy family is one that is well-functioning with respect to its end — the physical, emotional, and spiritual well-being of all its members. Malfunctioning in one sphere almost always affects the others, just as true healing in one usually requires healing in the others. The health "of" the family as a whole organism reflects itself in harmonious and re-enforcing relationships between its members such that each member can pursue his or her life with a minimum of discord, discomfort, disability, or disease.

The health of a family, like that of an individual, is a relative state, not the absolute freedom from disease. It is, in effect, an equilibrium struck between goals and aspirations, on the one hand, and the limitations imposed by heredity, social, and economic circumstances and the health of each of its members. The precise definition of health for a particular family will be unique to it, since each family's history and actual circumstances are unique. No absolute standard can encompass the multitudinous kinds of equilibria different families may attain consistent with the well-functioning of their members.

The health of a family is never static. Daily events — whether the members live together or apart — require continuous adaptation. The healthy family is characterized by its capacity to maintain its equilibrium state in the face of the many internal and external disturbant forces that threaten it.

Just as there is health "of" the family as a socio-biological organism, so can there be disease "of" the family, such that the family no longer nurtures but wounds its members. The whole and the part, the family and its members, are inextricably enmeshed with each other. Each can wound or heal the other.

While we may refer to the occurrence of illness in individual family members as disease "in" the family, any separation between disease "of" the family and disease "in" the family must be artificial. It can, however, be useful as a heuristic device precisely to demonstrate the indissolubility between health and illness, wounding and healing in the total organism and in its parts.

III. THE WOUNDING AND
THE HEALING FAMILY

We know, from the modern scientific study of the family, some of the factors in normal and pathological family dynamics. A wide variety of conditions can cause disordered family relationships, like divorce, separation, sexual maladjustment, alcoholism, drug addiction, child abuse, developmental, behavioral and learning disorders, and neuroses and psychoses of family members. These conditions occur more frequently in families where personal relationships are distorted or under tension. On the other hand, when they occur, they increase those tensions and distort the health of the family as an organism and of each member who is part of that organism. While many of these disorders arise also from socio-economic and cultural sources, the way they are perceived and adapted to depends upon the health of the family-qua-family.

Further examples of the relationship between family disharmony and the health of individual members are the common stress-related diseases as peptic ulcers, irritable colon, coronary artery disease, asthma, hypertension, and tension headache. When these disorders occur among family members, they can place severe stresses on family relationships. The same is true of any other illness which almost invariably tests the durability of the commitment of family members to assist and nurture each other.

Less obvious, perhaps, but just as important, are the effects of deleterious life-styles within the family such as excessive eating, smoking, misuse of alcohol and/or drugs, violence, or sociopathic or neurotic behavior. These disorders can be truly "contagious" in the sense that children raised in their presence are more apt to "catch" these bad habits, setting the stage for chronic, or even fatal disease and disability. When these children become adults, they refuel the cycle and "infect" their children with the same bad habits and bad health.

While the family can wound its members and its members wound the family, they can also heal each other. Indeed, the health of families and of their members are essential to each other's healing. Experienced clinicians know that most of the stress-related diseases cannot be adequately treated without some attempt to change the wounding environment of a disordered family to a healing environment. Since so many disorders have their origins in family relationships, healing requires attention to the health "of" the family. Healing must aim to restore not only the health or lost balance of the members of the family, but also of the family itself. To heal means to make "whole" again, to restore the balance that existed before the occurrence of illness, or if this is not possible, to help the one who is ill to adapt to, and cope with, the presence of a chronic disease or disability.

To heal the family as a family requires that we attend to its whole well-functioning — physical, psycho-social and spiritual. Modern medicine has much to offer in the cure and amelioration of physical illness and these measures are eagerly sought. Psychosocial and emotional adjustment are less frequently appreciated as integral to healing of the family itself and of its individual members. Catholic Christians, particularly, are fearful of over-interpretations of family life in psycho-social and cultural terms and may neglect, as a result, the significance of these factors in treatment. To accept the empirical validity of the behavioral sciences does not entail confusion of sociology and psychology with morality. The social sciences can provide empirically useful methods of treatment of the ill-health of the family. Christian anthropology, as adumbrated so well in three recent teachings of John Paul II — (*Redemptor Hominis, Familiaris Consortio,* and *Salvifici Doloris*) — is still the indispensable source for the motivations, meanings and spiritual resources authentic healing requires.[2,3,4]

IV. CHRISTIAN STEWARDSHIP
FOR HEALTH AND HEALING

Applying the two senses of Christian stewardship mentioned earlier to the family's stewardship for health produces obligations in three spheres: a) Obligations of each member for the health "of" the family; b) Obligations of the family and its members for healing those of its members who become ill; c) Obligations of the Church as an extended Christian family for the health of families and the members of those families.

A. Stewardship for the Health "of" the Family

Each member of the family is a steward of the health of the family to which he belongs. This means first that each family member must exercise stewardship over his own bodily, emotional and spiritual health because his health is integral to the health of the whole. This is an obligation in the natural order. When illuminated by the teaching of the Gospels it becomes an obligation in Charity as well.

Not only must each member seek attention for manifest disease in himself, but he must also attend to the prevention of illness of the family unit. Parents need a better grasp of the indicators of disordered family relationships, of the contribution they, themselves, make to these disorders by their own behavior, and of the causes and treatments available to restore health to the family as a family. The cultivation of health is always more important than its repair. Knowledge of the means available for the prevention of family disharmony and its prompt treatment should therefore be part of the education of young and old, as well as part of the preparation for marriage. Pastoral counsellors, physicians and other health professionals, whose stewardship for the health of others is specific, have special moral obligations to educate families and patients in the prevention of family disharmony.

Responsibility is not confined to parents. Children, as they become older, must also assume a role of stewardship for the health of their families. Often today, because of a growing emphasis on family dynamics in school, children may detect early signs of family disharmony. They should be afforded some opportunity to participate in prevention and to assist parents in promoting good health of the family.

Parents have a double obligation with respect to curing themselves of damaging habits like smoking, alcohol abuse, overeating, or violence. First as stewards of the health of their own bodies, but also to avoid infecting their children with the same habits. These habits endanger the security of the family by producing disease, disability, and premature death. Catholic Christians have taken too lightly the spiritual and moral obligation to correct these deleterious life-styles.

Parents are the stewards of their children — caring for them

as gifts of God to be nurtured; children have reciprocal stewardship for parents as they become older and dependent. A Christian
family molded in the spirit of *Familaris Consortio* is one in which
health "of" the family becomes a shared obligation in charity.

B. Stewardship for Sick Family Members

When illness occurs in a family member, the other members
of a family have an obligation to help and to provide a supportive,
caring, and nurturing environment in which healing of body,
psyche, and soul can take place. No hospital, and no combination
of professionals can substitute for the healing power of a loving
home. And, when cure is not possible, it is the family that can best
provide the consolation, reconciliation, and compassionate understanding needed to face death, dying, or dependency.

Even among Christians there is a growing disinclination today
to undertake the sacrifices required in the care of the chronically
ill, the disabled, the aged, or the retarded in their own homes. Certainly there will be many occasions when care in hospitals and
institutions will be indicated, and there need be no guilt if this is
necessary. But Christian Charity calls for a sincere effort to care for
the sick within the family environment.

No institution can substitute for the loving care of a devoted
family. Needless to say, however, an institution is to be preferred
to care given perfunctorily, begrudgingly, or simply to maintain
appearances. The sick need the charitable spirit of Christian
stewardship, not the superficial observance of its external for-
malities.

There is a special form of stewardship peculiar to our medi-
cally sophisticated times that requires particular emphasis. I refer
to the stewardship families are called upon to exercise in a formal
and explicit way when a family member becomes incompetent to
make his or her own decisions. This is increasingly the case as
medical progress permits dying or seriously ill patients to live for
long periods in non-sentient states.

Patients in coma, those with brain damage, the retarded, the
senile, and defective infants need surrogates and advocates who
can make crucial decisions in their behalf. Under these circumstances, family members assume stewardship for the very person

of the patient. They are charged with managing his or her worldly and medical affairs. Given the expanded capabilities of modern medicine, this is a kind of stewardship every one of us will probably confront at some time in our lives.

The ethical quandries encountered in decisions to resuscitate, to initiate, and to discontinue treatment in incompetent patients have been discussed at great length by medical moralists and need not be repeated here.[5] However, there are several features of surrogate decision-making that bear directly on the proper exercise of Christian stewardship by families and physicians.

This new form of stewardship requires sensitivity to several subtle dimensions of family relationships. Certain assumptions about family stewardship under those circumstances may not be true. For example, the family may not be presumed automatically to represent the patient's values, wishes, or interests. For one thing, families today are so often scattered and may not know each other's values, wishes, beliefs, or desires about death and dying. There may be subtle psychological tensions and resentments among siblings or between parents and children. These can lead unconsciously to unwarranted decisions on the one hand to undertreat, or, on the other, to over-treat to assuage feelings of guilt.

Also, even in ostensibly Christian families, conflicts of interest can obtain which militate against the patient's good. Expectation of an inheritance, a coveted property or article, or fear of depletion of an estate by excessive medical costs may move a decision in the direction of non-treatment. Similarly, anticipation of the social, emotional, physical, and financial burdens of raising a handicapped child may influence a decision toward institutionalization or non-treatment.

Christian stewardship in these circumstances calls for the most careful and sensitive analysis of the surrogate's motives by the surrogate himself, but also by those who may participate in the surrogate's decisions: health professionals, pastoral counsellors, friends, or family members. When a patient is incompetent, there can be a conflict of stewardships. The physician is expected to act in his patient's behalf, as are the pastoral counsellor and other health professionals. Each has a duty in charity, therefore, to evaluate the authenticity of the family's stewardship, its competence, possible conflicts of interests or psychological impediments to objectivity. If they are convinced that serious harm is being done to the patient or his values, those who cooperate with surrogates may have to intervene and even request court action if discussion and negotiation fail.

Individuals and families should anticipate the dilemmas of surrogate decision-making. Prudence calls for anticipatory discussions of how a person might wish his family to represent him or her in surrogate decision-making. Anticipatory discussions of one's preferences and even some anticipatory declaration — in the form of a Living Will — are desirable to protect one's own interests, to relieve the stress of one's family, and to guide pastoral counsellors and physicians when there is a conflict in their overlapping stewardships.

Christians, inspired by a concern for others, should more frequently make anticipatory declarations to avoid excessive and unnecessary expenditure in their behalf. Not only does the family have stewardship for the ill patient, but the ill patient is also a steward of the family and society's resources. Voluntary decisions to forego futile and expensive treatments is a form of charity Christian patients should contemplate more often. It may be one of the few ways to resolve the increasing dilemma of medical costs when no benefit can come to the patient from expensive technological interventions except prolongation of dying.

All these decisions must be made within the framework of a Catholic medical morality concerning life sustaining decisions, i.e. a "consistent" ethic of life.[6] But within those constraints there is considerable latitude of choice, provided the patient's wishes and values do not call for violation of a moral principle by the surrogate decision-maker.

Surrogate decision-making exposes some of the most difficult and sensitive dimensions of family stewardship for health. Prevention of conflicts between and among surrogates is a serious responsibility of families and their medical and pastoral attendants. In these circumstances, the customary dichotomy of patient care into care of body and care of soul with physician and pastoral minister each taking his assigned area is scarcely tenable. Each is forced by his or her moral obligations to enter the domain of the other. Each requires better knowledge of the other's domain and the humility to submerge professional territorial imperatives in the interests of the patient's welfare.

Recognition in the last two decades of the part the family plays in the genesis and the cure of illness has led to the growth of family medicine as a medical specialty. There has been an evolution from the general practice of medicine to the practice of family medicine — treating the family as an organism whose interactions as humans need diagnosis and treatment if the health of the whole and its members is to be safeguarded.

It is not unfair to say that family medicine is still striving to achieve a true medicine "of" the family. If this relatively new specialty can resist the temptation to mimic the technique-oriented specialties, it could provide that special blend of sensitivity to the interplay of psycho-social, physical, and spiritual elements that medicine "of" the family demands. In doing so, it could re-examine the family's stewardship for its own health.

Much of what is required for the health of the family is a motivation to the common good of the family. Spiritual and pastoral guidance are essential elements of the medicine of the family. This calls for a mutual willingness among physicians and ministers to work closely together. Physicians and clergy in fact share a common stewardship that they cannot responsibly ignore.

C. Stewardship of the Church

How do these observations about the family's stewardship for health apply to the Church — and the Bishops? If we take the Church to be a Christian community — an extended Christian family, then it has an obligation to foster health "of" and health "in" the families entrusted to it.

We have only to mention the example of Christ's own life to find the source of that stewardship. His public life was as much dedicated to healing as it was to preaching. His compassion and love for all the most vulnerable of humankind — the sick, the poor, and the outcasts — was extraordinary. He consoled, cured, and comforted them everywhere he went. Christ's deep personal and unremitting concern for the sick is unique in world history. If any message shines through in the gospels it is the importance of the healing ministry for the lives of Christians.

Over the centuries, the Church and the Bishops have followed Christ's example by establishing hospitals, hospices, homes for the poor, the aged, and the retarded. Everywhere the Church has evidenced its solicitude for the sick. That solicitude is as necessary today as in the Middle Ages when hospitals were first founded by the Church and its religious orders.

Today this age-old ministry is threatened by unprecedented forces — rising costs, competition, medical entrepeneurship, and a shift in national attitudes from health as a right, to health as a commodity to be bought and sold like any other in the marketplace. There are ample reasons why the Church and individual Bishops might consider abandonment of their health care ministry in the future — the threat of unsupportable costs to other essential ministries, the decline in religious vocations, and the difficulty of maintaining Catholic moral principles in a morally pluralistic society.

It would be inappropriate, and pretentious, to sermonize on the importance of the health ministry. I would, however, respectfully enter a plea for the continued involvement of the institutional Church in that ministry. It is possible, I believe, to survive today's eroding forces, and to do so without compromising the moral integrity of an authentic Catholic and Christian healing ministry. [7]

In that ministry, concern for the health "of" families and "in" families remains and, indeed, expands in today's uncharitable climate. It is an obligation that flows from the stewardship with which Bishops and the Church are entrusted for all members of the human family. The inspired teaching of the Gospels and the Pontiffs provide the motivation necessary to accomplish what is admittedly a very difficult task. That task is not only fully consistent with what it means to be a Christian in today's and tomorrow's world, but it is more necessary than ever before. While the Church's first emphasis must be on spiritual health, it cannot responsibly separate that obligation from the physical and emotional health of families.

Indeed, as we contemplate the current turn away from solicitude for the sick and the poor in our national policies, it becomes more obvious that the strongest "safety net" is the age-old dedication of the Christian Churches to the exercise of an authentic stewardship for health located first in the family itself, then in the health professions, and finally in the Church. This is a challenge, indeed, for the Bishops as they view the needs of families in the future of the Church.

Notes

1. Edmund D. Pellegrino, M.D., "Educating the Christian Physician: Being Christian and Being a Physician," *Hospital Progress,* August 1979, pp. 46-53, The Catholic Hospital Association, St. Louis, MO.

2. Pope John Paul II, encyclical, *"Redemptor Hominis."*

3. Pope John Paul II, apostolic exhoration, *"Familiaris Consortio,"* U.S. Catholic Conference, Washington, DC, December 15, 1981.

4. Pope John Paul II, "Encyclical Letter on the Christian Meaning of Suffering" *("Salvifici Doloris"),* U.S. Catholic Conference, Washington, DC, Feb. 11, 1984.

5. See especially, *Deciding to Forego Life-Sustaining Treatment, Ethical, Medical and Legal Issues in Treatment Decisions,* President's Commission for the Study of Ethical Problems in Medicine and Biomedical and Behavioral Research, U.S. Government Printing Office, Washington, DC, 1983.

6. Cardinal Joseph Bernardin, "A Consistent Ethics of Life: An American Catholic Dialogue", National Catholic Reporter Publishing Company, Kansas City, MO.

7. Edmund D. Pellegrino, M.D., "Catholic Hospitals: Survival Without Moral Compromise", *Health Progress,* May 1985, 42-49.

Chapter 10

Pastoral Concerns Regarding Institutions and The Family

PART I — DISCUSSION WITH FATHER ASHLEY AND DOCTOR DESTRO

Question: We're grateful to Father Ashley for clearly distinguishing the understanding of family in *Familiaris Consortio* from the traditional family of an earlier age. Too often our teaching is obscured by the false assumption that the Church's purpose is to restore an earlier society's realization of family. We found this helpful pastorally in proclaiming the authentic teaching of *Familiaris Consortio.*

We'd like to ask Father Ashley if he could spend a little more time in clarifying and developing the section on sex roles, for example, the role of the father as head of the family but in service and not in a domineering or dominating role. We would also like to ask if there is anything that is written in this area for our reading later on?

Father Ashley: I don't know what to suggest in the way of bibliography, but I do suggest we look at the New Testament again. Because of the emphasis on the rights of women, there is a tendency to explain away every text in the New Testament that is inconvenient. It's become even very embarrassing at the liturgy when we run across some of those passages in St. Paul.

What do you do with them? There is no doubt that they are conditioned by the historical situation in which St. Paul writes. We should not still maintain that women must cover their head in church or that they not be allowed to speak in church. Those were pastoral applications that were appropriate to St. Paul's situation and they can be explained in terms of the culture of the times. But that doesn't mean that those passages have no *meaning* for us any longer, that they're simply obsolete.

Back of St. Paul's pastoral application, which is time-conditioned, there are permanent principles. I think it's the business of exegetes and of theologians to take seriously what the Bible says and to try to discover the permanent principle behind the time-conditioned application. I think that principle is expressed in the New Testament and in the Old Testament, from Genesis onward, in the notion that the father is the "head" of the family.

Now what does that mean? The interpretation could be that the head of the family is simply the boss, or even worse that the family is his property and that he uses the family for his own ends and satisfaction, his own pride. I think that's the way a lot of people take that term "head." That's why those texts are offensive to many women today. They think that what is being advocated by St. Paul is patriarchalism in the sense that the head of the family has the right to treat his family as servants. He's the master and they're the slaves.

That is specifically answered in the New Testament by the famous passage in *Ephesians 5*. If you read that passage about marriage it says that Christ is the head of the body, and the woman is like the body of the family which at first sounds as if it's a relation of superior and inferior. But, then St. Paul goes on very much in line with Our Lord's own sayings about domination and servanthood. He says that the husband is to be to his wife like Christ, who sacrificed himself for the Church. In other words, the husband is to be the *servant* of the family. It's a reversal of role, a reversal of the sinful idea of domination.

I think we have got to communicate that to men today. The real answer to the problem of the oppression of women is to change the hearts of the men, to preach to the men what their role is. Yes, it's a role of great dignity, they are heads of the family. But for that very reason, just as the Bishop has to be the servant of the Church, the father of the family has to be the servant of his family. If we could communicate that idea, I think a large part of our problems about feminism would be solved.

Question: Is it possible that, if there were a family wage, the mother might be able to spend more time with the family, and the single wage-earner in the family, be it woman or man, might be able to live with more dignity and less struggle?

Prof. Destro: With respect to the family wage, at least in American law, unless you are very careful about it, you're going to find yourself up against civil rights advocates who would argue that you're discriminating against people who don't have families. Now, a statistic that I heard not long ago was that if the deduction that you get on your income tax for each child had kept up with inflation, it would have been about $3,600.00 per child. When you start talking about not taxing any wages if you have a family of 4 times $3,600.00 that's a fair amount of exempted wages. That may well be part of the answer to a family wage in our own system

Father Ashley: The social encyclicals have always maintained the idea of the family wage, it's been a standard position of the Catholic Church, however it's accomplished. We must realize that, when the woman is working at home taking care of the child, she deserves a compensation in some form. Without that compensation she is forced out of the home. We've got to keep saying that over and over again. This doesn't mean that there'll be compensation throughout her life, but only during the period of child care which is fairly limited. I can't think that this is economically impossible because, if the mother doesn't take care of the children, she has to pay somebody to take care of the children. Then we have the whole child care business which is a wasteful and not the best way of caring for children.

Dr. Destro: Let me just add one other comment. The American tax system is set up as a system of incentives and disincentives. The tax code would be very simple if it didn't have all that in it. Instead, it's a multi-volume set of very complicated laws and regulations. Keep in mind that there is a positive incentive for women to go out and work and not stay home. We give people a tax credit for child care expenses, but we don't give one for staying home. So the tax law apparently assigns greater value to the earning of income than it does to a parent's staying home and obviating the necessity for the extra income needed to cover expenses and child care.

Question: Father Ashley, how theologically correct is it to make an analogical comparison between the family of the Holy Trinity and the human family? Is the Holy Trinity reflected in the human family? John Paul II refers to the parallel between God and Father and the father in the family. There's also both unity and plurality of functions in each. Is it correct to say the family originates in a special way in the Holy Trinity? Mr. Destro, in Latin America constitutional law is not based on the Anglo-Saxon model, and it is therefore easy to correlate to Canon Law and easier to arrive at a common, that is, a civil and a religious, definition of family. In your investigation of systems of law, do you find this to be true? If so, would this easier correlation be of assistance in our North American struggle to understand family as it relates to both civil and canon law?

Father Ashley: There have been various efforts ever since the time of St. Augustine to find an exact analogy between man, wife, and child and the Trinity. Personally, I don't think that works out very well; it gets very complicated, and is not very convincing. I don't think it's very convincing, either, to argue that the Holy Spirit is the feminine principle in God, although there's some philological basis for that. The feminine Wisdom in the Old Testament as I understand it, is not the Holy Spirit but is the manifestation of God's order and God's law in the universe. It's more like the world soul, if you like, or the order of creation, rather than something within the Godhead.

But the connection between the doctrine of the Trinity and the family is that every human society is essentially a society of communication, of self-communication, a society of love. We form any kind of society by giving ourselves to others and putting ourselves in their shoes, being concerned about their interest, trying to take on their minds. The family, of course, is a special case of that, and even the primordial case. It is in the family we learn to communicate and to be self-giving. The Trinity, the very reality of God, is this total giving of self. The Father totally gives himself to the Son, and they totally give themselves to each other in the Holy Spirit. Thus every human society is an image of the Trinity and the human family is surely an image of the Trinity because it's the primordial society. But I don't think it does any help to try to work out who is the father, who is the mother, and who is the child. Analogies always limp, and that's the point at which this analogy limps.

Dr. Destro: In answer to the other question about American law, I think the point made is a very good one. The American system does proceed from an Anglo-Saxon tradition. If one looks at the American vision of the family, as traditionally understood, one sees a property-oriented approach. When we look at some of the other civil law systems which are still very strongly related to their Judeo-Christian roots, it is far easier to mesh their conception of the "family" with the Church's conception of "family". Because those systems have a very clear view of their starting point, it is going to be much easier to determine where their law is going.

The problem in the United States is that we are currently rejecting the traditional idea of "family" — in the name of pluralism. This leaves us with absolutely no idea of what our end point is going to be. We can learn a lot from the way other countries deal with family issues. American law has a "fortress-America" quality about it. Our cases do not even try to learn much from the approaches of the civil law systems. But this attitude is a problem across the whole area of law, not just in this area.

Question: Father Ashley, why do you not use the term Christian humanism which is common among some theologians? But our more fundamental question is on the Fatherhood of God. If you emphasize the mutual and total self-giving within the Trinity, then the mother seems to be as much a giver and sacrificer of life as the father. What really permanent principle can you derive from the Fatherhood of God?

Father Ashley: I think the reason the Scripture uses "Father" and not "mother" of God is not merely a reflection of the culture of the time, but it's because the Jews are radically monotheistic. For them the central doctrine is creation, that God made the world out of nothing. That underlies the whole biblical religion. That doctrine is not clear in other religions and many other religions have a mother goddess.

A mother brings the child out of her own body and she feeds the child at her own breast. She is not *other,* but identified with the child. So if you speak of God as a mother, you tend to be either a pantheist or a panentheist. You think of creation as coming out of God, as identified with God. I think that's why the Bible had to use the term Father, because that brought out more clearly the separation, the otherness of God from His creation.

You might say that that's no longer important to us, but I personally think it is still very important. I'm afraid the movement towards speaking of God as Mother is not going to do very much for the dignity of women but is going to do harm to our conception of who God is. There's a tendency at the present time to think of God as entirely immanent to the world, to overlook His transcendence. So I think at least we've got to realize that, if we change language on that point, this has theological implications.

160

Now, with regard to the other point about the fatherhood in the family, it surprises me that people think that to speak of father is somehow to emphasize that he's simply boss. The reason Our Lord calls God "Abba" is not to express that God is a despot, it's to take away from the idea of His being a despot. The Jews very seldom called God Father in prayer, because they thought of him as too great a power. The word father indicates the closeness of God, the intimacy, the care of God. God is like a father to us. He is other but very close.

I don't think the Biblical use of the term Father enhances male dominance at all, I think rather it's to bring the man into the family and to make him close to his wife and children. However, we're talking here about symbolic language and when you use symbolic language it depends how you see it, what you mean by it, and so on. I would prefer, though, to keep the Biblical language and to try to explain it to people rather than to try to change it in order to fit our particular culture and end up with very confused images.

The term "humanism" can mean a lot of things. There's the humanism of the Renaissance which simply meant that you were a literary person. Then there's Christian humanism as Jacques Maritain used it, to mean a Christianity that appreciates the value of earthly and human things. But I use humanism as a name for the philosophy of life, the system of values that grew up with the Enlightenment and which now tends to dominate all Western countries. The recent study of values in Europe shows that in most European countries the Christians are down to around 20% of the population. The rest of the people, however, are not without any kind of philosophy of life, or any system of ethics. They have a very definite system of ethics. The study of the media people in this country shows, too, that most of them are not religious in the sense of belonging to a particular thing labeled religion. But they certainly have a predominant world view and a set of values. So we've got to give a name to that.

A lot of people call this secular humanism and that term has been taken up by Jerry Falwell and some of our fundamentalist brothers. But secular humanism is like the term Protestantism, it is a pejorative name, it is an attack on a group. I would prefer to call them humanists in order simply to honor them as people having a different religion than I have. Their religion is the religion where the supreme rule in life is human reason and the hope of mankind is science and technology. It's a legitimate view, I can admire it and respect it, it's done a lot for the world. But it's not Christianity, it's a different religion.

Question: The traditional family has been described as void of romantic love. Is that correct?

Father Ashley: I really think it's true that the notion of romantic love that we take for granted, the idea that marriage should be based on falling in love with somebody, is rather a new thing. One of the Church Fathers discusses the Biblical text about a man leaving his father and mother and clinging to his wife and he remarks, "Isn't this odd that a man should leave people he's known all of his life to cling to a woman he never met before!"

Question: A first question is for Father Ashley. We're addressing ourselves to a counter-cultural response from our people when it comes to marriage and human sexuality. For example, we teach that every sexual act must be open to life, and yet the statistics show that more than 70% of our people at childbearing age use artificial birth control. How do we begin to present our ideal and help our people to accept it in some kind of a pastoral way?

The second question for Mr. Destro has to do with the protection of family rights against the focus of constitutional law on individual rights. Do we make our efforts at the state level or the national level and do we do it in terms of legislation in Congress or must we take our stand in the courts. Where are we going to deal with this problem?

Father Ashley: Well, the first question is a tremendously difficult one. The newspapers regularly report that Pope John Paul II again reaffirmed the stand on contraception or again reaffirmed the stand on abortion. But they leave out what he's really trying to do. As I see it, he's trying to restore our vision of the beauty and the importance of the family for real happiness and real fulfillment in life. If people saw that, then the teaching on abortion and contraception would begin to make sense. But until they get a glimpse of that vision, these other things don't make any sense.

I think we have to start from that end or goal. We should not leave out the teaching on contraception or abortion but put in the forefront the effort to rebuild this picture or image of the family. It can't be put just as a beautiful ideal either. We have to start from the actual difficulties that exist and then show that the only answer to those difficulties is the return to sound family living. We must work on communicating that image in the context of the very real difficulties that people have. Then the moral application can flow from that and be meaningful to people.

Dr. Destro: With respect to the question of where you should direct your energies, I think that there's a simple answer and then a more complicated one. I'd say simply that the first place you should direct your energy is the place where you have absolute control, which is in your pulpit. I think that you have to start talking about this with your congregations and with your priests. You have to develop a real appreciation for the family-centeredness of a lot of the Church's mission. Let's fact it, the judges and legislators go to church. You can always then say later when you go to lobby that you heard it in church first.

The second answer is that one of the reasons that the family is not protected in the American Constitution is that nobody ever dreamed that the state would get involved in it like it is today. And we do have the state involved in every-thing. Sometimes when there's a need you have to develop legislative responses. I wouldn't waste my time with the courts, I would go directly to the legislatures and do it at both the state and federal level. Also, how about considering another pastoral letter? You got a lot of attention on the last two, and you are certainly going to get a lot of attention on the next one. You might as well do one that will draw a lot of attention. It might not be supportive attention because you're going to be seen as going in the wrong direction, but it's still worthwhile to get people talking.

Question: Father Ashley stated that the Holy Father's ideal of the family has not been realized in fact, and indicated that this ideal is an eschatological model which the Gospel calls us to realize here and now. We are concerned about our prospects for fulfilling that calling.

Father Ashley: The Gospel invites us to peace, yet we've always had war. This doesn't mean, however, that the Church has not been effective in the past in doing something to bring about peace and to bring about care of the poor. We keep struggling at this. It's something that *can* be realized in this world and we realize it in part. I think the same thing is true with regard to the family. There will be a perpetual struggle to maintain the Gospel ideal in the face of a sinful world. But we have had some very real successes in the past. There were families in the past that were based on real Christian love, no doubt about it. So this is an ideal that's not up in a platonic heaven, it's something that can be essentially achieved here and now, but not perfectly. There are families where the husband and wife are really faithful to each other and really try to do their duty to their children out of the motive of love.

Question: Following upon Vatican II, the Church calls for a real self-giving in marriage to form a community for the mutual benefit of the spouses and the procreation and upbringing of the children. And marriages are declared null because such self-giving was lacking. Does this mean that marriages in the past where this self-giving was lacking were also null or not true marriages, or have the requirements of the Church for a true marriage changed?

Father Ashley: I think the easier answer, and I suppose its the right one, is that many marriages in the past were not real marriages. If you read the history of royal marriages, some of which were declared null by the Church, you really wonder whether those marriages could have been called real marriage in the Christian sense of the word. They fulfilled certain legal and external requirements, but whether theologically you could say they were marriages is another question.

But, of course, for a marriage to be valid doesn't mean that the people are perfect in their fulfillment of their obligation. The self-giving required for marriage to be valid means they can truly and freely assume a responsibility of self-giving. Now they may not carry that out very well and the marriage will still be a valid marriage. When we dissolve marriage what has to be proved is that the people were not capable or did not in fact undertake this responsibility at the beginning. It's not to prove that they haven't carried out their responsibilities well enough.

Question: There has been a new definition of marriage since Vatican II and the new definition has obviously been clarified and enlightened by the exhortation of Pope John Paul II. That new definition has been codified and expressed in legal terms in the New Code of Canon Law. Now obviously this is creating very serious pastoral problems. The average Christian brought up in a humanistic environment is either ignorant of his faith, or does not accept in practice that definition of marriage. On the other hand, we know that every baptized Catholic must be married before a priest and two witnesses for that marriage to be valid.

And so the pastor at the parish level is faced with a very serious problem. Does he refuse to marry a young couple, or refuse to accept the definition which we believe in and which we hold very dearly, or does he spend maybe several years trying to have the couple adopt our new definition, or does he leave it to the marriage court to decide what marriage is going to be valid or invalid?

Father Ashley: It does seem to me that we have the obligation to instruct the people as well as we can. You can't tell how deeply this is accepted, and whether their acceptance of this is nominal or whether it is real. But you've done your best to instruct them. They have a right to ask to be married by the Church, if they have taken the instructions, and the priest doesn't have a right to refuse to marry them. You have to take it that they understand and they're willing to go through with it.

Now later on it may be that they will try to have the marriage annulled and that they will be able to give good evidence at that time that for some reason or another the marriage was not valid and it can be legitimately annulled. After all, the Church is only witnessing their act of getting married. They have a responsibility there too. The Church has its legal procedures in order to protect the objective standards of marriage as well as possible, but the marriage court, like any court, can only go on external appearances, there is no way that they can decide the ultimate reality of the thing.

Question: I don't altogether agree with Father Ashley. There are times when people have the right to marry, but the Church also has a right to teach and preserve the meaning of marriage as we understand it in our society. So there are times when we can legitimately refuse to witness a marriage if people do not accept what is our understanding of that Sacrament or if they are incapable of fulfilling the marriage commitment.

Father Ashley: I'm not disagreeing with the fact that we have a right to refuse in some cases. I'm saying, though, that we don't have to feel that I have got to make sure that this person understands this because there's no way to make sure that the person understands it in a real sense. It's like students, they give the right answer but you don't know whether they have the right insight.

PART II — DISCUSSION WITH
DOCTOR D'AVIGNON

Question: The feeling has emerged that we are being asked to swim against the tide. We get the impression that perhaps we're not paddling hard enough. We would like Dr. D'Avignon, as a Catholic mother, to tell us whether in her perception the Church is too tentative and hesitant in her teaching, particularly of morals, but also of faith tenets. If we are to paddle harder against the tide, how can we do that?

Dr. D'Avignon: I know the harvest is abundant and the laborers are few, but I trust that, if we all go into the fields together, we will be productive. I do think that the Church has been very hesitant, especially in the area of religious education. I don't know why, except that I would attribute it to this whole phenomenon of the age of experts. Religious education directors come in with all their authority and expertise and I think often the parish priests are intimidated by them.

I find the situation in Catechetics has been appalling. I thought if I sent my children to parochial schools that they would really learn their Faith. That was the only reason I sent them to parochial schools. I didn't send them for structure. And yet I had the experience once of going to this PTA where we went to each class that the children had and the teacher told you the contents of the course. Well, in the religion class she was talking about teaching children to become persons, as if otherwise they were going to become cabbages! Of course, they're going to become persons. I asked what was the doctrinal content in this course. And she said, "We're teaching the children to become whole persons, to grow".

I don't know why this phenomenon exists but it does. I've also seen it in religious education when the kids went back to public school and went to CCD, I didn't have any better luck there either. I had one person tell me that they were teaching the Christian message: To reach out and touch somebody. That's the telephone company's message, it's not the Christian message! Yes, I think the Church has been very hesitant for some reason and I think it's probably intimidation by experts who claim they have the answers. That's the number one reason.

I think the best thing that the Bishops can do to help us is probably to start with the books used in religious education. Please look at those books carefully, especially some of the ones that are designed specifically to teach Catholic morality, and for Catholic sex education courses. Look at them! They're very explicit, they are almost how-to books. I was amazed to see chapters entitled, "What a young man needs to know about a young woman in lovemaking". The next chapter, "What a young woman needs to know about a young man in lovemaking". That's the whole emphasis, keeping sex in the physical realm. So I think we need to be really careful that these kinds of books don't become the best sellers in the diocese. We should demand from our publishers books that have content, books that teach Catholic morality. I think that's a real key area where Bishops can really be helpful to us. It is terribly frustrating to be a parent and to have your child argue for a secular value system that's been learned in their CCD class or in their religion class.

Question: Dr. D'Avignon, would your position, which we find so admirable, be shared by most of the peers in your parish? Secondly, you're not saying what we usually hear when a person who is a psychologist shows up and talks about these things. So we would like to know how much tension and conflict you may have found between your psychological training and your practical experience as a parent? And, thirdly, it seems that you were speaking of the good family, that their parental sense is to be trusted and should be listened to. But, in many of our parishes, maybe now half the people are those unmarried mothers or the single parents, and we're wondering about that teenage unmarried mother who keeps her child, can we trust what would be called parental instincts? Yet sometimes we see intellectual and well-trained parents failing while we find people, who would be described by some as primitive and illiterate, succeeding very well. So we are asking for some comment in that whole area of how do you know whether you can trust your parental instinct.

Dr. D'Avignon: Your first question was, is my position shared by peers in my parish? For the most part, yes. What I find happening is that when I talk to parent groups they know exactly what I'm talking about, yet they may not have the confidence to exercise their authority. They feel they have the right, but they don't have the confidence, because too many other parts of society undermine them. And, I think some people are more susceptible than others to this sort of phenomenon. But, I do think most parents do feel somewhat cheated. Because we really do feel that we could do alright if people would just stop telling us how we should do it better. There are courses for parenting and courses for everything you want to do, there are even prenatal training courses, believe it or not. But, we are getting to be too educational in our approach to things, I think.

168

The second question was about tension and conflict. Yes, I find that my position of being in the area of psychology and of being very committed to my Faith often causes conflict. It particularly causes problems for me professionally among my peers who do not see this as an issue that should be taken seriously at all, for most of them are not believers. That is a real problem and a real struggle for me personally.

In terms of your third question, I really don't have an answer. The teenage mother is not competent, she is still a child despite the fact that she has had a baby. She is probably more immature than the teenager who does not have a baby. The extended families were a wonderful resource. We don't have them anymore, we're too mobile as a society. We've all sort of lost touch with one another. Finally, I don't know how you tell who can be a good parent. Certainly, professional people who have lots of knowledge about child behavior sometimes cannot seem to get it right with children while other people do. My basic feeling is that it's a matter of faith and a matter of trust and a matter of prayer.

Question: Do you feel that our children today are handicapped in the area of sexual identity and the interrelationships of the sexes because they haven't really found out what it is to be a boy or a girl before they are suddenly thrust into mixed company?

Dr. D'Avignon: I think that is true. I think our children are really losing a sense of childhood, children don't play the way they used to play anymore. When I was a kid growing up, children played street games, children went outside. We weren't even allowed to go inside. We had to play outside. But children don't play as much as they used to, they don't play the same games that everybody used to play. They rely much more on television. That is probably the real number one problem in this society. From TV they learn to imitate very adult-like behaviors. Children are forced into positions that they just can't cope with. Their childhood has been dramatically shortened and the quality of that childhood has been dramatically diminished.

Question: You have noted the problem we have about vigilance over religion texts. What can we do really? The experts seem to be proponents of the secular values, the value clarification method and all that. Is there any more that you can say to help us with this?

Dr. D'Avignon: I know the major publishing companies have been pushing the books that really don't have much content. I haven't seen the new Sadlier books that are out. I understand that they have made an effort to include more content. There are some good books out there: I've seen some. There's a new catechism for adolescents by a friend and colleague of mine, Peter Kreeft, from Boston College: It's a Socratic dialogue approach to issues of faith. It's designed for the adolescent child, because it's an argument about the existence of God and some of the more theological questions. But, for the most part, all I can tell you is, just to avoid the books that you known are not teaching the Faith and to really have somebody research this area for you, and seek out the good books.

Question: With regard to the role of parents as primary educators in such a basic matter as teaching prayers of fundamental beliefs, can they, should they, and do they fulfill this role presently?

Dr. D'Avignon: Yes, I think they do. I said that moral values are not formally taught by parents. I never sat down with my kids and said, "Let me tell you, God made you and God loves you". I've never done that, but those things come up as children ask questions. "Mom, who is God and where did he come from?" I had to teach them traditional prayers. But when they were in first, second, or third grade, they came home one day and said they couldn't say the Hail Mary and Our Father any more! I said, why not? "Our teacher told us it's better that we pray just using our own words". I told them that sometimes we all have really bad times and we don't feel like God can ever hear us. When we have bad times we have to rely on words that we know, because we don't have any other words to say. That's really hard to explain to a child. But, yes, I think parents have to continue teaching the articles of faith but, for the most part, faith is learned as it is lived.

Question: Is it your perception that parents are doing that?

Dr. D'Avignon: Probably less so then they used to. But I do know a number of families who do do that.

Question: How can parents regain or take up their primary roles as teachers? Did you want to hand back to the Church the responsibility to restore the role of parents as primary educators?

Dr. D'Avignon: I think the Church can play a major role in restoring that perception by reinforcing parents' position. You have to realize that there is no other institution that is going to do this. We can go to child guidance centers and they will tell us that we ought to enter into a social contract with the child, which is nonsense. It is really only in the Church that our role can be affirmed and reinforced. So we need you.

Question: What can parents do in the home to encourage vocations to the priesthood and religious life?

Dr. D'Avignon: I really don't know, except that parents should really make the effort. Parents should be reminded that it's very likely that some of their children are being called to a vocation. If parents were more aware of the fact that this may be so, they could make this an option when they talk to their child about what he's going to do when he grows up. Vocations to serve the Church should be included. We can say, "You might want to be a priest. you might want to be a nun, you might want to be a lay missionary." A lot of parents just don't think about encouraging their children in that way.

Question: When you're talking to children in that way, would you single out the priesthood for the boys, for example, to let them know its importance?

Dr. D'Avignon: Yes, but I also emphasize that this is not his decision, that this is something that he has to respond to if that is in him. It's a calling, it's not something you can just decide you want to be because it suits you.

Question: It just seems, though, if parents list all the possibilities without giving some kind of an emphasis upon vocations to the priesthood, the child might perceive them all as equal.

Dr. D'Avignon: Yes, that's true. So I think you are probably right that there should be an emphasis on teaching our boys that they have to become aware of that kind of a calling.

Question: A good deal of what Dr. D'Avignon presented could perhaps be more applicable to the early adolescent and later childhood years rather than to that very difficult time of mid-adolescence. So many of our parents are really copping out at that time. They're afraid they don't know how to deal with their youngsters at that time. How can we help them to face up to their responsibilities, or to be more courageous or more able to handle that very difficult moment when the youngster not only feels that he or she can talk for him or her self, but everybody else is telling him or her that she or he can?

Dr. D'Avignon: I know what this is like, my own children are 14 and 13, and my daughter has really hit adolescence. It's very difficult sometimes. I have to remind myself that she is a sweet child. I don't always remember that, but I think the important thing would be to be able to have parents come together to address the issue of being a parent of teenagers. Parents at this point become so frustrated that they really need to hear from somebody. That is a difficult time. There are ways to get through it. You end up sometimes having to prioritize what is really bothering you. You make compromises, but you have to learn to do that during those years, otherwise you would be yelling all the time. So you settle for, instead of a clean room, a path from the door to the bed. That's good. Those are the sorts of little things that you have to learn to compromise on so that you don't lose it all when the big things come. Parents need to know that they can do that without losing authority and that they can still exercise authority when it is important to exercise it.

Parents just become intimidated by their own children sometimes when their kids are so quick with telling them what their likes are. Teenagers are very well informed today. They get a student bill of rights, they know what their rights are in school. My daughter asked me this Christmas to buy her a book called, "How to Sue Your Parents for Malpractice". You have to learn to laugh at these things.

Question: Dr. D'Avignon, we have a feeling that the modern day psychologists, by fearing to affirm as positively as you have

172

done the traditional values that are good and worth retaining, are doing a disservice to our society and perhaps leading us down the wrong path. Do you agree? Secondly, what percentage of professional psychologists and educators think as you do, or are you like a voice crying in the wilderness?

Dr. D'Avignon: I'm afraid there are not very many of us. I could barely count them on one hand. Most modern psychologists, I agree, are leading us astray. Perhaps this is because they feel very powerful. They know so much about human behavior and they think they can also predict human behavior. There is a lot of danger in much of what is being taught in psychology today. In Dr. Kilpatrick's book he talks about the sheep in wolf's clothing. Some modern psychology on the surface looks very Christian. The psychologists talk about loving one another. We must all love one another. But they don't talk about the real hard love, it's all very sentimental. It is very trivial compared to what love really is. Hence this love looks on the surface to be very Christian and it's really not.

We believe that God did create us as good people. We are graced by goodness, but we are also scarred by sin. This psychology refuses to acknowledge that we are scarred by sin, that there is evil within us as well as goodness, and that we are really not as autonomous and freely independent as we would like to think we are.

Question: We have noted the tremendous tension that arises when a permanent deacon or a catechist or evangelizer who is loyal to his or her family and who is committed to the Church seeks to balance family life and ministry. As a mother how do you think we could best integrate the familial and ministerial life so that they can enrich one another rather than be destroyed by jealousy?

Dr. D'Avignon: I think that it just takes sensitivity to the needs of the family in arranging schedules, for example. For me what is really difficult is arranging my schedule so that my children don't have to be home alone. In Church functions when you have people as lectors, don't have members of the family at separate Masses all day long Sunday!

Question: With regard to the whole problem of the media, how do you deal with the pressures from the secularized culture while trying to give your own children the values that you hold dear? Secondly, how do you get your children to internalize the values?

Dr. D'Avignon: I pray a lot! In my personal life, I'm not really big on censoring, but occasionally I won't sit through a T.V. program. It's not easy because it ends up in a fight and I know it's going to be a fight. I just have to keep saying, "I'm sorry, I don't want this stuff in my house". I can't control what our children do when they go to other people's houses. They could lie to me about what movies they go to and they could be in bookstores reading all the dirty books. I can't control those things. But there is the understanding in my house that these things are not acceptable. My children are very aware of that. It sinks in in time. Every study that I've ever seen shows that.

Question: One of the questions that was asked from our table was what is the validity in the education of children of discipline? The discipline of denying them privileges or affirming them and rewarding them. How valid is that in the education?

Dr. D'Avignon: That is a valid method of disciplining children, but this has to begin when the child is very young. Children should experience an intense reaction from parents when they transgress, when they hurt somebody else. That kind of reaction makes that behavior very clear to the child. It makes it a very distinct kind of behavior and a non-acceptable kind. But, in order to be effective, that reaction has to also be coupled with a kind of altruistic pattern of behavior in the parents. Children whose parents kiss their cuts and make them better and do that sort of thing tend to raise children who in turn behave altruistically. But, these two things have to be present, both the parents' involvement in genuine care taking of the child and the parents' conviction that hurtful behavior is not accepable. In terms of discipline it's important for parents to feel strongly about how they want their children to behave and to be examples of that behavior.

PART III — DISCUSSION WITH DOCTOR PELLEGRINO

Question: Doctor, what preparation would you suggest, psychological or otherwise, to members of the family when a member of the family becomes handicapped through drug abuse, alcoholism, especially when it might be the head of the household? Secondly, from your personal experience, what would be the pros and cons of proposed Living Will legislation?

Dr. Pellegrino: On the first question, when a member of the family becomes involved in one of the disorders that you outlined, we must try to bring to bear as many resources as we can and to take advantage of what the social and psychological sciences have given us in the way of empirical knowledge.

It is my own conviction, particularly with things like alcohol and drugs, that ordinarily the patient does not make a change until undergoing some kind of a conversion, not necessarily a conversion in the religious sense, but a change in the way of life. Unfortunately, that often doesn't happen until the patient hits the very "bottom of the barrel". We hope to get to those people before that happens with help from Alcoholics Anonymous or other community resources.

Certainly, if the patient is a believer, and a Christian, and a Catholic, we must draw on spiritual resources. I have been distressed by the fact that Catholic physicians, and I must say at times even the clergy, do not draw on spiritual resources as a part of the attempt to help such a person. We need to raise the question, what is it, as a Christian, as a Catholic, that God might want you to be, to do, under these circumstances? That may sound "unrealistic" to some, but the reality is that some patients do respond if we approach them properly. I think that what is needed more than anything else is the non-moralizing approach. This is the approach of charity, that makes clear that one doesn't accept that kind of behavior, but one is always open, willing to help.

On the question of Living Wills I would say the following: I believe that a Living Will properly executed may be morally valid under certain limited conditions. That would mean first that it ought to be executed when the patient knows that he does have an illness which has the potentiality for being fatal. To make a Living Will at age 20 and expect it to be binding at age 57 is to ask too much of anybody. We do change, we are different persons in that period of time. Secondly, the one who makes the will must be competent and clearly express his/her wishes and values. Thirdly, the patient must not ask the physician or the nurse or someone else to do something which runs counter to their moral beliefs. Under these circumstances I think the Living Will can be a morally licit and useful document. One must approach its use with great care. Obviously if there's any question about the moral legitimacy of that Will, then, one must presume that the patient wants to be treated.

Question: Doctor, we applaud your concern for the poor, how do we as Church provide health care for the poor in our general hospitals in light of government regulations and third party payers? Secondly, the question arises can we stay in the hospital business? Or, is our better option to stay in pastoral care in hospitals run by boards and administered by lay persons?

Dr. Pellegrino: Those are very good and crucial questions. They are intertwined as a matter of fact. I think we must stay in the hospital ministry and I think we can stay without compromising our moral integrity. First, we must put our resources together. We have too many Catholic hospitals in competition with each other, too little cooperation among them and some real inequities in shouldering the burdens of care of the poor. We need to organize Catholic hospitals on a national and a regional basis cutting across Diocesan lines and the boundaries of sponsoring religious orders. A multi-hospital, national network of Catholic hospitals and health care institutions is a tremendous resource with which for-profit hospitals would have to contend.

In addition, we must also increase Catholic health care philanthropy. We have an enormous potential here still to be tapped properly. The Roman Catholic community must ask itself where the health care ministry fits in the evangelical and apostolic mission of the American Church. Do we not have a serious responsibility of stewardship which must be translated into financial sacrifice?

We cannot abondon the health care ministry unless we ignore Christ's own example of daily healing. Nor can we do so at this time when the national temper is to retreat from equity of access, availability and quality in health care. If we abandon this ministry who will be there to pick it up?

Catholic health professionals must also do more for those who cannot afford care. Catholic communities must mobilize to help as volunteers to care for the sick at home, to provide home making services, to supplement hospital and outpatient care. Often what is most lacking is not technical, medical assistance but the help of a pair of willing and caring hands.

Catholic hospitals will increasingly come under lay control, since the religious orders do not have the requisite man and woman power.

The Catholic laity must replace them, not as part of a health care "business," or health care "industry," but as part of a genuine ministry. There are too many Catholic hospitals that are yielding to market forces because cost containment and competition can become ideologies, self-justifying, self-perpetuating principles. But our ordering principle has to be different. We have enough hospitals; some will have to close; functions will have to be partitioned among them. Everybody can't do everything. With a truly cooperative network we could continue to operate not-for-profit hospitals and not be overwhelmed by the for-profit hospital chains.

The day will come when the abuses inherent in for-profit medicine will be a public scandal. Then we will see hospitals as public utilities with the most stringent regulation we've ever conceived. Catholic hospitals can answer that health ministry is not a business, medical care is not a commodity transaction. People are waiting for that kind of statement to be made by us. We can mobilize people behind that kind of an idea. But for how long, if we too succumb to the marketplace in our misguided attempts at survival.*

177

Question: Is it time for us as Bishops to promote and support socialized medicine?

Dr. Pellegrino: I must know precisely the definition of socialized medicine. If we're talking about a system which would make available health care to those who need it, irrespective of their ability to pay, then the time is here. Does that mean a government-operated system? Not necessarily.

What I am concerned about is the major issue, i.e., can we provide for those who need health care? We cannot turn our backs; we can't make health care a matter of the market place because the market place will not distribute it. Inevitably, as far as I'm concerned, we are going to come to some kind of system. We've turned away from it for awhile. But, I do think the American people will become aware of the abuses that are already occuring under a competitive system. We will be moving in some other direction. So is it time? I thought it was time a long time ago. As a physician I see the assault of illness on the whole person, on the very humanity of a person. If one doesn't have health one can hardly do any of the other things in this life. Health is a fundamental human need. I'm not talking about health care as being a right. I speak of it as being an obligation for which a civilized and concerned society must make provision.

Question: There seems to be a significant percent of men who now want to enter the seminary who have psychological problems or of those who, despite greater screening, become priests and then have psychological problems. Do we simply say that we don't want to accept any of those people because of this problem or is it something that we simply have to live with and accept the fact that counseling is a way of life?

Dr. Pelligrino: People have been sensitized to these issues today. It's my guess that these problems existed in every society and every era. We are more aware of them. I cannot say what psychological aberrations would constitute an absolute impediment to entry into the seminary. I do not think you can avoid bringing in a number of person with emotional problems. I think that they perhaps can function very well with help. They'll be helping others. Here is where the problem lies because their own problems may interfere with their ability to help others. Nonetheless, one would hope that by supporting them as seminarians, we can make them helpful and useful to other human beings. I don't think that the situation in recruitment is such that one has to take a grossly aberrant person. But, somewhere in between there's a line that perhaps one may stretch a little bit.

We must also, however, educate the laity to the acceptance of some minor aberrations. They've had an unreal and romantic notion of the clergy at times, and have not been willing to accept their humanity.

Question: Our Mexican Bishops tell us they have socialized medicine and they view it with a bit of reservation, although perhaps that's the only practical way for this social medicine to be administered. They have regulations governing which medicine you give for which illness and the doctors say that these parameters that are specified by regulation are not always effective. The doctors often ask patients to come to their own office to get a more effective medicine.

Dr. Pellegrino: That's why I was very cautious when the question of socialized medicine was raised. I would want to have a full definition of just what is being suggested when one uses that term because there are many many patterns and plans. Take for example, the socialized medicine of the Soviet Union. One of our scholars at the Kennedy Institute has been studying from the Russian medical literature published. The health of the Russian people is on their own accounts, atrocious. They are 20 to 30 years behind the times, using treatments and facing problems which we've discussed.

The emphasis I would put is on the end first, and then work back to means which facilitate that end. The end is a system which would provide the capacity to provide health care for those people who need it. I'm not convinced that the American people have agreed that 10% of the gross national product is all that one should spend for health. We do want efficiency and effectiveness and productivity, but they should not be ends in themselves, as they seem to be at the present time. Everything needs to be looked at from the point of view of some ordering principle, the criterion against which you judge whether a means you've suggested does, in fact, bring you toward the end which you've defined.

What I'd like to see is not a government-run program. That I think would be the worst in the world. I would like to see a financed insurance program that would provide at least, first, protection against catastrophic illness. We're seeing people wiped out today, selling their houses, wiping out their savings because of illness.

Question: With the rise of the industrial revolution new social needs arose, among them health needs, and the Church responded with hospitals and new congregations. Do you see, Doctor, some present unmet health needs that the Church can and should address?

Dr. Pellegrino: I think the most important contribution of the Church is to operate institutions that provide care because that's the most urgent need today for people who have no place to go to, or turn to. There's another reason as well. We need places where persons can come who seek protection for their values, if they are Christian and Catholic values. Likewise, we also need places where we can evidence to the world that it makes a difference to be a Christian. That difference only comes when you're making some kind of an act of sacrifice and help to a human being who needs it. That's our contribution. How we do it would depend on our resources, and how much sacrifice we want to make.

---

* For a fuller explication of these ideas see E.D. Pellegrino, Catholic Hospitals, Survival Without Moral Compromise, *Health Progress,* May, 1985, Vol. 66, No. 4, pp. 42-49.

PART III:
FAMILY PROBLEMS TODAY

OVERVIEW
OF PART III

This final part of our volume singles out four specific problems of families today. Chapters 11 and 14 discuss, respectively, migrant families and the aged members of families. Chapters 12 and 13 discuss family violence and parental roles in transition. Chapter 15 concludes Part III with the pastoral concerns which these problems generate.

Mario Paredes has carefully organized his analysis of the problems faced by migrant and alien families as evangelical, cultural, and socio-economic challenges. His Chapter 11 could be a handbook on ministry to these families.

In Chapter 12 Bishop Ricard draws on his scholarly understanding of family dynamics to paint a disturbing picture of conjugal violence and child abuse. His chapter, too, meets a current need as public attention is drawn toward sexual abuse of children and the fate of missing children by the mass media.

Clayton Barbeau, well-known throughout the U.S. for his lectures on marriage and the family, divides his reflection in Chapter 13 between historical observations and the contemporary experience of marriage as relational. His comments on parental roles stem from his own life experience and his ample experience as a marriage counselor. Readers will find his style refreshing and his insights down-to-earth.

Chapter 14 returns to the problems of aging family members which Dr. Soldo introduced in Chapter 3. Msgr. Charles Fahey, Director of the Third Age Center at Fordham University, writes from considerable background in geriatric studies. AFter reviewing the demographic facts about the aging and some seven aspects of aging itself, he explores the Church's responsibility in the areas of service, values, and spirituality.

Finally, Chapter 15 brings the four authors into dialogue with the Bishops at the Workshop. Readers have the opportunity to give second thought to many specific points raised in the previous four chapters as the authors develop them more fully.

Chapter 11

Ministering to Migrant
and Alien Families

Mario J. Paredes, M.A.

I have chosen to present a reflection on my topic rather than a scholarly essay. There are, therefore, no footnotes and no bibliographical references attached. The work of the scholars who make up the majority of this conference's speakers more than compensates for my option.

I begin with a disclaimer. It involves the topic assigned to me which is identical to the title of this chapter, ministry to migrant and alien families. The topic is far too broad. Leaving aside whether we could reach an adequate understanding of the word "ministering," I doubt that we could ever embrace the variety presented by migrant and alien families in the United States today.

I take migrants to be people who wander from place to place in a region or nation in search of livelihood. In the United States, the most well-known and largest migrant group is the farmworkers. But, the truth is, farmworkers are themselves diverse. They include, among others, Southern blacks, Chicanos and undocumented and documented Mexicans. Gypsies are migrants. Other migrants are carnies and the dozens of groups of seasonal and occasional workers that wander about. Properly, too, the word should apply to Puerto Ricans who come to the continental United States. They are native citizens, even if, in fact, they are aliens or strangers in most of the English-speaking North.

Aliens are those from any and every other continent and nation in all their differences, with or without proper documents.

I am obviously not qualified nor prepared to approach so global a topic, not even in a reflection.

A brief description of the aim of this chapter was circulated in advance. It narrows things somewhat by giving considerable limits to the word "ministering" and, to a degree, reducing the compass of "migrant and alien families":

> An examination of the special challenges to family life among peoples uprooted from familiar surroundings in pursuit of their economic well-being, discussing viable approaches to these families and efforts being made or projected for the Church's assistance.

"Ministering" now assumes the particular sense of serving people challenged in special ways — ways we shall have to describe. The words "migrant and alien families," however, still embrace too broad a diversity for me to claim any competence.

My experience is intense within its boundaries. It is, however, only from within these boundaries that I can offer comment. I am not a sociologist or whatever be the particular kind of student who would have a universal view. I have worked in the Catholic Church for and with the Hispanic migrant and immigrant communities of the Northeast for the past fifteen years. I am myself an immigrant to the United States. Considerable involvement nationally with others working in the American Catholic Church for its Hispanic membership has given me a wider perspective, as has an increasing association with the bishops, clergy and people of the Church in the countries from which Hispanic newcomers to the United States mainland derive. Nevertheless, my real experience with migrant and alien families remains the Hispanic Northeast.

I shall write, then, about special challenges to family life that I know exist among Hispanic migrant and alien families now living in the United States, viable approaches to these families and the Church's efforts at assisting them. I think that most of what will be put forward has validity for other populations elsewhere, but judgment on this rests with those who know those situations better than I.

One more clarification is demanded, one which extends to more than Hispanic families. The families of migrants and immigrants are not all the same. Within the composite are families of every social and economic class and of every other sort. Some are families of highly educated professional persons, others are families of illiterates. There are the wealthy, the middle class and the poor. Some are extended families, others nuclear. There are two-parent families and single. Generalizations need to be governed in their acceptance by these facts.

With Hispanic families, a further caveat stands over generalizations. Hispanic people come from the Mexican Southwest, Puerto Rico (United States citizens both by birth), and from each and every Spanish-speaking nation. Each ethnic group, while sharing language and some traditions with the rest, has its own cultural peculiarities which affect family life.

In short, "special challenges" are ultimately real only in individual families. No abstract "special challenge" belongs necessarily to all families of any group and not to any individual family precisely in the same manner as to any other.

For my purposes, I classify the challenges to family life that I perceive under three headings: evangelical, cultural, and socio-economic. After listing the challenges that stand out for me under each heading, I shall immediately discuss what viable approaches I see, and the Church's efforts.

I. EVANGELICAL CHALLENGES

Everyone is challenged by the gospel. Everyone of us receives the contrary challenge of sin — whatever its etiology — the anti-challenge from what John's gospel calls the "world." Persons in the relationship of a family have before them the evangelical call to approach that relationship of self-giving love exhibited to us and Jesus, the only Son, by the Father "from whom every family in heaven and on earth is named" (Eph 3:14-15) and from Jesus our Lord who gave himself on the cross "to gather into one the children of God who are scattered abroad" (John 11:52). Clearly, this challenge is met only by supernatural grace. Yet, in the mystery of God's plan for us, he demands that we nourish one another for it through the spoken and witnessed Word and through the great signs of his love that Jesus has left his Church.

This challenge is a special one for those in new and different places, in homes where they are not at home. Leaving the required room for individual difference, I see my migrant and alien Hispanic people carrying a cultural tradition that strongly emphasizes the Christian ideal of family, even if it is not always pursued in all its aspects. Their understandings generally are those of our Catholic Church. The majority, however, do not have a tutored knowledge of faith demands nor are they accustomed to regular assistance in the formal worship of the Church.

The anti-evangelical message resounds in the United States. Some details of that message appear below. For now, it is sufficient to say that for many Hispanic people of every class and background, the Christian proclamation of family is heard less in their new home and the contrary proclamation sounds loudly.

Viable approaches to this problem must have objectives like the following: effective preaching of the gospel; affirmation of Christian family values already possessed by newcomers; their strengthening through clarification; drawing people according to their needs into communities of affirmation, above all within their native Catholic Church; demonstration of the falsehood of the anti-evangelical message; association with the sacraments.

Rather facilely, I list these approaches for accomplishing the objectives just stated: the use of Christian propaganda; outreach through a trained, compatible, empathetic and — to the the extent possible — racially, ethnically, culturally and linguistically matching ministerial cadre; and welcoming communities that pre-exist the newcomers but are ready to adapt themselves in order that the newcomers may feel comfortable.

Much has been done by our American Church in many places in line with these approaches. In some dioceses with large migrant and alien populations, there are and have been vast efforts at recruiting and training personnel and volunteers, organizing and encouraging programs and movements that attempt appropriate evangelical affirmation and development, publicity and media-use to meet the demands. The details are either well-known or available readily to anyone interested.

Rather than linger on these positive elements (which I fully acknowledge and praise), I think it is more valuable that I consider items which require more attention. I suggest three in light of the special spiritual challenges posed to migrant and alien families within our ministerial scope. These are, first, the attitudes apparent within some of our parishes and institutions, then, the intensity of our proclamation of the appropriate gospel values and, last, the evolution of lay leadership and its association in ministry.

Attitudes, views, biases, prejudices — whatever one properly calls them — determine much of what we do. These are usually unreflective assumptions out of which we act in daily life. There is no room to expect that the vast majority of American Catholics, white and English-speaking, will not reflect the preconceptions and outlooks of the dominant society. Yet, consequent behavior is frequently such that it offends rather than welcomes the migrant and alien. Those of different color, physiognomy, language and customs receive a message that declares "stay away." That behavior, which really says the "not-like-us" foreign-born or wanderers should be prohibited from being with us, shows itself often, explicitly and implicitly, among our clergy, religious and fellow Church members, in parish and institutional practice and gatherings. "Physician, cure yourself" should, in my mind, become a priority in the years to come. We are told, and repeat to ourselves, that we are salt for the world, its light, its leaven. All of us who are actively the Church must engage in the conversion necessary if we are to support family life in our society in general. In particular, our attitudes must reflect the gospel if we are to sustain the family life of those most confused by the world in which they find themselves.

Is the economic prosperity of a particular church facility worth more than its being a place where poor families are welcome? Are schools operated by us fulfilling the mission of the Church when their cost excludes large families and the poor? Are our institutions acting properly when they do not pay family wages to employees? Are parish congregations in evangelical conformity when they omit to do that extra which will attract the presence of strangers or, worse, when they choose to do what will keep them away?

My second item for comment is the intensity of our proclamation of the gospel values which will meet the spiritual challenges relative to family which face our migrant and alien brothers and sisters. This is not unrelated to what we stated above on the attitudes among us. Again and again liturgical and scriptural texts refer to the Church as God's family. We call God our father, Jesus our brother, Mary our mother, one another brothers and sisters. Yet, there is, in my experience, something missing and even inconsistent. I doubt if there is much in the gospel message more basic than the Joannine statements that "God so loved the world that he gave his only son" (John 3:16) and that "if God so loved us, we also ought to love one another" (I John 4:11). If this were truly accepted within a Christian community, it seems to me that belief would create the conditions which would affirm every family and reach out to welcome the stranger.

In our propaganda, in our media efforts, in our preaching, it would be so welcome to see these values the pervasive theme. When it is necessary to deal with the secondary, the peripheral and the mundanely practical, such as money, why can we not be made to see clearly that the purpose of it all is to expand and make more effective the essential message? One of the delights many Hispanic people find in Pentecostal congregations is this precisely. Although they are asked for money, are bothered with the secondary, nevertheless, the constantly restated theme in word and practice is God's love and the sustenance of a community of brothers and sisters, a family.

The third and final item concerns the evolution of lay leadership and its association with the ministry. Clergy overall have decreased in number, as have religious, the two traditional cadres of apostolic workers among us. Appropriate clergy and religious for migrant and alien peoples exist in a proportionately even more diminished state. Efforts at developing lay involvement, the involvement of whole congregations, even of whole dioceses to compensate for the loss and replace it with effective ministry are either individual or sporadic. The diaconate is not the answer. A campaign is demanded which will seek to turn over the minute to minute tasks of gospel ministry to laity and groups of laity. This especially applies to migrant and alien peoples who do not enjoy attachments to the institutions and forms of the American Catholic Church.

Enthusiast sects, such as the Jehovah's Witnesses, are not to be imitated, but they do provide lessons. Simple people engage themselves readily and well for their cause. How are we to do similarly? How are we to become evangelical and missionary communities in our parishes? How are layfolk to lead and do? We must.

II. CULTURAL CHALLENGES

Elements which challenge all family life are legion in American culture at the moment. Many of these elements impact more upon migrant and alien families because of their newness to them, their passivity and vulnerability as strangers and because of their insecure condition as persons bereft of their former cultural support systems.

It is this situation of the migrant and alien which is the special challenge to us who are concerned about ministry to them. Shortly I shall list off some of the many things which hinder the proper existence of families in our society. The difference between a mainstream American family confronted with them and the newcomer, however, is immense. Two examples suffice. To come from a society where relatives or as-if relatives are on all sides with help and concern in moments of difficulty to a society which prides itself on individual independence, with neither relatives nor as-if relatives, means equivalently to be thrown into the sea without a life-preserver. To come from a place where ownership of something as ordinary among us as a color television set is either unknown or extraordinary to a world where this is not just a commonplace but an expectation is itself fantastic. To be exposed constantly through

191

that television set to a mentality that says, "you are to buy, buy and buy more," creates in the stranger, particularly the poor stranger, a disastrous condition, one which causes conflict and personal disintegration.

In some place, Church institutions have stepped in here. They provide the conditions wherein migrant and alien families can find a community of support for their positive family values and can evaluate what they face. Unfortunately, the extent to which this is true is relatively minimal.

As people go from extended to nuclear families, from group existence to individual existence, as they lose their roots through migration, as church, religion and community become unfamiliar and unresponsive because alien in their externals, they suffer. Those who would minister to them must be aware of this and make the effort to counter the losses.

Among the items in present-day American culture that I find most dangerous to family life among our migrant and alien families are individualism, consumerism, the valuing of things over persons, immediacy of satisfaction as a goal, escapism, the structuring of roles in the American family, sex as pleasure and separated from marriage and love, the ease and acceptance of divorce. As I intimated, these are challenges to family life for all, but they are especially so to those for whom they are so new. Individualism, consumerism, valuing things over persons are the very antitheses of Hispanic cultural values, at least. Although we Hispanics are notorious for dropping everything for the sake of a fiesta, our equally notorious devotion to *manana* belies any appreciation of the "I must have it now, without work" of immediacy. Our cultures teach us the reality of suffering, the difficulty of the human condition. We look at the Sorrowful Mother and her crucified Son. Escapism with its emphasis on entertainment, alcohol, drugs and sex is appealing, and we are vulnerable.

Our family cultural patterns are, at least theoretically, patriarchal. Moving to a society which says equality of man and woman and even hints at equality of children with their elders is a tremendous shock. Hispanics are no less subject to concupiscence than others. The United States, however, has now culturally reduced sex to recreation without thought. It is removed even in ideal from its

192

hallowed place as an exchange of love in marriage, open to the begetting of children. Finally, the acceptance of divorce for virtually any reason in American society is incredible.

Every bishop in the United States can recite the various steps that his diocese and the Church nationally has taken to try to respond to these cultural tendencies. I could enumerate those that have been taken to answer them among the Hispanic people whom I particularly serve. All would have to admit that the results of our efforts are not overwhelmingly successful, at least on the surface. (Perhaps success is there but hidden from us.)

Again, I choose to plead for something else, the same plea I have already made. We need to be convinced and grow in our conviction of the central elements of the gospel as they affect life. For the time, at least, the consequences of this conviction cannot be the center of our preaching and propaganda. Communities of support, uniting in the shared values and welcoming others, are a primary necessity. Lay leaders and doers must carry the weight of evangelisation. The weapons of those with whom we must disagree are mighty. They have the media and the promises of the earthly paradises. Yet, if we rely on our true weapon, faith working through love in brothers and sisters, we are mightier.

III. SOCIO-ECONOMIC CHALLENGES

In preparing this reflection, I made lists of all the challenges to family life I could think of. As may have been evident in what I have tried to say about cultural challenges to family life among migrant and alien families, what eventuated was that the challenges that face migrant and alien families in the United States are all but totally the same as those that face all other families. The chief difference seems to me to be the newness of many of these challenges to newcomers and the lack of supports with which to confront them. This is especially so with the socio-economic challenges to family life. Little is unique to migrants or aliens if we remember that they are of every economic and social class and of every type of family. Most migrants and aliens are poor, however, and they share with the rest of the poor, in their own ways, the challenges to family life as these receive them.

Employment, housing, governmental welfare systems, ghetto existence, schools, urban existence, racism are all challenges to family life for the poor. (They are challenges to the other social and economic classes as well, but one assumes that those should be more resourceful in coping with them.) The wages of the migrant and alien poor, particularly the undocumented, are known by everyone to be insufficient for family support. Everyone also is well aware that, except for occupations others do not want, the migrant and alien poor have difficulty in obtaining and retaining employment.

The housing conditions under which migrant laborers are frequently forced to live deny humanity, let alone appropriate family existence. The costs of housing and the conditions of it for the poor in our cities are scandalous. In New York, at present the housing shortage for the poor is so severe that nearly a fifth of the children in foster care are there only because their parents (usually single parents) cannot find housing. Thousands are in temporary shelter and more thousands are without any shelter at all.

Governmental welfare and dole systems mean to supply basic needs. The fact is that, although they may sometimes succeed in this, they dehumanize the recipients. In other cases, especially since the changes in federal policy of these past few years, they actually work at destroying family existence.

The ghetto existence of the poor in our cities means now the breeding of hopelessness, the despair of the disenfranchised, bombarded constantly by the television images of the rich and powerful outside. Families disintegrate as humanity disappears.

The schools that serve the poor have been the targets of enough criticism without my adding to it. Migrant and immigrant children do worse. They do not have the same starting place as other children in the United States. A large number come from families whose adults have only minimal education, if any. Those whose household and street language is other than English live in supreme confusion. Migrant children obviously lack continuity in schooling.

Urban existence is itself a problem for many migrant and alien families who come to live in our cities. Those who come from rural societies, especially those from warm climates, are untutored in urban living as we must do it. There are skills involved which we take for granted. If, for example, the chief purpose of shelter is to sleep, since climate and culture say one is to live out of doors most of the day, then it is difficult to adjust to a winter with the requirement of a large number of people crowded constantly into two or three rooms.

Racism and other forms of unjust discrimination, including a xenophobic hatred of those who speak other languages and the de facto economic inferiority of women, add to the difficulty of many.

I have emphasized only some factors of the socio-economic challenges to family life, and these basically only as they affect the poor.

I am proud to say that the Church nationally and in many dioceses has taken the lead in trying to alleviate these negative realities. We could enumerate effort after effort by national offices of the Conference of Bishops, diocesan agencies such as Catholic Charities and individual parishes. I am certain these efforts will continue and multiply.

Still, there is need for a conversion in our whole Church that will result in a community of people attempting to correct all that hinders proper family life and trying to establish what will further it. This conversion requires a serious and intense on-going effort at the evangelization of all the in fundamental demands of the gospel. The effort at evangelization requires lay leaders and doers.

CONCLUSION

Ten chapters have preceded this reflection, In them, scholars and experts have discussed many aspects of the family in general and in the United States today. I avowed at the beginning that I could not possibly treat the whole topic of ministry to migrant and alien families, that I could speak only from my experience as one working with Hispanic newcomers in the Northeast. I made a deliberate choice not to provide statistics, data, and so on, even on the areas of ministry to Hispanic migrants and aliens with which I am conversant. Rather, I chose to review an immense problem and make a simple plea for a future direction in resolution of it.

Chapter 12

Pastoral Responses
To Family Violence

The Most Reverend John H. Ricard, S.S.J., D.D.

Introduction

That acts of physical violence are common, even typical of American families, has been well documented. What is not well known is why violence occurs in families and what to do about it. The available research seems to identify two common misconceptions about violence among family members. First, that it is an infrequent occurrence and, secondly, when violence or abuse does occur, the family member who resorts to it is thought to be psychiatrically impaired. Neither view seems to be correct. If we put aside the most violent forms of social disintegration, war and riots, we find that physical aggression occurs more often among family members than among any others. Moreover, the family is the predominant setting for every form of physical violence and abuse, from slaps to torture and murder. In fact, some form of physical violence in the life cycle of the family members is so likely that it can be said to be almost universal. If this is the case, then violence is as typical of family relationships as is love.

The available evidence also suggest that with rare exceptions, family members using violence are not mentally impaired. Instead, violent acts by one family member against another are the result of socially learned and socially patterned behavior.

Our first task is to identify the components of family violence which include: conjugal violence, child abuse and neglect, and incest.

Conjugal Violence

Certain difficulties arise in an attempt to identify conjugal violence. One difficulty is that of definition, the other is that of measurement. In the first instance, when one attempts to define conjugal violence, it becomes immediately apparent that it is a political rather than a scientific term. For example, wife beating, as a form of conjugal violence as presently understood by the courts and law enforcement agencies, refers only to those instances in which severe damage is inflicted. Operationally, the other violence is treated as "normal" or trivialized. This suggests that a certain amount of violence among couples is "normal violence" in the sense that it is unavoidable or deserved, and that contrary to society's position on violence outside of the home, there should be no state or civic intervention. This point of view maintains that what goes on in the home is exempt from public scrutiny or jurisdiction. If the husband beats his wife or if parents abuse their children, that is a private matter.

If we accept the first two premises, then it becomes clear that family violence goes beyond the span of any single episode, it is not the end product of occasionally taking leave of one's senses. As indicated, the research of the last decade has demonstrated the frightening degree to which family violence is cyclical in nature, with violence in one generation begetting violence in the next. As a socially learned and patterned behavior, children in violent

197

homes "learn" violence in much the same way they learn any other behavior. They observe that violence is a normal way for people to treat one another and a normal way to solve problems. The family violence that occurs today is a time-bomb that will explode years later as abused children become abusers of their own children or other children, and as children who watch one parent hitting the other repeat the example in their own relationships or the community.

The costs of this violence and its transmission through the generations are intolerable, however they may be counted. The human costs in suffering are the most obvious and the most immediately tragic. But there are other costs as well for society as a whole. The family is the fundamental unit upon which society is built. When families are unable to function as the healthy, protective, nurturing institution that America has always depended upon, it should come as no surprise that community problems, crime, drug and alcohol abuse, dropouts from education and from the workplace abound.

Students of family violence recognize that certain cultural norms and civic codes permit violence between couples. In 1521, an Englishman, Mr. Justice Brooke, is quoted as stating that if a man beats an outlaw, a traitor, a pagan, a villain or his wife, it is unpunishable. John Stuart Mill decried the conditions in English law whereby a man could commit almost any atrocity against his wife without punishment, but she could not escape her total dependency upon him. Murray Straus, a leading observer of family relationships, observes that the effect of law and cultural patterns make the marriage license in effect, "a hitting license." It is suggested that this may well reflect the residual effects of the very early understanding of male-female relationships, when women pledged obedience and fidelity to their male protectors who saved them from being carried off by the enemy for their value as breeders.

The present position of women in light of the above is succinctly summed up by the statement of Mary Saltzman, the author of *Victimization of Women,* who observed: "Female victimization could be viewed as a problem with manageable boundaries, amenable to specific solutions if the perpetrators were aberrant

198

and if the criminal justice process could be effectively employed." "But," she continues, "there is a widespread network of attitudes and social codes that provide a firm foundation for the enactment of violence on women by men."

Our second concern, that of measurement, is evident as the significant and continuing obstacle to understanding and eliminating violence, that is, in the inconclusiveness of reliable statistical data. Such data, which may reveal the magnitude of the problem — when and where the violence occurs, the extent of repeated acts, and the circumstances preceding and during assaults in the family — are difficult to obtain. Numerous studies have verified that a basic reason why accurate data is not available is that the victims of conjugal violence do not feel safe and protected in reporting freely their victimization.

Nonetheless, reliable national estimates on the extent of conjugal violence indicate that of the approximately 54 million couples in the U.S., 4.7 to 15 million reported abuse in 1982. Other estimates provided by judges, attorneys and domestic relations counselors suggests that fifty percent of American wives are battered. Among those couples where beating occurred, it was typically not an isolated instance, violence was almost a daily or weekly event. The range being from about one-third of the couples, where beatings occurred once a week or more often. In addition, it is now well documented that cases of abuse occurred at all levels of society, not exclusively among lower socioeconomic groups.

Factors Relating to Conjugal Violence

Sigmund Freud's early theories suggested that aggression is instinctual, this was also asserted by Konrad Lorenz in his study of animal behavior. Later theorists, including Brownmiller and others, challenge this view and claim that human aggression resulting in violence is learned behavior. They maintain that sex-role socialization is the chief cause of male violence and female submission to it. Marvin E. Wolfgang offers this general definition of socialization: Socialization — is the process of cultural transmission of relaying through the social funnel of family and friends a set of beliefs, attitudes, values, speech and habits. Sex role socialization conditions the woman to submission; the male to dominance.

With respect to the influence of sex role socialization, Mason observed that:

> Boys are increasingly expected through the middle childhood and adolescent years to be dominant as they relate to girls and in times of stress to suppress fear and to control expressions of emotions. In contrast, expressions of fear, hurt feelings and general emotional upset are considered more acceptable for girls. While boys are expected to deal more pragmatically, calmly, and to dominate stressful situations, helplessness and submission is expected of girls.

Charles Seligman developed the construct of "learned helplessness" in studying human and animal behavior. This construct implies that if individuals believe that they cannot control the outcomes of their actions, they soon stop trying. Women are more often encouraged to think of themselves as helpless than men. This is borne out by objective research which shows that a significant number of battered wives continue to endure the pain and humiliation inflicted by a volatile husband for extended periods of time. Fully one-third of the reported cases in 1982 reported beatings to continue for one to three years and slightly less than fifty percent of the abused wives returned to their husbands after brief separations. Furthermore, a large proportion of family violence is committed by people who do not see their acts as crimes against victims. One indispensable step in preventing family violence is to ensure that abusers and victims alike are aware that these acts are morally and legally wrong.

Battered wives report a variety of reasons for staying with their husbands: a) a significant number reported that there was no place for them to go, economic constraints and discrimination in employment allow some women little choice other than to remain with an abusive husband, with the alternative being poverty: b) many report remaining in the home because of the children; the burden of child care keeps women out of the job market and thus dependent on the abusive husband.

Finally, all studies of conjugal violence report that the husband or wives who observed violence between their parents were more likely to engage in conjugal violence than those who had never witnessed physical conflict between their parents. In such instances, the individual learns that physical violence is an accepted method of conflict resolution and carries this into adult life and finally into his or her marriage. In this way, violence in the marriage is a socially learned and patterned behavior rooted in learning patterns established early in life.

Child Abuse

Child abuse and neglect continue to demand increasing national, legal, moral and medical attention as the number and severity of cases become public. According to the available official reports, cases of child maltreatment more than doubled between 1976 and 1982, with 929,310 official reports involving an estimated 1.3 million children being filed. Of those children, it is estimated that approximately 60,000 will die, prompting the National Institutes of Health to report that abuse and neglect represents the major cause of death in children. Another 400,000 children will be permanently injured.

Although the number of reported cases increased by 123 percent from 1976 to 1982, there is a remarkable consistency to the characteristics of reported families over time. Most studies indicate that the children who are victims of abuse and neglect are often very young, with an average age of 7.1 years compared to the national average age of children of 8.7 years. More than half of the children would have been abused from one to three years before they are discovered to be victims of parental violence. As many as one fourth die under the age of three and the sex of the children does not seem to be a significant factor; only slightly more than one half of the victims are boys.

As in the case of conjugal violence, however, we face a basic problem of definition. For in our society parents or guardians are given the right to inflict forms of physical punishment upon a minor child in a disciplinary effort, and this remains commonplace and widely acceptable. However, it is also recognized that any form of physical punishment inflicts injury and this injury can

201

be potentially severe resulting in maiming, bloodletting or crippling. Thus, the question arises, when does physical punishment which inflicts some form of injury become "child abuse?" It is currently recognized, of course, that mild to moderate nonmaiming, nonbloodletting, and noncrippling physical injury is not considered abusive, but an injury which requires medical treatment would. However, questions such as, who makes this determination — physician, the courts, the parents or the child — remain unresolved. Further, it is recognized that societies which allow physical punishment have far higher rates of child abuse than societies which do not use physical punishment as a form of discipline of children. This is especially evident when one compares Japanese society to American society. The Japanese have a far lower rate of child abuse than the American families; they also do not generally use physical punishment as a disciplinary measure.

Definitions

Proposed and present moral or legal definitions of the same child abuse entity require emphasis on different features of the same problem. Presently, neither physician, sociologist, psychologist or legislator, either separately or together, agree to the descriptive definition of child abuse or neglect. Federal law, passed in 1974, defines child abuse and neglect as meaning physical or mental injury, sexual abuse, negligent treatment or maltreatment of a child under the age of eighteen by a person who is responsible for the child's welfare, under circumstances which indicate that the child's health or welfare is harmed or threatened thereby. State laws are very similar. In the same year, all 50 states had, in effect, an almost identical definition of child abuse as the federal law.

As to the forms of child abuse, there seems to be a general consensus that the three following elements should be included:

(1) Physical Abuse

The basic definition relates to the nonaccidental injury of a child. However, in current society, the right of the parent or guardian to inflict forms of punishment upon a minor child in a disciplinary effort remains commonplace and widely acceptable. Mild to moderate nonmaiming, usually nonbloodletting, noncrippling physical injury, remains a form of enforcement of discipline in the schools and home. However, any injury which requires medical treatment would appear by consensus to be considered as excessive to the acceptable corrective measure. Additionally, the description should include the act or acts of physical or emotional persuasion such as binding or closeting that force or place the child in a potentially dangerous situation in which subsequent and significant physical injury severe enough to require medical treatment has resulted.

(2) Physical Neglect

Physical neglect may be defined as a failure to provide the necessities of life for the child. Such neglect includes inadequate or insufficient medical care, nourishment, clothing, supervision, housing, or the like. It is recognized, however, that such factors as the economics of the family as well as the immediate day-by-day availability of these "necessities" must be taken into consideration. Legally, the failure to provide must be "willful."

(3) Sexual Abuse

Definitions of sexual abuse suggest reference to any sexual activity between an adult and a minor. Here the definition breaks down further into presence and/or degree of physical injury and whether any associated trauma is severe or less severe, present or future in appearance. More will be discussed on this topic later in this chapter.

Demographic and Psychosocial Profile of Families of Abused Children

There is no distinct profile which would fit all families of abused and neglected children. However, an all-inclusive nationwide report covering 1976 through 1982 identified with remarkable consistency a number of characteristics of reported families that differ from those of the general population.

a) Demographic Factors

1) A disproportionate number of reported families were headed by single females. Such families made up 43 percent of the reported cases, but accounted for only 19 percent of all U.S. families.

2) 43 percent of reported families received public assistance, compared to about 12 percent of all U.S. families. In 41 percent of the reported families, no caretaker was employed.

3) Reported families were larger than the average family. They had an average of 2.2 children, compared to the national average of 1.9.

4) Sixty-nine percent of the reported families had some serious familial crisis relating to finances, difficulties with housing, or domestic friction.

5) Over eighty-nine percent of the families reported some form of health problems either of the mother or some other family member.

b) Psychosocial Factors

As with conjugal violence, the question remains as to why only some female-headed, low income, or large families, resort to violence in the form of child abuse. The answer may be found in other factors, which taken together, gives us a composite picture of what we might want to look for in our discussion of child abuse and neglect. They include the following:

(1) An unwanted or unplanned pregnancy, or the child having been born out of wedlock.

(2) The experience of serious medical difficulties during pregnancy and the perinatal period.

(3) A complicated childbirth, which is also seen as an unpleasant experience.

(4) A complicated neonatal period which may interfere with the establishment of the mother-child bond. Most children who are separated from their mothers in the earliest period after birth have a tendency to develop unresponsive and difficult behavior and, because of this fussiness and unresponsiveness, the child can be at especially high risk.

(5) Child rearing techniques which are rigid and exemplified by the approach to toilet training which is commenced early and likely to be punitive. This factor of rigid/punitive toilet training is found in all studies of abused children.

(6) Socially isolated families, with few contacts with other adults outside of the family, and infrequent opportunities to be relieved from the burdens of constantly caring for a child who is seen as unrewarding.

c) Abuse as a Socially Learned and Patterned Behavior

A final factor which is of interest is the background of the abusing parent, that is, a significant number of whom experience harsh and cruel punishment at the hands of their own parents.

Incest as a Form of Family Violence

In the past, most studies considered incest extremely rare, and the taboo against it was so strong that those involved in it were pathological and driven to the relaxation of inhibition as a result of high levels of stress. More recent scholarship has revised estimates of incidence upwards, but retained, on the whole, the view that unusual stress and/or psychological pathology were key causal factors. Exact estimates as to the rate or incidence of incest are difficult to find; however, numerous studies do present us with enough of a composite picture to bring light on this phenomenal disorder.

The several studies reviewed indicated that incestuous relationships are predominantly heterosexual. The age of the male perpetrators in most studies was mid-thirties (35.2) years; the median age 38. This is approximately 25 years older than the mean age of the child participants (10.2) years. These figures indicate that incest relationships continued for several years. In most cases, the children became incestuous sexual partners of older men at least four years prior to puberty. This finding becomes important for considering the hypotheses that girls' developing bodies and sexual interests were causal in stimulating incestuous relations.

It was also possible to examine from these studies the duration of the relationships, which indicated that 76% continued for years; 18% continued for one to three or more years; the remainder for one year. Five percent continued for months; 17% occurred "several times", and 10% just once. The incestuous relations were terminated either by the girl's moving away from the household, by discovery by some outside authority or, least frequently, as a result of discovery by another family member.

When kinship relationship is considered, biological fathers represented slightly more than 80% of all incest assailants, while "social fathers", that is, non-biological father, a mother's boyfriend or lover, or the victim's stepfather represented 18% and the remainder were represented by other male relatives. The findings also indicate that women virtually never sexually abused children, and that non-biological (social) fathers indeed were overrepresented in incest in comparison with their presence in studies of other types of abuse.

A relevant factor in most studies is the degree of the father's (non-biological as well as biological) upbringing of the child. This factor is evident by a qualitative analysis of the cases involved in the studies in which one of the striking characteristics of the incest assailants was their lack of empathy with the distress they caused their victims. In addition, male presence in the child's household did seem to provide greater opportunity for incest in cases where there was no mother present. Male-headed single-parent households were overrepresented among incest cases.

The absence of the mother may have other meanings than simply the creating of opportunity; one study found absence or weakness of a mother to make a girl psychologically as well as physically more vulnerable to sexual assault.

In the Hermon and Finkelhor study, many of the mothers of the victims were or had been victims of physical abuse themselves, usually at the hand of the man who also was the incest assailant. A number of the mothers were ill or had some disability. Many had weaknesses such as alcoholism or drug dependence, were rejected by their own relatives, were recent migrants to the U.S., or unable to speak English. Many were in several of these categories. Did the mothers know of the incest? This is difficult to ascertain, however, because mothers often felt pressured to dishonesty in talking with social workers or investigators for fear of losing their children, shame, or fear of prosecution, for example. Still, in the analysis of most incest case histories presented in the studies, there seems to be a noticeable inaction on the part of the mother. Fifty-two percent appeared to know about the incest. Some 32% interviewed admitted this knowledge, and only 28% intervened. Mothers of the victims were likely to be the complainants bringing social workers or police intervention into their families.

By way of summary, incest was almost always a sexual relationship between an older man and a younger girl. The evidence suggests that this type of incest is coercive, when one considers the age of the girls and the age differential between the girls and the men.

Many incest victims have low resistance; many studies indicate that shame and guilt felt by the incest victims made it difficult for them to tell or seek help; there was a further dis-incentive to complain or resist because to do so might cost them their family. In addition, incest victims, because of their imprisonment, often played the role of surrogate mothers.

There is evidence that incest more than any other type of family violence is calculated and premeditated, not a result of a sudden loss of control. The typical incestuous relationship continues for years. In none of the studies was there indication that the older participants (the males) break off the sexual relationship, as one might expect if they were vulnerable to recurrencies of shame and/or guilt. Qualitative analysis of the data shows that in most cases the process of obtaining privacy for the sexual activity also required premeditation.

The pattern found to be most consistently associated with incest was extreme male dominance of the family. It was evident, quantitatively, in the various indicators of the weakness of the mother — her death, her illness or disability, or her own victimization from wife beating. It was evident qualitatively, in the victim's and wives' expression of submission and fear toward the male assailants.

Theories of Family Violence

During the early years of family research, theoretical approaches to family violence in the United States were characterized largely by psychological models, which focused on the psychological state of the abusing parent or spouse, especially on early childhood experiences. Gradually, these theories gave way to the broader approaches to family violence which emphasized the social environment as well as psychological factors.

1) Family Violence and Environmental Stress

A descriptive analysis of the stress-producing social situations that are involved in family violence would reveal that poverty and social deprivation are highly associated with child abuse and neglect as well as conjugal violence. From the evidence provided, families where abuse occurred are disproportionately poor, female-headed, of low employment status and low education. Many of the family heads of households are on public assistance. On the basis of these findings, many researchers place emphasis on the conditions in society that lead to abuse and neglect as well as the abnormal psychological characteristics of individual parents or spouses. Stressful conditions such as finances, housing, and health problems have been linked with high rates of family violence, thus a composite picture of this subject would need to include stress as a factor.

2) Aggression as a Cultural and Structural Pattern

Aggression as a pervasive cultural pattern is shown in numerous studies. An interesting starting place is Sipes study of the relationship between aggressive sports and warfare. He showed that both cross-culturally and in a time series analysis for the U.S., the higher the level of armed combat, the more common are aggressive sports. A study by Archer and Gartner of 110 nations find that, contrary to the "catharsis theory," homicide rates increased with the occurrence of war. In respect to the mass media, the nations or periods with the most actual violence are those with the most violent popular literature. Finally, in respect to husband-wife violence itself, Steinmetz studied the families of university students in an American and a Canadian city using identical instruments. She wanted to compare Canadian and American families because these two societies are alike in so many ways, yet Canadian rates for homicide, assult, rape, and other forms of violence, are only a fraction of the rates in the U.S. The Canadian families, it turned out, have a considerably lower frequency of husband-wife physical aggression.

I concluded from these and other studies that each modality of aggression in a society, or paradigm for interaction in other spheres of activity, rather than serving as a means of "draining off hostility" serves as a means of learned aggressive roles and as a kind of cultural and structural "themes" template.

3) Aggression as a Family Pattern

The same theoretical principle also applies within the family. That is, violence in one family role is associated with violence in other family roles. Thus, studies of child-abusing parents in three countries found that such parents had themselves experienced severe physical punishment as children. At the macro level of analysis, although child abuse statistics can best be considered only as educated guesses, there seems to be some correlation with the frequency with which physical punishment occurs in a society. Goode, for example, suggests that child abuse is rare in Japan because physical punishment is rarely used. Finally, the study of Steinmetz of U.S. and Canadian families found that couples who use physical force on each other use physical punishment more often than other couples. Moreover, their children, in turn, use physical aggression against siblings more often than do the children of parents who do not hit each other.

In addition, Gelles also examined the patterns of family interaction and the very structure of family life and offers the following observations as possible factors which may be associated with family violence:

1. Time at risk, i.e., the fact that in many societies, family members spend considerable amounts of time with each other. Other things being equal, they therefore are more likely to engage in disputes and conflicts with each other than with those whom they spend less time. But of course, other things are not equal, and particularly:

2. Range of activities and interests — family members are likely to share a wider range of activities and interests with each

other than with others with whom they may also spend much time. This means that there are more events over which a dispute or failure to meet expectations can occur.

3. Intensity of involvement and attachment — not only is there a greater probability of hurting family members than others because of the greater time exposure and the greater number of spheres of overlapping activity and interests, but in addition, the degree of injury experienced when the problem arises with a family member is greater than when it arises with someone else because of the intensity of involvement and attachment that is typical of family relationships.

4. Sexual inequality and the typical pattern of ascribed superior position for the husband has a high conflict potential built-in because it is inevitable that not all husbands will be able to perform the culturally expected leadership role and/or not all wives will be willing to accept the subordinate role.

5. Privacy — the privacy of the family in many societies insulates it both from assistance in coping with intrafamily disputes and from social control by neighbors and other kin. This factor is, of course, most present in the conjugal family of urban-industrial societies, and least present among societies such as the Bushmen, where virtually all of family life is carried within the small circle of the Bushmen camp and is open to immediate intercession by others.

6. Cultural norms — cultural norms legitimizing the use of violence between members of the same family in situations that would make violence a serious normative violation should it occur outside the family. In Western societies, to this day, there is a strong, though largely unverbalized norm that makes the marriage license also a hitting license.

Each of the above, together with other factors, merits detailed consideration. However, within the confines of this chapter, there is room only to consider those causal factors that have been empirically studied. Although this is not adequate, the theoretical basis for selecting it has the merit of being appropriate for the focus of this volume and of reducing the range of materials to be considered to what can be fitted within the chapter.

Bibliography

Chester, R. and Streather, J. "Curley in English divorce: Some empirical findings." *Journal of Marriage and the Family* 34 (November, 1972): 706-712.

Curtis, L. *Criminal Violence: National Patterns and Behavior.* Lexington, Mass.: Books, 1974.

Dobash, R., Wilson, M., and Cavanagh, C. "Violence against wives: The legislation of the 1960's and the policies of indifference." paper presented at the National Deviancy Conference meeting, 1977.

Elston, E. Fuller, J., and Murch, M. "Battered wives: The problems of violence in marriages experienced by a group of petitioners in undefined divorce cases." Unpublished paper. Department of Social Work, University of Bristol, 1976.

Gelles, R. J. *The Violent Home: A Study of Physical Aggression Between Husbands and Wives.* Beverly Hills: Sage, 1974.

Gibson, E. *Homicide in England and Wales 1967-1971. Home Office Research Study No. 31.* London: Her Majesty's Stationery Office, 1975.

Gibson, E. and Klein, S. *Murder 1957 to 1968. A Home Office Statistical Division Report on Murder in England and Wales.* London: Her Majesty's Stationery Office, 1969.

Goode, W. J. "Force and violence in the family." *Journal of Marriage and the Family 33* (November, 1971): 624-636.

Levinger, G. "Source of marital dissatisfaction among applicants for divorce." *American Journal of Orthopsychiatry 36* (October, 1966): 804-806.

Lystad, M. H. "Violence at home: A review of the literature." *American Journal of Orthopsychiatry 45* (April, 1975): 328-345.

MacDonald, A. "Death penalty and homicide." *American Journal of Sociology 16* (July, 1911): 88-116.

McClintock, F. *Crimes of Violence.* New York: St. Martins Press, 1963.

Martin, D. *Battered Wives.* San Francisco: Glide Publications. 1976.

Moran, R. *"Criminal Homicide: External restraint and subculture of violence." Criminology 8* (February, 1971): 357-374.

O'Brien, J. E. "Violence in divorce prone families." *Journal of Marriage and the Family 33* (November, 1977): 692-698.

Pitman, D. J. and Handy, W. "Patterns in criminal aggravated assault." *Journal of Criminal Law, Criminology and Police Science 55* (December, 1964): 462-476.

Simmel, G. *Conflict and the Web of Group-Affiliations,* New York: Free Press, 1955.

Steinmetz, S. K. and Straus, M.A. "The family as a cradle of violence." *Society 10* (Sept/Oct., 1973); 54-56.

Straus, M.A. "Sexual inequality, cultural norms, and wife beating." in *Victims and Society,* pp. 54-70. Edited by E. Viano. Washington, D. C.: Visage Press, 1976.

Von Hentig, H. *The Criminal and His Victim.* New Haven: Yale University Press, 1948.

Voss, H. L. and Hepburn, J.R. "Patterns in criminal homicide in Chicago." *Journal of Criminal Law, Criminology and Police Science 59* (December, 1968): 499-508.

Wolfgang, M. *Patterns of Criminal Homicide,* Philadelphia: University of Pennsylvania Press, 1958.

Chapter 13

Parental Roles In Transition

Clayton C. Barbeau, M.A.

I approach the topic of parental roles in transition not as a demographer, sociologist, statistician or historian, but as one of ten children, the now-widowed father of eight children, and a Marriage, Family and Child Therapist with a scheduled thirty to forty client hours a week. In addition to these credentials, I have experienced the questions of young people and the parents of young people in various parts of the country when I present myself as a lecturer on family topics.

HISTORICAL OBSERVATIONS

I'd like to begin by making a few historical observations. At the turn of the century most of the people in the United States lived on farms. Marriage had, for everyone, a strong economic base with a heavy emphasis on the contractual. A man tending a farm from dawn til sundown, seven days a week, had great need for a wife who would separate the milk, make cheese, bake bread, put up preserves for the long winter, tend his house, darn his socks and otherwise meet his housekeeping needs. The woman, *sans* too many occupational choices, had equally strong need for a husband, spelled Good Provider, who would keep a tight roof over her head, food on the table and provide her with a modicum of Social Security. There was a quid pro quo in this sort of relationship of mutual economic need: "you're going to do this, I'm going to do that — and that's how we're going to survive!" Husband and wife roles were very clearly defined in such a situation.

In this rural setting children were likewise an economic asset, for at a very early age they were able to feed the chickens, milk the cows, help with feeding and tending the farm animals and weeding the garden. As they grew older, of course, their economic value increased, they could be of more help in the running of the farm.

On the farm, the father's authority was usually unquestioned and unquestionable. He was, after all, the more experienced farmer. It was up to him to make the decisions regarding when and where to sow, when to harvest, when and which animals to slaughter. Children could clearly see the relationship between his labors, the sweat of his brow, his decisions, and the food on the family table.

In 1900 only seven out of one hundred children in the United States attended high school. Only four out of one hundred U.S. children went on to college. Where were these ninety six out of one hundred out-of-school children? They were full time workers on the farms or in the mines and sweatshops of the nation. As late as 1928, 85% of the U.S. population lived on farms.

In the cities, at the turn of the century, immigrant families were struggling for survival and parents were seeing that the "Old World" ways were shed so that their children would be "American." The same children were expected, as early as age eight, to put in their 12-13 hour days in the mills, the mines, or the industrial plants to aid in the survival of the family and, indeed, to help the family "get ahead."

213

These youngsters were joined by those others who, at age ten or so, decided like Thomas Edison to leave the farm and make their way in the larger world. Beniamano Bufano once told the story of how his mother, in the Italian ghetto of New York, on the occasion of his twelfth birthday, patted him on the head, presented him with one thousand dollars she had saved and said: "Today you are a man. Good-bye, my son." Two years later, having arrived in China aboard a merchant ship, he found himself fascinated by a Chinese potter at work and thereupon decided to become a sculptor. Bufano's story is not too much different from that of numerous other members of his generation, except that his mother had somehow been able to save one thousand dollars with which to launch him on his adult life.

The novels of Horatio Alger are unrealistic only insofar as his young heroes always made it to the top. Dickens' *Oliver Twist* is much more truth than fiction in its depiction of the life of the young in England in the latter half of the last century.

The Depression years of the thirties saw the exodus from the farms of America. It also saw the shift away from the contractual, quid quo pro, marriage, to the cohabitational. "Two can live as cheaply as one," became the slogan of those who had discovered shared interests or mutual sexual attraction and decided to found their marriage on these. Still, the Depression found many families like my own, where all of us children sold magazines door to door, collected and sold papers, brass and rags and bottles to the junk merchants (we didn't call it "recycling" in those days, it was simply making money) to help support a family whose breadwinner was unemployed or on WPA. And, as soon as we had collected enough "Brownie" or "Greenie" coupons (given as premiums for our magazine sales) we got a bicycle so that at 4:00 a.m. in the morning we could carry two paper routes and at 4:00 p.m. carry another newspaper route to aid in the same cause of feeding our large family. Material cares loomed large. "Cash and Carry" was the watchword with merchants and it took a college diploma to get a job with one service station chain in California.

On the parental level: breast-feeding was actively discouraged by doctors and milk company propagandists; home delivery of children was shifted to hospitals, thereby excluding family participation; while mother's work was highly visible and her role little changed, Dad's work became removed from family contact and he became a "wage-earner", a "bill-payer."

World War II saw the final rupturing of the extended family; the exodus to the cities for jobs in the defense effort was in full swing. The end of that war found millions of young men who had learned the lessons of the Depression: a good education was a necessity to make one's way in the world. The college diploma, formerly reserved for the rich, was made available by the GI Bill, a legislative attempt to keep the flood of veterans from hitting the job market en masse. The new credit economy even allowed many to marry while they went to school — and many, wanting to "make up for lost time", did just that. Their wives, many of whom had left the hearth of home for the hearth of the factory during the war, continued in their outside-the-home-work in order to aid their husbands in the pursuit of higher education which was seen as an economic (rather than an intellectual) goal.

The extended family having been shattered — one out of three persons in America changes his/her "permanent residence" each year — the new mother-father couldn't turn to parents or experienced relatives living nearby in order to get advice about child-rearing problems, so they trusted in the theories of the spate of "experts" — experts in child-care who were following the trail blazed by Dr. Benjamin Spock's phenomenal best-seller.

Some experts counseled rigid feeding schedules, no matter how loud the child's cries of hunger; others took a firm stand on potty training. Because both parents were busy — father at school or just starting in his profession, mother working to help pay for the education or to support them while he got established in his work field, baby-sitters were in as great a demand in the nineteen-fifties as were the "expert" authors.

But the baby-sitter which took over most often, even when the parents were home was the new marvel: television. Today, by the time a youngster graduates from high school, s/he will have spent eleven thousand hours in a classroom and fifteen thousand hours in front of a television set. According to one report, the child will have seen in that fifteen thousand hours eighteen thousand murders, over one per hour, witnessed uncountable rapes, beatings, robberies, arson fires, car crashes, and assorted other forms of violence against persons and property. The same report states that during that fifteen thousand hours the child will have been subjected to over a third of a million commercial messages — 55% for edibles, 65% of these heavily sugared edibles. Many of these commercials are designed to provoke the young to urge their parents to buy something for them. "I am convinced," wrote psychiatrist Michael Rothenberg in that report, "that television advertising encourages confrontation and alienation on the part of children toward their parents and undermines the parent's child-rearing responsibility."

> Walt Whitman wrote:
> *There was a child went forth every day*
> *And the first object he looked upon, that*
> *object he became.*
> *And that object became part of him*
> *For the day or a certain part of the day*
> *Or for many years or stretching*
> *Cycles of years.*

It was in 1940 that another major change took place which bears heavily upon the matter of parent-child relationships. In 1940, the teen-ager was invented. Prior to 1940, nearly every attempt to limit the exploitation of child labor had failed or been declared unconstitutional. Often enough, it was church persons who opposed such legislation, apparently thinking that "idle hands are the devil's playground." It was economic rather than humanitarian motives which got the first Federal Child Labor law passed, a law which Franklin Delano Roosevelt signed in 1940, thereby promptly rendering over 800,000 boys and girls unemployed and unemployable. There would never again be a Thomas Edison leaving home to find work in the big city at age twelve, a Beniamano Bufano working his way to Asia at the same age, or any of the other stuff of which Horatio Alger stories are made. It was against the law for such youths to be gainfully employed.

So that these unemployed young persons would not be merely littering up the streets, legislation was passed in many states making their attendance at schools mandatory. The high school, previously a place of education for the privileged few able to enjoy the luxury of learning, had now become a warehouse for youths legally required to be there. Since it was now compulsory, it had to be made pleasant, which meant the dilution of academic content and intellectual discipline. To make sure that they attended school and had someone taking care of their materials needs, other laws were passed holding parents legally responsible for the behavior of their children, and the welfare of their children, up to a certain age (depending upon the individual states).

For the first time in history, young men and women were forced to stay at home without gainful employment, forced to attend schools (mostly coeducational), and parents were forced to cope with them.

The early 1960's saw many of the parents of such young persons now trying, with material gifts, to make up for their earlier neglect. Having succeeded in attaining their material goals, they tended to offer things rather than time and attention. It was not uncommon for the young men and women entering the freshman class in my university in 1955 to be heard comparing the make of automobile which their parents had given them upon high school graduation.

It was from such materialistically-oriented homes, for the most part, that the "Beat Generation" and later the "Hippy" came. Both dropped out of a spiritually dead scene. The latter boldly announced they were looking for "love" and, in the earliest phases of this sociological phenomenon, lived as simply as possible.

When these became parents, they reacted against the impersonal bottle-feeding of their infancy and the tight scheduling of the experts their parents relied upon. Natural childbirth and breast-feeding (both still considered novel when we had our first child that way and Myra breast-fed him) began to grow in popularity. My appearance in a delivery room in 1960 was a first for the great obstetrician we had, and for the hospital. It is today taken for granted in educated circles that the father will be involved in Lamaze classes, and "birthing rooms" are commonplace, as are father's assisting at (even televideo-recording) the birth of their children. Sometimes the whole family is involved in the birth. Home delivery is not uncommon, and breast-feeding is no longer considered exceptional practice.

Indeed, today the infant is stimulated by all manner of educational toys, toys which Myra and I in the 1950's had to purchase through mail-order and which today are available in any self-respecting department store. These same infants are taught to swim before they can walk and the parents seek out nursery schools which will encourage learning. Indeed, Joseph Menosky reports that some private preschools are offering four year olds computerized tutoring. Many of these same parents are already saving money and planning on the college their child will attend. The danger in this is that such parents may identify too closely with their child's achievement or lack of same and will not leave room for that process of individuation which is part of growing up. Some are over-compensating for their own parents' lack of emotional closeness. Many seem to keep their children (and themselves) so scheduled with sports activities, dance classes, social events, that there seems little time for a youngster to cultivate the fine art of "doing nothing", the lazy day-dreaming or gazing at clouds which is the stuff of the contemplative or poetic spirit.

It was the sixties also that saw the so-called "sexual revolution" during which time many young persons who had rejected their families also rejected the notion that marriage was necessary if you wished to cohabit. Cohabitation without vows became widespread — with many Hollywood stars and popular singers serving as "hip" role models in this. The desire to cohabit or even to parent was no longer seen as synonymous with the desire to marry. Perhaps the example of divorced parents — for whom the vows proved no lasting bond — contributed to this. (It needs to be pointed out, however, that cohabitation without matrimonial vows was not limited to the young. Many senior citizens, facing loss of widow's pensions or other economic problems should they legally marry, choose to do without the religious and civil benediction on their cohabitation.)

We all are aware that every marriage is, indeed, a contract and a contract which normally involves cohabitation. But no man any longer marries to get a housekeeper or cook in order that he can survive. No woman in the United States needs a Good Provider in order to have economic security or social status. So, if survival and maintenance are no longer a valid reason for marriage and no longer define marital roles, and if cohabitation is no longer viewed as requiring a marriage commitment, where are we?

MARRIAGE AS RELATIONAL

In the past twenty years another aspect of marriage has moved into the forefront of consciousness: the relational. Yes, Grandad was related to Grandma, they did have a relationship, sometimes a very strong and beautiful one. However, unlike the husbands and wives of today, they did not spend their time fretting about the quality of their communication, debating the question of how fulfilling their sexual lovemaking was or was not, or seeking a perfect emotional bonding. They were usually simply too tired from the burden of maintenance and survival chores to worry about such matters of quality. Yet it is precisely such matters of quality that form the major concerns of many married couples today who married because they felt that in this relationship each would be able to be more than s/he was alone, would experience life in a richer way, and would come to know emotional, spiritual growth through their union in love.

"When two people are under the influence of the most violent, most insane, most delusive, and most transient of passions, they are required to swear that they will remain in that excited, abnormal and exhausting condition continuously until death do them part." So wrote George Bernard Shaw in his preface to "Getting Married." There is an unfortunate ring of truth to GBS's statement, for all too many do seem to expect from marriage what it cannot deliver. The failure to move to a more mature understanding of love and what it can ask and what it can give in a marriage — as well as what it cannot deliver — accounts for many of the divorces which we deplore. The mean age of a marriage at the time of a divorce in the U.S. is 6.8 years. Ten years ago, one out of six children in the U.S. was single-parented. Today that figure is one out of five. Ninety percent of these children will be living with their mothers who are separated or divorced or simply never married. Any consideration of the changing roles of parenting in our day, any attempt on the institutional level to deal with parenting problems in our time, must take this into account. Also, we must be aware that fifty percent of all children in the U.S. will be single parented at some time before they reach age eighteen — because of separation, divorce or the death of one parent. In talking to any congregation, any group of "parents" or any classroom of youngsters, this reality must be taken into account.

The emphasis upon the relational aspect of marriage in our time has spilled over into the parenting role. Until recent years, it was assumed that parenting skills simply came with the plumbing. One biologically produced a child and the "parent" came into being with all the necessary know-how to handle the child's needs on all levels. Today it is more widely understood that parenting is an art. More educated parents seek out all the help they can get in this task, paying to attend courses in parenting, reading books on the topic, taking Parent Effectiveness Training, or Systemative Training in Effective Parenting courses. It has been my experience, as I tour the country, that there is an enormous hunger on the part of parents for all the help they can get in coping with the challenges of parenting in our time. Among the better educated, both parents involve themselves in this educational process — a change from the days when the mother parented, dealt with the emotional and religious upbringing of the children and the father felt his role was fulfilled by paying the bills and occasionally dealing out the physical punishments which, today, would be labeled as "child abuse." My first book, written in 1958 and published in 1961, titled *The Head of the Family,* was considered rather novel in its thesis that the Christian father was called upon to do more than pay the bills.

Still, for all the talk of shared parenting, and for the increasing numbers involved in it (and, to my knowledge, more fathers are involving themselves in this way), we have some evidence that we are far from having the majority of American men sharing fully in the parenting and housekeeping tasks. The talk and the books and articles may be the cutting edge of the wave of the future, but at present a lot of it seems to remain mere wordage.

Recently, ten thousand engaged couples were polled by Glamour magazine about their marital expectations. They expected a marriage of "friends and lovers" with equal rights and shared parental and housekeeping duties. Eighty percent expected most household chores (as well as parental responsibilities) to be shared equally — though, for reasons unexplained, only sixty percent felt that doing the laundry should be shared.

Contrasted to these expectations, we have a McCall's magazine survey of 40,000 working wives/mothers. On the average, these women contributed 43.7% of the family income but most contended that they were still left with a full-time second job: child-care and housework.

So, despite all the talk and feature article publicity, the roles would not seem to have changed dramatically, save that one bread-winner is doing most of the work. My wife educated me out of such nonsense early in our marriage. I recall one day early on, when we were both working, prior to the birth of our first child, when I chose to surprise Myra by mopping the kitchen floor while she was out grocery shopping. When she came home, I pointed with pride to my handiwork and said, "I mopped your kitchen floor." She responded: "Whose kitchen floor?"

"Yours," I said.

"I thought you ate out of this kitchen also. I understood that this was our kitchen, so why shouldn't you mop it when it needs mopping?"

A number of years later, I came home one day and casually remarked, "Wow, the front room looks like a tornado hit it."

"I know, " Myra replied. "It wasn't high on my priority list today. If it bothers you, clean it up."

Thus are egalitarian roles in marriage and parenting brought about.

Another personal note: I recall when my son, Michael, now thirty, was nineteen. He was already living independently. On his birthday, I took him aside and apologized to him for all the mistakes I had made. I wanted him to know that I realized that I had over-supervised him, been over-strict, very authoritarian and otherwise uptight — but that he had turned out well in spite of me. I just wanted him to know that I had been doing my best to be a good parent — my own father, an alcoholic, not having been a very good role model for me. After his initial surprise at my little speech, Michael commented: "Yeah, Christopher gets away with things I wouldn't have dreamed of doing. He does them right in front of you and you don't bat an eye."

"Christopher, " I commented, "was the eighth. I would hope that I had perfected some skills and a more relaxed approach by now."

In point of fact, with Christopher now nearly eighteen, I've just gotten this parenting art down pat — and I've run out of kids to parent. I have checked informally with other parents of my age group and I find they too moved from a more authoritarian approach to parenting, to a more personable one as they matured and as they gained more insight into their parental roles.

Parent, as you know, comes from the word *parens* which means source. As a parent, one faces the same challenges, no matter what culture, educational level or era in which one lives. The challenge is to supply a growing child with adequate love — which lets the child know something of God's love as well as providing the youngsters with a sense of his/her own worth. It is a challenge which includes the need to meet the material needs of the child for food, shelter and clothing; to provide that sort of parental discipline which will, hopefully, lead to the young person growing up self-disciplined; the sort of education that teaches right from wrong not only in spelling or math, but more importantly in the area of the great moral issues confronting us in our time and the personal choices we all make daily; and which instills, as much through example as preachments, the moral courage to confront the problems of mature life with sound principles and personal integrity. It also means providing the young persons under our care with a role model/s for the man-woman relationship, for married life, for their own later parenting challenge.

Those tasks haven't shifted much through the years. They were once easier to handle. Parents were, once, the major educative influence on their children's lives. Today it takes about eighteen years for a child to mature physically, while adolescence is being extended in some cases to age twenty-five.

The television tube and the commodity merchants who want to get their share of the billions of dollars in the "youth market" have a vested interest in keeping the young at odds with their parents. Further, the commuting father, or the uninvolved one, carries very little of the authority his grandfather or father had on the farm. Moreover, the television presents other role models all day long — most of them rock stars with dionysian impact:

Item: eleven million teenage girls in the U.S. are sexually active. One million of these will get pregnant this year. One hundred and forty thousand of these will have miscarriages. Two hundred and seventy thousand will have abortions — most without their parent's knowledge. Over half a million will have live births.

Item: The suicide rate for teen-age mothers is seven times that for other girls the same age.

Item: Venereal disease is rampant among teenagers — again usually without parental knowledge. Gonorrhea and Chlymidia will sterilize many of these young women prior to their marriage.

Item: While I've been writing this, another teenager was killed in an alcohol-related auto accident. The national rate for teen-deaths in alcohol-related accidents is one per hour.

Item: The suicide rate for teen-agers has tripled since the "sexual revolution" of the 1960's. My personal dealings with suicidal teen-agers tells me that many of these are related to premature sexual activity, that and drug abuse — or a mixture of the two.

Item: Some studies show that 1 out of 10 school children attempt suicide and by high school age 1 out of 2 has seriously considered it. Two weeks ago, a television news program carried the information that a survey had disclosed that 70% of high school students polled had seriously considered suicide. Over four thousand youngsters did kill themselves last year, and most authorities feel this figure is very low since many coroners, doctors and police (especially in small towns) seek to spare the families of such children and class their suicides as accidents.

Item: There were two million runaways in the U.S. last year. Half of these were girls, some as young as 13 or 14.

Is it any wonder that Anna Freud should comment: "The most difficult role in life is to be the parent of an adolescent child."

I know of no parents who aren't striving to do the best parenting job possible. I find, as I travel to parishes from one coast to the other, from Florida to Alaska, from Hawaii to Massachusetts, that they crave all the help they can get. I've been convinced for years that the Church has been in the forefront of defending and nurturing the family. It insisted on premarital counseling, if only the old canonical three hours, long before any other body, religious or civil, saw the need. I find, increasingly, as the forces of the secular world intrude more and more into the home, that parents turn ever more hopefully to the Church for help in building healthy families. This is where instruments like the Cursillo, the Engaged Encounter, the Marriage Encounter, Search, Beginning Experience (for the separated, divorced and widowed), Teens Encounter Christ, and Family Retreats, are so useful. But so are Alcoholics Anonymous, Al-Anon, and Al-Teen and so are those counselors which some parishes are beginning to supply on a full time basis to do family counseling.

For, let's face it, if we have some people who can't comprehend the loving fatherhood of God, it may be because they've not experienced a loving father on earth. If we have some who do not appreciate their brotherly/sisterly ties with all the human family, it is because they never knew such familial love at home. If we have alienated persons who are not at home in the world, it may just be because they have never had a real home in the world.

However a man and a woman seek to work out their relationship as husband/wife, father/mother — and every marriage, and every family, like every human being, has always been and always will be, unique — they need all the support that we can give them; only with such support can they be the "little church", that community of faith, hope, and love which all Christian families are called to be: "beacons to the world, upholders of the message of life."

Chapter 14

Toward The Autonomy
Of The Aging

The Reverend Monsignor Charles J. Fahey, M.S.W.

The first theme of this chapter might be characterized as, "it has never been this way before." Modest increases in life span coupled with an extraordinary increase in life expectancy have combined to present a human reality different from that of any other in history. It calls for both discernment and action in every sphere of life.

While there are many aspects of society which influence the art of living, the length of life is one which is not appreciated sufficiently as both a cause of and an effect on life-styles, values and social processes. It affects profoundly the way we perceive ourselves, our relationships, our family life and our public policy. The dramatic increase in the amount of life to be lived calls for new anthropological understandings as well as for serious theological reflections.

THE DEMOGRAPHIC REALITY

We are experiencing profound changes in the amount of life each person can expect to live. This in turn effects relationships within an age cohort and among age cohorts.

Ironically, scientists have become committed to the notion of a biological clock ticking inexorably with the inevitability of death a certainty. Life span is perceived as limited. However, we have experienced increased life expectancy for individuals. This has been achieved as a result of decreases in mortality and morbidity in every age cohort throughout the population with dramatic improvements at least in mortality among the old old.

We have increased average life expectancy in the United States by 60% since 1900. In that year the average life expectancy at birth was 46.3 years. In 1982 it was 74.6 (Statistical Abstracts).

Half of those in the human family who have been blessed with living 60 years are alive today.

What is the explanation? Largely, it results from an accumulation of factors associated with living in relative affluence. They touch persons' lives at every age. Our long lives result from improved maternal and child health, from immunization, from a less dangerous environment, from better nutrition, from more healthy life-styles generally as well as from better understanding of how the body and its systems work, more precise diagnostic tools and effective therapeutic interventions; all more readily available to an ever greater number of our people.

This phenomenon is associated with the developed countries but the trend is to be observed worldwide. As noted on the occasion of the World Assembly on Aging, a majority of those persons in the human family who have achieved 60 years of age live in less developed lands (Vienna Plan of Action). As public health measures and other positive elements of the developed countries are introduced, spectacular gains in life expectancy are achieved.

Neighboring Mexico gives an illustration of the spectacular growth in the older population. The over 60 population was

1,387,000 in 1950. Based on conservative estimates it will be 17,511,000 in 2025. In 1950 there were 86,000 persons over 80. It is anticipated that this figure will grow to 1,271,000 in 2025. It should be noted that both projections are based on persons currently alive and upon trends now evident in that country.

We can expect that 2/3rds of us will live into our 80's with 90% to live within a span of 77 to 93. (Fries)

It should also be underscored that there is a dramatic difference in life expectancy between that of men and women with the latter living an average 7 years longer than their counterparts. The reasons for this are not entirely clear.

Black Americans have shorter life expectancies than their white brothers and sisters though the sex difference prevails with black women living longer than white men. In 1900, the average life expectancy of black Americans was 30. In 1982 it increased to 70 (Statistical Abstracts).

Statistics such as these can be quite deadly but behind them there is a story and inherent in them a tremendous challenge.

Simply stated, the generations alive today have been given a gift of life not only fuller in a human sense than that of any period in history but also longer. We will live lives that are at least twice as long as those persons who lived at the time of Jesus when less than half the persons born lived to be fifty. Most of the increase in life expectancy has occurred within the life time of persons who are alive today: persons who have experienced and caused to happen more social change than any cohort in the history of the world.

It is within this context that I suggest we must struggle to understand the meaning of the gift of aging and rethink its place in the divine economy, in the life of every social institution including that of the family and every individual.

We cannot put new wine in old wine skins or sew old cloth with new thread.

Like many other social institutions, the Church has tended to think of older persons only within the context of frailty and vulnerability. Indeed it is fitting that in accord with our preferential option for the poor we have special concern for those whose poverty is exacerbated by age even as for those who become dependent because of infirmities associated with old age.

However our analysis must be more extensive and intensive as we take cognizance of this reality that is uniquely the challenge of this generation. There is a new ethical agenda to be identified. What values sustain persons in this new milieu? We need a better understanding of its effects on population and development. How will work, wealth, power, status and resources be shared equitably?

When one is in the midst of rapid social change it is difficult to fully understand or deal with it; yet those who would be moral leaders cannot escape the effort to try.

We study aging not only to understand the process and to help older persons but also to better understand the human experience and to inform other parts of the developmental process. We study the aged and the aging experience to help both the old and those growing old but also to understand from the old and their interaction with social institutions lessons about life at every stage.

While there may be an aura of objectivity and otherness about such a reflection, it is intensely subjective and personal. We are considering our own lot as well as that of others. We are all aging and we aspire to a rich old age, if we have yet to achieve it.

While Divine Revelation formally ended with the death of the last apostle, in another true sense it continues and discernment is a factor of our personal and collective lives as long as there is something to be learned about our intrapsychic functioning or about the stars. The gift of a prolonged life is not only something to be appreciated but also to be understood.

Neither Tradition nor Sacred Scripture has a great deal to say about aging.

Given the age structure of the population of the time, it should come as no surprise. The references to persons of extraordinary age are likely to be literary devices and the use of the word "elder" likely refers to relative age, i.e., length of time in a given community as compared to others.

Life in Scriptural times was not only hard, it was short and uncertain. The paucity of references to or reflections about the old are understandable but should challenge us in our time. Similarly the moral teachings which viewed life as both uncertain and brief must now be reviewed in the light of the new reality of a much longer life. Such an analysis must not only reach the old but also all social structures in the light of a generally much longer life.

TOWARD AN UNDERSTANDING OF AGING

At first glance "aging" and "aged" may seem like simple concepts; the former referring to the process through which one passes over time, and the latter, the state which one achieves after having lived a substantial part of one's life. While these are sound, there are other ways of looking at them which may help in our discernment process.

TYPES OF AGE

It is useful to distinguish a number of ways in which "age" is used as a concept:
1. Chronological
2. Biological/Physiological
3. Risk
4. Demographic
5. Longevity
6. Cultural
7. Role/Status

1. Chronological Age

This is the straightforward concept which most persons think of when the word is used. However, insights from various disciplines have helped us understand some of the limits of using it as an exhaustive discriptor of human potential and behavior. Chronological age is useful in broad sociological terms but is a poor predictor of individual health, attitudes, values or behavior.

2. Biological/Physiological Age

The aging process begins at conception. Until the late 20's it is a process of growth, a strengthening and maturing of the various systems. At this period there begins a general, gradual decline. However, there is considerable redundancy and we are able to function in a satisfactory manner until the end of our lives, barring serious and incapacitating illness.

"Aging" and "illness" are not synonomous. However, the gradual and uneven decline in systems makes persons susceptible to certain types of debilitating diseases, many of which are chronic in nature.

The "decline" in systems is not tied, lock step, with chronological age nor do all systems age simultaneously.

It should be noted that "senility," as dementia is often called, is not inevitable nor is it caused by any one agent. Often Alzheimer's disease is characterized incorrectly as premature senility. More accurately, it is a type of dementia often seen in older persons which is a result of disease rather than aging itself.

3. Risk Age

Some persons can be said to have the prospect of a shorter life span than others. They are "at risk" of debilitating or death-causing conditions. The risk which they face is the same as that which would normally be associated with persons older than they. Thus they can be said to have a relatively high risk age.

Some risks are involuntary, while others come into being as a result of conscious choices.

A man has a higher risk age than a woman; a black person, higher than a white; a person whose grandparents lived shorter lives and died from natural causes has a higher risk age than that person whose grandparents lived longer lives. These are examples of involuntary risks.

On the other hand, those who smoke, who are obese or who abuse substances such as alcohol or drugs voluntarily increase their risk age.

4. Demographic Age

This concept includes the notion that a person ages both in relation to the numbers of persons of his or her age and in relation to the number of his or her age cohort to that of other age groupings. The total number of persons of similar age has significance to the way in which the rest of the population relates to them. Large

230

numbers of older persons may be a "political force" in a democratic society. On the other hand, in some societies, the few surviving older persons may accumulate both wealth and power and thus contribute a societal reverence for older persons.

The number of persons in each age cohort relative to other age cohorts will be a factor in the distribution of jobs, wealth, status, political power and cultural influence.

5. Longevity

Longevity refers to the length of time a person is in a given place or social circumstance. It is frequently and appropriately linked with age. However, they are distinct though related concepts. Sometimes a person may be in a social location for all of his or her life and the two ideas are realized in the same person. In some instances we may attribute the way a person acts or feels to age when in fact it is a result of length of time in that particular role or relationship rather that the person's age.

Particularly, in our period of prolonged life we have some older persons in social locations for a short time and we have younger persons in locations for long periods.

In terms of longevity we may identify an 80 year old who is a neophyte and a 40 year old who is an elder.

We find evidence of "curves" in learning, productivity and satisfaction. Were people's learning, satisfaction and productivity to be charted over time, the chart would evidence a steep ascent at the start of an activity, gradual plateauing and decline as time passes.

While formerly these "curves" were associated with age, they are more accurately associated with longevity in particular circumstances.

This phenomenon poses challenges for both the married and religious states since persons find themselves in these "social locations" for such long periods of time.

6. Cultural Age

According to "role theory," the behavior of people results not alone from their values, capabilities and the opportunities afforded them, but also from the expectancies which people have of them.

In some instances this social pressure may seem to be beneficial and at others inimical to human dignity. The latter condition prevails when a person is inhibited from exercising his or her potential because of some irrelevant characteristic. Our society has seen such oppression of persons on the basis of religion, sex or color. In his Pulitzer prize winning book, *Growing Old in America: Why Survive?,* Robert Butler MD coined the expression "ageism." It identifies the tendency to negatively stereotype older persons and thus preclude them from continuing to utilize their gifts.

7. Role/Status: The "Three Ages of a Person"

Persons are involved with various roles and achieve status in accord with the way in which they fulfill them.

It is useful to think of the life cycle in this way. We have three main cycles each involving a central theme. We might characterize this as the "Three Ages of a Person."

The first part of life is centered in the role of a "learner." It is the time to grow in the use of "head, hands and heart;" to grow "in wisdom, grace and age." While these are lifelong activities, they are the primary task of the first age. One's status revolves around the way one fulfills them.

The Second Age is marked by greater autonomy and changing relationships with persons and with society. A person makes several fundamental choices: what I am to do, who my friends are to be, who is my special friend, my spouse, children, where we will live.

While persons make many other decisions, they tend to be related to and even subservient to the activities associated with the basic choices. One's status is achieved by fulfilling the roles inherent in these fundamental choices.

For most people in history and for many persons in less developed countries, death would intervene before this phase of life was completed. One or another parent would die before the children were adults. Work to sustain a family would continue until one was unable to continue because of disability or death.

However, for the developed countries, with prolonged life span, the tasks, roles and status associated with the basic Second Age choices are completed with a significant amount of life, often twenty or thirty years, still before a person. This is the challenge of the Third Age.

Currently the Third Age tends to be organized around a twofold paradigm: work/retirement and family life. There are increasing number of indicators that these are inadequate as "organizing factors" for this new facet of life.

We at the Fordham's Third Age Center are forwarding the notion that this period of life should be marked by consciousness and intentionality. Having exhausted the primary roles of the Second Age, it is time to examine one's values, life-style, friends, work, where one lives, one's use of leisure and the place of money in one's life and make deliberative choices in affirming or modifying the way one "comes at life."

For all too many, a kind of inertia sets in which precludes a creative approach the rest of life. We need to discover organizing principles for the Third Age as there were for the First and Second Ages.

Paradoxically, it is a time for greater interiority and, simultaneously, of greater social concern. It is a period to further develop one's spiritual life and at the same time to be more concerned about the whole human family. Freed of Second Age obligations, it should be a time of concern about broader human issues. It is a time for greater commitment to the Beatitudes.

THE CHURCH AND THE THIRD AGE

The Church has a threefold responsibility in regard to aging: service, values and spirituality.

Service

Services may be characterized as those activities which help persons to function to their maximum capacity and with as much autonomy as possible. They are on a continuum from those involving low technology and formalization to those which are high tech and intensely formalized. The services may be on a congregational, regional, diocesan or national level.

The most extensive and, perhaps, significant is that which takes place informally, at the congregational level; that is, the parish serving as a place affording identity, meaning and belonging on an intergenerational basis. Many older persons are suffering what the sociologist would speak of as anomie. Their children have moved. They may have lost a spouse. The parish is a place where they can be at home.

Such an observation leads to an important consideration on the part of parishes. Is our community of faith hospitable to older persons? Does our concern manifest itself both in the physical and psychological features of the parish?

Is our church free of barriers which may inhibit persons who are disabled? Have we eliminated those things which may be hazardous to people? Do we have a good sound system? Do older persons feel at home? Do we have affirmative action programs to encourage their participation?

Parishes should be aware of activities to enhance the lives of older persons; both of those who are independent and of those who are frail.

Of all the persons in the United States who are disabled and aged, two-thirds are cared for by family, friends and neighbors rather than by formal systems. The Church has special opportunities to support and enhance this informal system.

Those who have not had the occasion to care for the frail speak of the need for financial assistance when asked what help they would need if ever faced with this issue. Those who have the care of frail persons speak of the need to have respite, technical assistance, professional backup and knowledge. Parishes are logical places to provide or to see to the provision of such support.

An important element in the institutionalization of a person is the presence or absence of a "significant other." It is virtually impossible to maintain a disabled, older person in the community if there is no caring person nearby. Whether the parish community can provide such support is problematic. Some congregations do so in individual instances. Whether this could become an intregal part of parish life is questionable.

The Church's history is resplendent with the work of religious communities which have devoted much of their apostolic effort in the service of frail elderly persons. Dioceses have entered this field only of late and without a clear concept of what they can or should do.

One of the most promising approaches is the "parish outreach" movement encouraged by the National Conference of Catholic Charities. This initiative has seen a greater commitment of Catholic Charities' resources to enable the parish to meet the human needs of their constituents both directly through a series of services and indirectly through various social action activities.

Similarly, the Catholic Health Association is encouraging and assisting its member agencies to reach out to parishes in meeting the needs of their frail.

Catholic agencies are involved in programs ranging from those designed to meet the leisure time needs of older persons to meeting their needs for food, clothing and shelter. Some parishes sponsor housing for the elderly and a few have developed nursing homes. They do so as single parishes, or with others of a region and frequently as part of a neighborhood and/or interfaith coalition.

The Third Age Center at Fordham is in the midst of a nationwide study of religious congregations and the frail elderly.

Values

The Church would seem to have two important roles in the area of values:

1. The transmission of insights from an integration of gospel values and an understanding of a prolonged life span.

2. The initiation of an intentional, systematic process of discernment to understand the meaning of a prolonged life span and its impact on individuals and social structures including the Church itself.

There is little "intentionality" about the Third Age. Persons tend to drift into it and through it without realizing its meaning and opportunities.

The Church has many approaches to education and personal development. Virtually none of them have the Third Age on their agenda though significant if not disproportionate numbers of our congregants are in the Third Age (to say nothing of those who are priests and religious).

The changing demographic reality poses a series of new questions concerning the meaning of life in the Third Age, the role of family in a four and five generational milieu, the just distribution of benefits and burdens, particularly through the political process, in a multigenerational society and changing personal responsibilities in the light of the prolonged life span. We have given little thought to these matters.

A related but distinct and important consideration is the impact on Sacred Scripture and our religious tradition of a relatively short and uncertain life span. We have become more attuned to our religious tradition by understanding the cultural milieu within which it has developed. One of the elements which is inadequately understood is the impact of "longevity" on this tradition. Did the reality of a relatively short life span cause a certain emphasis and give rise to certain insights which need to be rethought in the light of a longer life span?

Spirituality

Spirituality as used here refers to one's struggle with the mystery of Salvation and the development and maintenance of a relationship with God.

Simply stated: is there a unique spirituality of the Third Age? Do life experiences, changing social roles and relationships, modified physiological capabilities and approaching death have such impact that older persons have a distinct way of approaching the Lord? Are there pastoral implications about the Third Age?

We simply do not know at this time. Few persons have reflected upon it. There has been virtually no systematic approach by the Church in this area. The New York State Catholic Conference has initiated a Commission on Elderly which has identified this area as one of its priority considerations.

The potential of older persons as ministers has only begun to be exploited though they would seem to be an important source of leadership if given the opportunity and support. There are sufficient examples of such as to give rise to the expectation that more older persons will find themselves in various ministerial roles.

The state of the art in pastoral care of the frail elderly seems to be in its infancy. While there are charismatic individuals and isolated places through which good care is rendered, these seem to be the exception rather than the rule.

There are more than 1,400,000 nursing home beds in the United States. Unfortunately, we have perfected neither the techniques nor organizational patterns for addressing the religious needs of their residents nor for those with similar disabilities in their own homes.

THE FAMILY

The family is profoundly influenced by the prolongation of life, and the gift of the Third Age.

Four generational families are normative in our society and five generations are common. Most couples will live together longer with no possibility of having children than with the possibility. Many couples will spend the major part of their lives having completed their primary parenting role.

Seventy percent of women over sixty five are single by reason of divorce, separation or the death of a spouse. Seventy percent of men over sixty five are living with their wives.

Virtually all of the Church's reflection and education has taken place within the context of a three generational, relatively short-lived human experience.

We are in need of a rethinking of our perspective in the light the gift of the Third Age. Such a rethinking is not alone about the nature of marriage in the Third Age for the sake of older persons. It should also be geared to further understand the purpose of marriage in the Second Age. It should help us discover the reciprocal roles of husbands and wives throughout the whole span of marriage. It should help us better understand intimacy, sexuality and the independent/interdependent roles of men and women who are at the same time husbands and wives, individuals as well as a couple even as they are mothers and fathers.

The current theology of marriage is understandably defective in failing to recognize the post-parenting phase as an essential part of marriage as well as instructive about the role of intimacy and sexuality throughout marriage.

The reality of a prolonged period of infertility coexisting with active sexuality should give pause to our almost exclusive focus on the physically generative aspect of sexuality.

As in other facets of this new era, we should reflect on the gift of the Third Age for the benefit of those who are older, to learn about growing old gracefully and to understand the whole life cycle more profoundly.

RELIGIOUS AND PRIESTS

Religious

The consideration of the Third Age and the family would be incomplete without some reference to those parts of the Church family who serve God's people in the religious life.

We are approaching a crisis in regard to the sustenance of older religious. With the median age of religious in the United States having passed sixty and with an appreciation of the economic realities of religious life, it is clear that numerous religious communities will be unable to care for their frail older members. They will have neither the financial nor human resources to do so. It is not a problem for religious communities alone but for the whole Church that has benefited from their ministerial activity. We are in desperate need of a national strategy to deal with the question not only for those who are already frail but for those members of communities who see the necessity for all their creativity to be utilized in support of their older community members with little prospect of them having anyone to care for them. It is a problem of such dimensions that is almost less painful to ignore it, but it will not go away.

As in the instance of marriage, a deeper analysis of the graying of religious communities will assist those who are growing old in the service of the Lord as well as sharpen our understanding of religious life in a period of a much longer commitment than that in previous centuries.

Diocesan Priests

The graying of the diocesan priesthood presents other challenges. The diocesan priesthood is "maturing" at a dizzying pace. For those of us who are part of this reality, the challenge is to devise techniques so that the learning, satisfaction and productivity curves which tend to level and dip do not do so in the instance of priests. However it is not a challenge easily met. It cannot be met if not faced.

Another facet of graying of the clergy is the fact that it tends to mask the impending shortage of priests. Analyses done by Fordham's Third Age Center are similar to those reported in *Catholic Church Personnel in the United States*. While we have virtually as many priests in service today as we did in 1963, many have grown old in the service of God's people.

The significant factor is the seminarian ratio. In a study of 20 representative dioceses we found there was .82 seminarian for each priest in 1960. In 1963 it had risen to a ratio of one for one. In 1983 there was .15. While it is difficult to establish an accurate replacement rate (i.e., the number of seminarians needed, on average, to replace the priests who would become unavailable for ministry by reason of disability, of having left priestly ministry or death) it is likely that the 1963 figure was below it and the 1983 figure is in the magnitude of 6 times less. It is certain that the number of priests in active ministry will drop dramatically in the next ten years, undoubtedly generating its own dynamic. The face of the Church is about to change radically at the parish level.

Conclusion

It has never been this way before. It might be said with equal accuracy that it will never be this way again.

It has become increasingly apparent that in our quest for personal holiness we must be involved in discernment as well as prayer and behavior consonant with the Gospel message. The metaphor "a pilgrim people" readily comes to mind as we realize the gift and challenge that the Lord has given us and the Church in a prolonged life and a Third Age. It has and will profoundly influence understandings of ourselves, our families and even of the Church and the precious inheritance of the Tradition of Faith.

Bibliography

Butler, Robert N. *Why Survive? Being Old in America.* New York: Harper & Row, Publishers, Inc., 1975.

Fries, James F. "Aging, Natural Death and the Compression of Morbidity." *New England Journal of Medicine* 303 (July 17, 1980): 130-135.

Statistical Abstracts of the United States. 1984 Bureau of the Census, December 1983, U.S. National Center for Health Statistics.

Vienna International Plan of Action on Aging. World Assembly on Aging, United Nations publications, (Sales No E. 82.I.16) New York, 1983.

Chapter 15

Pastoral Concerns Regarding Family Problems

PART I — DISCUSSION WITH MR. PAREDES AND BISHOP RICARD

Question: Mr. Paredes, in the section of your topic dealing with evangelical challenges, you mentioned that we should involve lay people in ministry. We agreed with that and we wondered what kind of collaboration you have in mind, and what kind of preparation should we favor so that they become responsible for sharing ministry with us? Bishop Ricard, we were impressed with the survey you mentioned about violence in Canada and in the United States and the relation between violence in the family and violence in society, and we feel that the relation is probably reciprocal. We are wondering about capital punishment? We feel that both in Canada and in the United States there is an increasing support for capital punishment. We as Bishops have some influence on public opinion. Should we remain silent about that trend, or should we speak out in order to decrease violence both in society and in family?

Mr. Paredes: In order to respond to the first question, I truly believe that we as lay people have an important role to fulfill in the Church because of our Baptism, not just because of the absence of clergy. To describe what type of program, what type of preparation we should have, let me speak from my experience in the Hispanic community. The Dominican Republic is a country in the Caribbean with a program which is called the "Promoters of the Word." These promoters are lay people who have been given 2 or 3 years of preparation through small communities. This is a model that with certain adaptations we could use in many of our communities.

I referred above to the question of the diaconate as not an alternative for us. Many people feel that we can solve our problems with a lot of Hispanic deacons. I'm not saying that the diaconate is not a good ministry, it's a ministry the Church needs. But not everybody is called to serve the Church as a deacon. There are many other ways to serve the Church. In the urban centers, in housing developments we need people and families that can witness to the Word. One of the greatest hungers of Hispanics is to learn the Word of God. They have a devotion, a real devotion for the Bible. Now, there are no people that guide them in reading the Bible and finally they end up with the fundamentalist sects and that breeds distortion and confusion and we lose them.

Clearly there are models of lay ministry and a very successful one is the one in the Dominicn Republic. The training will have to vary. We have to work at various levels. Intellectual training must be given, but also we have to take into account that, because of culture and economic limitations and conditions, we have to adapt these programs. We cannot demand a whole ambitious curriculum that immigrants have to follow before we give them permission to minister. We have to be flexible in that area. The role that this lay minister will play is the role of witnessing. They will witness to their peers and their brothers and sisters that the Church opens her arms and welcomes them so that the Church is their home. These lay people will play an important role by being the bridges between our people already here in the dominant culture, and those who are immigrants and migrants. Preparing these lay ministers requires funds, programs, and personnel.

Bishop Ricard: In reference to your question about capital punishment, I think a proper response to that would be to look at all forms of punishment in a society. The people who study family violence look at punishment not only in terms of capital punishment but punishment of children in the home and schools and they see a clear link, a clear correlation, between the uses of physical punishment and violence; one seems to be very clearly associated with the other. So, I would think, logically that we can say that if we look at capital punishment as a form of a violent punishment, that's one area we should very seriously begin to explore as we seek to decrease all the levels in violence in society.

Question: We have several clarification questions for Bishop Ricard. Could you say that your figure of 50% of wives abused includes almost minimal forms of violence? The second clarification deals with the Canadian/U.S.A. difference. What are some of the factors that create high levels of difference between these two geographical areas, although culturally they are quite similar in many ways? Thirdly, you mentioned the incest question of older men and young women. Are there any studies done in terms of older women and young boys? Are there any studies to indicate that the victim incites violence, the masochistic factor? Do certain types of personalities seek to be abused or to be violated in some way? And, finally, are there any real pastoral suggestions that you might offer us for pastoral letters and homilies? What can we do as Bishops in dealing with the question of violence today?

Bishop Ricard: I could give another talk! To begin, the 50% estimated abuse in American families is provided by judges, by social counselors, by lawyers and so forth. This is an estimate and admittedly this is an upward estimate from the actual reported cases. Hard data is very, very difficult to obtain in this area because so many people fear reporting this and much of it is not reported. I know very clearly in Maryland, for example, if the police respond to a call of domestic violence and if the wife refuses to go with the police in the police car to the precinct or if she refuses to press charges against her husband, they just leave it alone.

The factors why Canadian cities tend to be less violent are not really known. Perhaps it is because the Canadians have a more stable society. It's often pointed out that the Canadians have lower rates of street crime, of violent crime, murder, homicide, robbery, and so forth, than American cities, therefore, the lower rates of family violence are linked to that. I would suspect that it's because Canada is a more stable society, it's a smaller society, more manageable than you see in U.S. cities. In the U.S. we have migrations to cities and disruption and that's highly correlated with violence.

As far as incest is concerned, there was only one study out of all of those listed at the Academy of Sciences that had a mother and son engaging in actual incest. What they have found is that some mothers permit some type of fondling, the child sleeping with the mother and some type of non-penetrating activity occurring. But that is not too frequent and many times it happens either because the mother is an alcoholic or the mother is in some type of drunken stupor where she allows a young child to sleep regularly with her.

As far as pathology is concerned, very often there's some psychological evidence that victims, in effect, do provoke violent situations. If a wife, for example, grows up in a home where she sees violence occurring between her parents, then the acceptable mode of relationship to a husband is one of accepting violence. She may develop a type of psychological pattern, and in effect she may look for the one who would inflict violence on her. That's a kind of a masochistic approach to relationships, but some people do with words and gestures seem to provoke that type of violence.

244

The pastoral suggestions I would offer in this area would certainly deal with how we handle and how we respond pastorally to conjugal violence and child abuse. I think what's happening now is that when the child is abused your own social workers that operate your Catholic charities tend, by and large, to take the child out of a home or to remove the battered wife from the home and this in effect doubly punishes the child. The child is not only abused or the wife is not only abused, but they lose their families. Many times children don't report abuse and wives don't report abuse because they fear losing their families, especially the children.

I would suggest that we see the family as a treatment modality, that is, we treat the family, we keep the family intact at all cost, provided other things are provided for. We must treat this family as a pathological entity. That would be one approach to that, another would be simply to inform our Catholic people that this danger does exist and that we should find a way to diminish our propensity for violence. We should clearly point out that violence is systemic. That is, we see it at one level, and it's going to follow at another level and so on.

Question: The U.S. Bishops are now debating the pastoral letter on the American economy. We would like to suggest that we strengthen the sections on the family which still seem to us to be somewhat weak. This is something we can act on. In reference to the school questions, we'd like to suggest a couple of things. First of all, in view of the fact that we have lost in the Catholic schools of the United States 2½ million students in something like ten years, it's obvious that the Church is not able to provide the schooling that we would like to provide. In other words, we are for a true pro-choice for the minorities and for everybody else to choose the schools they wish for their children. It seems that perhaps the opportunity is with us for the minorities to lead us to this solution. This suggestion should be reflected in our pastoral letter, that we believe in true pro-choice for schools for our families.

Secondly, perhaps one of the solutions for family violence should be moving towards a family allowance. We have here with us the Canadian Bishops and Canada has had a family allowance for many, many years. There is some correlation between poverty and violence. In this family allowance the mother would usually receive the money to use for health or for education or other needs. Surely we would agree that the family allowance is not socialistic or tending towards socialism, although this could be one of the objections.

Mr. Paredes: I fully agree with the need for Catholic education. One of my criticisms to my Hispanic peers in the nation is their reluctance to join in the effort to fight for tax credits or for tuition credits. This is not the complete solution to the problems of schools, we have to be aware of that. But I'm a strong defender of Catholic education and I think we have to fight as minorities for tuition tax relief. It is a battle that must continue and we have to have our minorities speak out strongly and loudly on this issue.

Regretfully, some of the Hispanic leaders, I don't know about the blacks, are not Catholic militants. They are Catholic by Baptism, but somehow they are not really directly in touch with the leadership of the Church. We have nine Congressmen in Washington, and rarely are they in touch with our Catholic agencies. But the large archdioceses like New York, Philadelphia, Los Angeles, Chicago, and Brooklyn are doing a fantastic job on Catholic education and providing education to minorities, particularly to Hispanics. I believe that 40% of the Catholic population in parochial elementary schools in New York is Hispanic and 30% of the school population in Brooklyn is Hispanic.

Bishop Ricard: I think the pastoral letter certainly needs to stress a great deal more about family because disproportionately more single-headed families, as well as families on public assistance, report conjugal violence, child abuse, as well as other social stresses such as problems of housing, financial problems, problems with health and so forth. One very concrete way we can address the alleviation of this problem is to strengthen those families and remove those stressors, remove, in effect, the stresses that come with housing and finances, health-related problems and so forth, to strengthen the female-headed family.

Question: Mr. Paredes, many of the problems enumerated by you exist throughout Latin America due to migration. In other words, there are people moving in great numbers from Haiti to the Dominican Republic, from Columbia to Venezuela, from Mexico to Guatemala, etc. In some cases perhaps some of this migration should be discouraged by the systems to avoid so much of the dehumanization, would you agree with that? And, secondly, Bishop Ricard, what would be your thinking on the influence of the media on family violence? Does the data you have studied show that the religious preference has a greater or lesser bearing on family violence?

Mr. Paredes: My initial reaction is absolutely to discourage all types of immigration to the United States. When I see how immigrants come here, particularly from the area I know, Latin America, and how they're confronted with this society that is so vastly different from theirs, the shock is so incredible that certainly I would like to tell them to stay home. I'm sure that some of you saw the movie "El Norte", "The North", an interesting movie and a very moving one. It's a story of a brother and sister from Guatemala who had a dream to come to the North and finally, after the great adventure, arrived in Los Angeles. And, they had to find jobs. When she found a job she was employed by this lady in a wealthy family. She was a housekeeper who found herself in front of all types of new equipment with all types of buttons that you had to push. But never had she ever in her life pushed one single button for anything, because she was an Indian from Guatemala. The lady taught her how to use every machine in the house in order to do things well. But she just went berserk with all those machines. Finally, when she had to wash the clothes of the house, she decided to go out to the garden and do it by hand as she used to do it in Guatemala. She thought that was much better and the clothes more beautiful and much more clean.

This movie certainly gives us a lesson that indeed we have to discourage this immigration because of the cultural shocks and the violence that the people are suffering by coming here. On the other hand, who can stop this process? Do we have to build walls on the frontier? Do we have to tell the people to stay out when they are running away from brutal dictatorships? The crisis of Guatemala is incredible, the persecution and killings that go on there. Now we have a leftist regime in Nicaragua and we have people on the other side getting out of Nicaragua. We have the question of El Salvador where the right wing and the left wing are fighting each other and killing each other.

How do we stop this? Truly, I don't have any specific answer. I personally will discourage immigration; I don't think it's a way of being human to come here if you are not prepared. If only through the Church we could prepare immigrants in a rational way, that would probably be the logical thing to do. But who prepares for catastrophes, who prepares for war, who prepares for revolutions? They all of a sudden explode, you don't know what to do and you suddenly have immigrants at your doors here. They will walk in, no matter what you say, no matter what you do. So the responsibility is that they're here, let's receive them, let's work with them, and let's integrate them into the life of our Church and of our society.

Bishop Ricard: To respond to the question about the impact of the media on family violence, let me say that certainly a child who repeatedly sees acts of violence on television is going to be conditioned to violence. That may be overly simplistic but it is a psychological truism. When I was in Washington, the school that we had was in a ghetto neighborhood. In one of the eighth grade classrooms the police were chasing after this guy who had reportedly snatched somebody's purse. He ran into the classroom and all of the kids were very startled by this. This policeman had a gun in his hand and the first thing the kids did when they saw him was that they all gave him their lunchboxes, or at least were prepared to do so. And, I thought this was very striking when it happened, it was almost a spontaneous response. Most of the kids who had reacted this way said, "Well, that's the way they do it on television." They had been simply responding to what they had learned. I believe there's a very clear correlation between what they see in television and what they will actually do when circumstances arise.

Secondly, in the question of religion, certainly you would find fewer incidents of conjugal violence and perhaps child abuse among Catholics because you have fewer Catholics who would be on public assistance. On the other hand, there seem to be higher rates of abuse and violence among recent immigrants to the United States so that where they would be Catholic you would find a higher incidence there. Those two factors seem to relate to the question of religion. But, generally, the Gallup poll of about three months ago stated that Catholics and other believers, as far as their values were concerned, did not seem to differ significantly in many ways from those who profess no religion.

Question: What happened to the proposed legislation regarding immigration? And, what are the pastoral consequences if this legislation is approved under the criteria that have been presented?

Mr. Paredes: I am not an authority on this field, especially in front of Bishop Bevilacqua, who is the expert on this matter. I think it's better that Bishop Bevilacqua himself answer this question.

Bishop Bevilacqua: The immigration bill of last year just died in Congress, it never got any place. It died because the bill tried to offer too much to too many people. As a result you had too many isolated groups fighting about different parts of the bill so it pleased no one in trying to please everyone. I feel that's the major reason for the defeat of the bill. It is possible that in a new Congress it will be presented again, I would hope that we could present it in such a way that the various elements within the country, Hispanic elements and other elements, could have a unified support for whatever is presented. It might be better to present it in segments because there are some excellent proposals in the bill, particularly on the question of amnesty. It was a very generous amnesty that was being proposed, and that would have been a great benefit, particularly to the Hispanics in this country. But the part on Haitians and Cubans was also excellent. So in the defeat of the whole bill these very beneficial elements also were defeated.

Mr. Paredes: May I add a word to the comment of Bishop Bevilacqua? I am personally very grateful for the role Bishop Bevilacqua is playing on this very crucial matter for us Hispanics in this nation and for all the immigrants that are here illegally. There are people who have been here 12, 15, or 20 years, they have families, they have already established roots here, but they are in limbo, they are no entity in this society because they are not legal. So amnesty is a crucial question. Our Bishops' Conference and Bishop Bevilacqua have been fighting strongly for that. We are very proud of what the Church has been doing in this regard.

Question: Knowing the problems affecting the migrating family, either within a country from the countryside to the city, or from country to country whether legal migration or undocumented migration, how can we more effectively coordinate efficient assistance and evangelization within an episcopal conference?

Mr. Paredes: I am not a Bishop and this question should be answered by some of the members of the college of Bishops. But I will comment in general. It is my belief that our Church in the United States is moving more and more in a new direction which is very positive. This is that the Bishops of the U.S. are establishing commissions and committees with Bishops of neighboring countries, like the United States and Mexico. They should do this at various levels and more often so that dialogue could be established. Bishop Bevilacqua's committee is working very hard on this matter and we support very strongly what he is doing. We are trying to do the same thing with the Dominican Republic, with Columbia, and with Ecuador.

Commissions should be developed more and more even though you Bishops are very busy and are all overburdened. There's no way of developing effective pastoral programs without a direct dialogue between Bishop and Bishop. When I look back and see that in 1981 in Washington, D.C., we only had no more than 15,000 Central Americans and today probably we have more than 100,000 in a few years, I realize that this is a phenomenal problem.

250

Our episcopal conferences should work out programs of cooperation. For example, contracts or agreements could be signed between episcopal conference and episcopal conference with regard to pastoral agents. I think Bishop Bevilacqua is moving in that direction. That has been done with Poland, it also could be done with Columbia and with Mexico and with all the countries. So in order to respond specifically, Bishop, I encourage and I see now as a very positive trend what our episcopal conference is doing, establishing commissions. These commissions should include members of the hierarchy of both countries and they should be working commissions, not just visiting commissions. They have to be very effective and operational.

Question: Mr. Paredes, can you cite positive efforts on the part of the migrating family to enter into and integrate themselves into the American culture? And then, the second question, in ministering to immigrant families how do we handle the distinction between those here to await a political change in their own country and those who have come here to remain and start a new life? Bishop Ricard, are there any statistics on emotional abuse on the part of parents towards their children, or towards one another? Secondly, are there any statistics concerning the elderly being abused by adult children? Thirdly, recognizing as we do the violence of abortion, what other violence arises within the family circle as a result of abortion?

Mr. Paredes: The two questions you asked me, Bishop, are not easy to answer. You ask first for some positive values that the immigrant families bring in order to contribute to the society or in the process of integration in this society. I can only speak of my own culture. I believe that Hispanics, due to the history of their American Catholicism that is coming out of the experience of the Reformation and the Counter-reformation, which came from the Iberian peninsula in Europe, have given us a view of life and existence that is very, very rich. For example, we accept suffering, we accept sacrifice, we accept a self-giving of oneself to others for service, we accept a family that is extended in every sense of the word. These are very evangelical and very beautiful Christian values that we

251

could contribute to this society. These are positive elements that, if we are helped to establish ourselves well in this country, we can contribute to enrich this society since we have inherited these values from the long, rich tradition of Catholicism in Latin America.

The second question about classifying temporary and permanent immigrants is also very complicated. We have new waves of immigrants coming from Central America as in years back they came from South America. Salvador Allende of Chile was overthrown in 1973 and from 1973 up to the 80's we have had a turmoil in Latin America. Dictatorships sprang up and a lot of political refugees began to move up North. Then in the late 70's, we had the turmoil beginning in Central America where people began to get out of those countries by the thousands and thousands, literally.

In both experiences, from South as well as from Central America, we are receiving people that, with the exception of Chile, probably have had very little experience of a democratic process or a democratic society. There has often been a chain of revolutions. Look at Bolivia — that country has had almost as many coups and presidents as years of history. They have 160 years of existence and they have had 90 presidents! So we Hispanics have that type of history behind us. In addition to that we should note that the Spaniards impregnated in Latin America a desire to establish all these small countries, sometimes with the mentality of a small feudal castle with a moat in front of it. All this has affected the way of viewing this society when a Hispanic immigrant arrives here.

So what to do? We have to implement programs at various levels. At the very local level, when we're receiving immigrants from political areas that are in turmoil, we have to minister to them, take care of them, to see that they can adjust themselves in the local churches. At the national level, I think, our Church should be well-informed about the causes why these political turmoils are taking place and what our Church should say and do with regard to these political questions in Latin America.

Specifically, I am thinking right now about El Salvador and Nicaragua. Our own pastoral agents are divided about the views that we should have on the question of these countries. A lot of nuns and priests and sisters and some Bishops are in full agreement with a number of things that are taking place in Central America whereas others are in complete disagreement. Apparently, both sides have some truth and there is no clear direction where we are heading now with this complex question of Central America.

So, in summary, I suggest simply that you in the local Church should instruct your pastoral agents to care for those who have arrived and somehow to assist them to view this society that has a different way of life and a democratic process that many times they are not used to. On the other hand, I think at the national level, our Bishops also should try, through the various agencies that they have, to obtain clear information and views and take public stands on matters so delicate as the ones that are taking place in Latin America.

Bishop Ricard: You asked for statistics for the emotional abuse of children. I would respond to this in a general way by saying that you would find that most people who are recipients of psychotherapy today, especially the variety that would last six months or longer, would maintain that they were victims of psychological abuse of their parents. They blame the proverbial Jewish mother or Catholic mother who did not provide adequate nourishment, adequately positive feedback, the feeling of being loved, and so forth. Actual statistics are very difficult to find.

With reference to your other question on abuse of the elderly, there's a phenomenon which has been identified as "granny bashing." This refers apparently to an increasing problem of children abusing their parents, especially elderly parents. This reflects the failure to understand proper stewardship of the family's role in caring for its sick members. Again the actual data is very difficult to come by, but increasingly social service agencies are going to the homes, especially of elderly people, to investigate this. They find that those who become impatient with their aging parents are at high risk for abusing them. But statistics are difficult to come by.

Relative to the question of abortion and violence, my own reaction to this is that a society which tolerates abortion, tolerates violence. There seems to be some connection there. When you have this attitude towards life which is that life is expendable, it's expendable at all levels, whether it's the unborn or the children or wives or whoever. So it seems that this is a systemic difficulty. It certainly is tied in to our basic attitudes towards life itself, at all levels.

PART II — DISCUSSION WITH MR. BARBEAU AND MONSIGNOR FAHEY

Question: Msgr. Fahey, can you expand on the particular needs of aging religious and priests as you understand them?

Monsignor Fahey: I'd like to speak about each separately and then the common thread between the two. In regard to religious, and particularly religious women, although there's also the challenge for religious men, the median age of religious women in the United States at the present time is 63. That poses enormous challenges to us and we might as well recognize it. First of all, it raises questions in regard to apostolic decisions and the use of resources that are involved in apostolic decisions. Each diocese will have to be prepared, whether they have large concentrations of religious motherhouses or not, to deal with this issue, and it should be a shared one. Unfortunately, more and more religious communities perceive themselves as being forced into making decisions about the apostolate based upon economics. Often they are selling ongoing operations, or having persons go into high-paying jobs.

The second aspect, with this median age of 63, is that clearly we have the care problem ahead of us. While some religious communities are well able to take care of this, a number will not be able to take care of it, requiring unparalleled inter-community cooperation often through the brokerage of the local diocese. The third and related aspect that I would draw to your attention in regard to religious, particularly of religious women, though increasingly religious men are recognizing it as well, is the liability that the community has when it is unfunded in regards to the care of those who are retired or near retirement. And, while many dioceses have taken some steps in this regard, it is of such a breadth in scope that it will require us to take some sort of national action.

Just two weeks ago we convened virtually all the cast of characters from throughout the United States at the behest of a number of foundations that are funding the national efforts or are funding individual communities with retirement problems, with the participation of the USCC, the Leadership Conference of Women Religious, The Conference of Major Religious Superiors of Men, etc. Some 30 of us put together the state of the art which will be reported to the Executive committee of the USCC and the other groups. A white paper will be prepared on this that will be sent to all religious communities and to all dioceses, describing where things stand at this moment, and the kind of challenge that faces us all in that regard.

Now, let me switch to priests for a moment. In regard to priests, in 1969 the Commission on Aging of the National Conference of Catholic Charities convened a meeting on the retirement of priests. Frankly, all that could be talked about at that conference was, first, let's have some finances to take care of older priests, and secondly, how do you get the old men out? All I can suggest to you is that it is time that there be much more cooperative activity in regard to older priests.

The fundamental issue for priests is not retirement, although retirement is an issue. The basic issue is that we have priests serving much longer periods of time, being expected to perform many more tasks in social locations that are very demanding and we must develop skills among us all of sustaining and enriching the lives of priests in the third age. When it comes specifically to the frail among older priests, I'm saddened to say that many dioceses are going at this whole question piece-meal, one by one, they are all reinventing the wheel. There is a need for some sort of convening and some sort of joint activity to deal with the question of older priests generally, specifically with the care of those who are frail. I would suggest a number of resources exist, but so many of the dioceses are going through this very same process with few people consulting with them. So, I would beg for that consultation.

Now let's look at a common factor in regard to both priests and sisters. I would suggest that out there there's terrible anguish on the parts of many priests and sisters about caring for their frail older parents. In many instances, it's older priests and sisters who are caring for very old parents. There's nothing I'm called upon more to do recently then to go to dioceses to talk with priests and sisters about caring for their parents. And, ironically, particularly religious women are being asked to care for a parent as the unmarried daughter used to be. They are told, you're not doing anything important, you ought to take care of them! On the other hand, in some instances, they're totally excluded from participation in family decisions in this regard. So this is a big issue in almost every diocese and there has to be a way of dealing with it.

Let me note that we have many Sisters, particularly second career ones, who are out there working for the support of their communities. But this is never going to happen that way again and we can not be too dependent upon these second career nuns. We ought to learn from what they are doing because many of them are doing things in a creative fashion outside of ordinary structures. We at least should learn from them and what they're about.

With regard to the number of priests, I may be bringing bad news that you already know, but doing it now from a more cumulative point of view. Looking at a number of dioceses there is a relatively small shrinkage in actual priests working in parishes at the present time. It's an unusual phenomenon. Why? It's largely a function of aging in place. We have far more older priests working than were working a generation or two ago, and in some instances this is masking the enormous personnel challenge that is ahead of us.

We've done some statistical analysis that is only a first cut at it, and I would wish and hope we will do more. In 1963, which was sort of a high water mark, we had one seminarian for one priest. Today in a series of dioceses in which we're studying the facts, we have .15 seminarian per priest. I've tried to figure out what the replacement rate is in terms of priests. Frankly, there are too many variables to do it. My instincts are that even one for one is not replacement rate. We are likely to see in a very short period of time, within the next 5 years, not just a gradual but a radical decline in the number of priests that are out there. Unless faced head on and somehow within the context of the Spirit this will create its own dynamic, its own involutional and negative activity. I don't like to be the person bringing bad news, but this is a reality that somehow we in a prayerful way, not in a survey way, but in a discerning way, must try to struggle and deal with.

Question: Mr. Barbeau, do you have any suggestions for countering the bad influence of the media on our children? Also, you suggested several programs like Marriage Encounter and Search that help parenting. Do you know any others that you would recommend? Thirdly, what is the cause of the prolonged immaturity of adolescence. Fourthly, what do you see as the future of the family? Father Fahey, how do we best minister to people in the third age? What should we be doing?

Mr. Barrbeau: I would hope that schools would offer, just as they offer literature appreciation classes, classes in critical evaluation of TV programs. One could tape them, and play a program and you could literally help the child or young person take that program apart, including the commercials. We did that in our home. If they'd have a beautiful bikini-clad girl sitting on a hood of a car to advertise the car, I would turn to one of the kids and ask what she had to do with that motor or what does she tell us about the quality of the car? In a certain drama, I would ask, why did they move the camera over to that person, do you know? We can try to teach them some critical ways of looking at this.

With regard to program selection, I used the principle: "Don't let little children see anything on TV you wouldn't let them see in reality." Up to the age of 8, children make very little distinction between what is on that tube and what else is going on in the front room. It's all reality to them, including the commercials.

Now, in regard to parenting programs I mentioned Marriage Encounter and Search and so on because there's a great hunger right now. One of the things that the Search program or TEC or other weekend retreat programs of Christian inspiration do for youngsters is to challenge their idealism. Adolescence is a time of great idealism and there are a lot of kids out there who are not being challenged in their idealism in regard to Christian principles or Christian life style.

The Engaged Encounter is wonderful. I found many couples who had to rethink their marriage decision in the light of the communications that went on in that Engaged Encounter weekend. They learned that they hadn't gotten around to discussing whether they shared certain values, or how many kids they wanted, or whatever. All they knew was that they were busy gazing into one another's eyes. Engaged Encounter and many other intensive marriage preparation programs designed by different people in different parts of the country encourage an important kind of premarital communication. They help people to overcome projective love, an immature form of love where I project upon you that you're perfect and you're going to fill all my needs and so on.

The other infantile form of love which such programs help counteract is object-centered love. The little tiny tot has his security blanket and people say he loves that little blanket, we can't separate him from it. He doesn't love that blanket, he loves what the blanket does for him: it makes him feel secure. Or the teenager in love with his car doesn't love the car; he loves the power, the speed, and the fact that it's a portable shelter for the seduction of other people's daughters. He loves all kinds of values the car brings him, he doesn't love the car.

When I talk in high schools there are all these kids who think they're in love. They get a lot of sex education and very little love education. I go in and I talk about love. I say if you're in love, your grades have gone up one grade point average this semester. Because love energizes, sharpens the wits. If you're in love, your parents have complimented you on how wonderfully helpful you've been around the house lately. You have made 10 new friends. They're stunned. I try o get across the difference between love and infatuation.

At any rate, our teenagers are hungry for information about where they are, what's going on with them, and for some challenge about what contribution they can make to the quality of their family life style. Many of them think that they're acted upon rather than that they make an active contribution. I've had kids come up to me after a talk in a high school or a classroom situation and say that a veil was lifted from their eyes. One girl said she thought when her parents yelled at her all the time and nagged at her about where she went and who she went with, they just hated her. Now she realized they are doing that because they care about her. Teenagers are as interested in improving the quality of the relationship with their parents as the parents are with the kids. I found that teen programs that bring the two of them together in the same room and facilitate communications help a lot.

The reason I mentioned Beginning Experience is because when we talk about the single parents out there — most of them women, most of them not receiving support payments from their husbands, therefore, having to work full time — you have a group of women who have young children, who have a 7-day week, unshared responsibility for children, and very often have practically no recreation time and no support group. They often feel totally alone, totally isolated in this parenting context. The Beginning Experience not only helps them to heal some of the wounds from their loss of a love but also gives them a support group and gives them people in a like situation. It reassures them that they are not going crazy, that other people feel the same way that they do, have anger, have denial and depression and all the phases of death and dying that Kubler-Ross describes. That confusion of feelings and that resentment at being alone in the world can be helped, can be overcome if they have such a program.

With regard to the prolonged immaturity of adolescents, it is a result, I think, of the fact that we have no puberty rites. By that I mean that many cultures (and Hopi Indians to this day) have a rite in which one day you are a child and the next day you are taken in by the women or the men, depending upon your sex, and you're put through a ritual. When you finish this ritual, however long it is, depending upon the tribe or the culture, you are today a member of the male adult community or the female adult community. We don't have that.

When we invented teenagery, the kids had no economic function in the home and now had this task of identifying themselves, without getting to experiment out there with different kinds of work. Many parents are focusing a lot of attention in a child-centered way, making the children all important in their lives and not wishing to relinquish that dependency status. They are not moving fast enough towards allowing them to get out.

I can give you one example of a couple who came to me very depressed to talk about their "boy." He was at home all the time, not going to school and not working. He was smoking pot and sleeping all day and he would borrow the car at night and be gone until four in the morning. I found out the "boy" was 25, and asked the parents how long they intended to subsidize his drug habit? I strongly urged them to sit him down and say that they were renegotiating his contract of residence. Many parents don't do that. When I talked to these parents they looked shocked. I told them they could have a discussion with their son about entering a drug program, looking for a job, going back to school, or in other words, shaping up his life, or getting out. They could do that now, or wait until he would be 26, 27, or 30, because until they did it, he was not going to change. So the prolonged adolescence is very often occasioned by the parents, either their unwillingness to confront the issue or their neurotic neediness for the child to be still dependent because their meaning in life comes from being parents. Sometimes parents are afraid of what will happen when the last one leaves the nest; they might not have anything to say to one another.

Now let us look at the future of the family. The family has always been in transition. Indeed, there is no better institution for the humanization of people or for the raising of people that we know of. It constantly has been undergoing transformation in terms of roles. My feeling is that we are in one of the greatest periods of renaissance of appreciation of what marriage and family life is all about since the dawn of creation. We have come down to seeing the marital union and the family not so much as an economic unit but as a place of nurturing people to full spiritual and emotional maturity. We are focusing on the family as an organism of humanizing and christianizing its members.

Parents are christianized and humanized as much as children, that's why I can talk to kids about raising parents, because they do. When I talk to parents that way, they understand immediately what I mean. The children are occasions of virtue for us. We have to learn patience and long suffering, humor and all kinds of things. So I think the future of the family is going to be relatively healthy. We are going through a lot of upheavals because of the cultural impacts upon it, but we have found a resurgence of marriage going on again, and of people regularizing their live-in relationships, etc.

Monsignor Fahey: In terms of ministry to third age persons, I think one task is just to define that it is a ministry to be aware of, to define it broadly so it isn't just the old old but it's the young old as well. We must do this at each level, on the parochial level and the diocesan as well.

Question: Msgr. Fahey, what do you mean by a distinct way of holiness in the third age? And for Mr. Barbeau, how has the feminist movement affected parenting and is the phenomenon of homosexuality a product of the disruption of the family, or what do you think would be its principle cause?

Monsignor Faber: I raised the question of whether there is a distinct spirituality in the third age and, frankly, I place virtually everyone of you as well as myself in the third age. I simply ask, do you perceive God in the same way as you did 20 years ago? I suspect as we accumulate experiences throughout life, and we have more of a base to function from, our internal psycho-

261

logical functioning changes. By the same token, the way in which we are in relationship to other persons or circumstances or jobs also demands from us different kinds of interaction. I suspect that our very familiarity with sacred things can be negative or can be positive. Being nearer to death than one might otherwise have been and being more conscious of that can drive persons towards different kinds of responses.

Let's look at other aspects of spirituality. There will be those who say, isn't it too bad that older people have not responded to Vatican II? But it has been my experience, quite broadly verified, that older persons who receive an adequate catechesis and the opportunity to understand liturgical reform are the most enthusiastic about it. Older people are being introduced to the opportunity of not just being intellectually engaged with scripture, but also using it as a tool of prayer. I suspect this is a development that from a pastoral point of view we should examine more closely. Focusing on the spirituality of older people might serve older persons well. But it also may give us hints in terms of spiritual formation of younger people, whether lay persons, married or single persons, or whether it be in terms of priests and religious.

Mr. Barbeau: In terms of the parent-child relationship, *Ms.* magazine did a survey of its readership a few years back, which we can assume to be mainly feminist-oriented. It found that women were raising their girls to be more independent, more assertive, to feel that there was no occupation not open to them and so on. But they were raising the boys just the way they'd always raised them, to protect their little sister, to be aggressive, and so on. They were raising them with all the macho ideals. They apparently felt that the boys were going to face a tougher battle out there than the girls. In terms of the parental tasks, I think that there are more men who are co-responsible for the tasks that used to be definitely the woman's domain.

One of the nicest things that the feminist movement did was to liberate the female in every man to the degree that it reached them. By that I mean it allowed more men to feel that it was okay to be tender, soft, caring, sensitive, and open about certain softer feelings without feeling that their wife would reject them if they did so. That also meant that they were going to be more open, tender, soft and caring towards their kids. They no longer felt that that was somehow a feminine thing.

The homosexual question is a difficult one. We have 70,000 male homosexuals in San Francisco. I don't necessarily think homosexuality is due to the disruption of the family. I don't see many homosexuals as clients, I've seen 2 in the last 2 years, and one of them was really bisexual. My conjecture about that, and it's only conjecture, is that a number of people on the homosexual scene have been seduced into it. Kids, in a city like San Francisco or New York, find themselves without money, and they start hustling or they are hustled by somebody in a big Cadillac who takes them to a swanky home and introduces them to the gay scene gradually. Having been seduced once into it, they find it very difficult to get out. There's a good percentage of people who are that way, I think, who aren't what I would term true homosexuals.

One of the problems I found in the 60's and early 70's was that numerous schools, Catholic as well as public, were inviting people from the homosexual community to come in to talk about homosexuality as an alternative life style to kids in their adolescence. Some of these kids were at that time going through what Freud called the homosexual phase of their growth. In other words, they were boys who were in gangs with boys and girls who thought boys were "awful" and they ganged with girls. Then somebody comes in and tells them that that means that they are homosexual. I think some kids got very confused at that time by that kind of presentation. They were really going through a normal phase of growth, the phase of identifying with their own sex.

I do think, though, that there are individuals who are true homosexuals. There is a lot of dispute about this in various ways, but when you talk with them, when you get close to them in terms of finding out what motivates them, you find that these were never attracted to women, have always been attracted to males and some of them come from very firm home backgrounds, with 3 or 4 heterosexual brothers and sisters and with a good family background and so on. Yet here they are on the homosexual scene. Some of them even went into marriage thinking that would be a way out of this, and then all they did was saddle some woman with a homosexual husband, and eventually they have affairs with men and finally break that up. So I don't think homosexuality is necessarily related to the break-up of the family, the dislocation of the family in our time. The absence of a father's love seems important to many — but this is all conjecture.

Question: Mr. Barbeau, what do you feel about corrective discipline with regard to children, adolescents, and parents? Msgr. Fahey, how do we prepare ourselves and our priests for retirement and where do you feel it is best for retired priests and Bishops to live?

Mr. Barbeau: You ask about corrective discipline for children, adolescents, and parents. When a child is before the age at which a parent can gently remonstrate with him about the difficulties of reaching his hand up and trying to pull the boiling kettle of water over on himself, one may have to slap a hand and say "no" very, very firmly. One may even have to slap a bottom, if a kid is doing something that's dangerous to his health or welfare before the age of his understanding. But after a certain while, those methods really are not useful. Archbishop Roberts had a beautiful line. He said, "Authority, if it expects to be obeyed, must commend itself in love". Kids really respond to loving correction, so I don't think physical violence is really necessary nor do I feel it's necessary to shout at kids. Systematic training in effective parenting can teach a parent how to communicate what the parent needs and wants. The child's respect for the parent, respect for the rights of others, and respect for himself are so useful and they are there. Those tools are there for the corrective discipline of children in a way that not only doesn't harm the child's self-esteem or the relationship of parent and child but actually enhances both.

In the case of discipline for adolescents, let's use an example. I had a woman come to me who was yelling from the moment she arrived at the door and all the way up the stairs to my office about her 17½ year old sugar-junky daughter. She screamed about this daughter, when she ate too much sugar there was sheer pandemonium at the dinner table because of the angry outbursts. They punished her, grounded her, took car privileges away, took away her allowance, and so on. I asked her, "Do you love your daughter?" "Of course I love her", she shouted. I said "I think that message has gotten lost in the last year or so."

I told her what I wanted her to do, and I think this is an example of what I mean when I say punitive measures are not necessarily helpful, but other measures can do things. I never saw the daughter. I told her to get very calm and to focus on the fact that she really loved this girl and that's why she was so agitated and so full of fear and anger about what was going on. Then when she was calm enough, she was to take her daughter to the park and to sit down with her someplace where she wouldn't be interrupted. I told her to take both her daughter's hands in hers and to look her right in the eye and say, "I love you very much" and then to say, "I love you so much that when you abuse your body with the overindulgence in sugar it just drives me kind of crazy and I've been making a terrible, stupid mistake of thinking I can control your sugar consumption and I can't do that". I instructed her in turning responsibility over to the daugher.

I made an appointment with the same lady for 9 days later, and on the 8th day she phoned me. Her daughter had since their talk been at dinner every evening and they had had no upsets whatsoever.

I'm not sure what we mean by corrective discipline for parents but I have talked to teenagers on how to manipulate their parents more properly. I don't know of any parents who aren't trying to be good parents, but the normal issue that comes up from kids is that their parents aren't letting them be responsible for their own time, like on Friday evenings or something, and they won't expand the curfew. I usually give the kids some clue. I say, you think you are talking about curfew and daddy's talking about sex. They look wide-eyed and I say, well, you normally talk about it at the wrong time. If you want to correct your father's intransigence about the curfew time, you don't do it while some lunk is leaning on a car horn out there and daddy's looking out over your shoulder as you're going out. You get him right after Mass, when he's rededicated himself to the task of being a good parent. You tell him that for 18 months you have had this curfew time, and you would like to expand it by another hour because you think you have been very responsible and all.

Anyway, I'm not sure what corrective discipline for parents means, but adolescents do have a lot to do with the quality of their relationship with the parents. They can set things up so that the parents are angry or upset, but the parents have to collaborate in it if it's really going to be an uproar situation. If parents don't collaborate in it and try a different method they can very often bring peace and harmony to the situation.

Monsignor Fahey: There's a degree of frustration because the question of growing old in priesthood is such an important one. And that's the question. It isn't the question of retirement. We have had some discussions already about the Church and culture and which influences which. Frankly, in the question of growing old in the service of the Lord, we are dominated by culture rather than developing our own internal culture. At the very same time that the secular society was doing away with age discrimination in employment and with mandatory retirement, we were instituting it.

Retirement is part of the armamentarium that we should have available to us as individuals and that we need to have as administrators. But, particularly in regard to religious life, it ought to be tied into disability. When Social Security was developed in this country, the idea was it was an indicator or a proxy for fraility. It really was an outgrowth of the notion of unemployment insurance. It has changed, so retirement in the culture now is seen as though it creates an entitlement to people to be able to withdraw from active participation in the community whether or not there's any disability. Frankly, that analogy may be valid in the broader society or it may not, but I don't think it applies to religious life. I think we are ordained for life, or we are religious for life. Some of us may have to go off the job and it's easier administratively to deal with mandatory retirement, but it isn't particularly just.

Having said that, I think that the preparation really is the question for growing old in ministry and that question really hasn't been raised in many dioceses. We have to raise it more carefully and clearly, whether we anticipate rust out or burn out or whether it just be diminished physical capacity. We may have to alter our participation in ministry, but it should be an altering of our participation, not an abrupt, "now you're active, and now you're retired" situation. This is the secular society's rather impoverished way to go about the issue of retirement. In the literature with which I'm familiar apart from Church there's all kinds of things about flex time, part time, modifications, etc. By and large this is not available to people in secular society but it should be available to us within the context of religious life.

In terms of the place where people live, it's a generic principle that people tend to be satisfied where they live to the degree in which they felt they were participant in the decision of where it might be. People tend to be satisfied where they end up living to the degree in which they felt they were a participant in the decision. So, for example, in the broader society, of those who live in retirement facilities, some are very happy and some are very unhappy. But, the variable that's most significant, did they have some role in making that decision?

Having said that, I do feel, not on grounds of a scientific study, but on pretty good professional experience, that most dioceses are well served, if there be a place for the frail but physically active older priests in group living. That is not the solution for all priests, but it is a useful alternative for many priests. This should be a place where freedom and autonomy is emphasized as opposed to being regimented. Someone once said that the sign of institutionalization is whether you can lock your door or not. If a person can lock their door, it's often well to have this.

I hope this is understood correctly, but it is helpful to have an understanding woman as the person who runs that facility with sensitivity. I think most dioceses are ill-served in trying to build a facility for those who are sick and in an infirmary. It's almost impossible for dioceses to do this. Some religious communities can, and indeed it may be worthwhile to explore with communities some sort of a joint facility. However, I think that even there, just as we use hospitals generally when we're acutely sick, if our degree of disability is such as to require institutionalization, we probably in most instances will have to use community institutions rather than build them specifically for priests.

The Family
And The Father

Paul C. Vitz, Ph.D.

PART I

I assume by now that we are all one big happy family, although, from many of the chapters of this book, I'm afraid that the "happy family" seems to be in short supply. Except for one important issue that I'll mention later, I am not convinced that things are quite so bad on the family front as it might appear. At least, there is important good news too, and so I plan to organize most of my comments around the familiar motif, "the bad news — the good news."

My first funcion is to review some of the major points of the chapters you have already read. After the review aimed at drawing out important common themes and integrating concepts, I will add some of my own analysis of today's family crisis.

Professor Glick gave us many useful statistics on recent major changes in family life, and in the process he gave us much of the bad news. For example, the divorce rate has tripled in the last 30 years, and there are now roughly one million divorces a year. Another way to think about this is to note that this means that approximately one million children go through the pain of divorce and losing one parent each year.

The proportion of babies born to unmarried women is now up to a staggering 19% — almost one in five (as of 1982) — while the fertility rate has dropped to 1.8 babies per woman — a figure well below replacement. And, of course, as most of us already know, there are one and one-half million abortions a year in this country.

Other statistics relevant to family change are that probably 12% of today's young women will never marry; and likewise, an increasing proportion of men won't marry. There are going to be lots of lifetime singles. Because of these statistics, plus increased divorce and longevity, the average household size is down to 2.7 people.

Where, you might ask, is the good news? Well, first Glick predicts that most of these statistics have levelled off. Such a stabilization may at least give us a breathing spell to try and take stock. Moreover, I am slightly more optimistic than Glick on these numbers. Very recent statistics for 1984 have reported some slight *drops* in the number of divorces and in the number of abortions. Thus, I'm willing to predict that most of the preceding grim statistics will be at least slightly lower by the end of the decade. Of course, such optimism is highly qualified by the bad news — the enormous absolute level of suffering that such statistics represent, even if there is a modest future decline.

But there is other good news, and Glick made this clear when he emphasized that 73% of household members still live in homes managed by a married couple and that roughly half of our population lives in a traditional family of father, mother, and children; another 25% are married but have no children or their children have grown up and left home. We should not lose sight of Glick's comment, "the central core of family life continues very much the same as it has existed for many generations."

270

More important news on the family, but again mostly bad news, was provided in Bishop Ricard's chapter on violence in American families. Physical violence, however defined, has clearly become a serious and all too common problem. Perhaps as many as 250,000 cases of child abuse are now being reported a year, and possibly as many as 10,000 children a year will die of such abuse. Wife beating is also disturbingly high, although whether this is an increase over previous years is hard to judge because of inadequate statistics. Likewise, sexual violence, in particular father-daughter incest, is now known to be considerably more common than previously thought. The increases in divorce and in pornography are almost certain to have made incest more likely today than in the past.

Unfortunately, there are still other forms of family violence that Ricard didn't mention, probably to keep his chapter focused and to spare us too many gruesome statistics. (Even those who have heard thousands of confessions can only take so much sin at a sitting!) Here are some other examples of family violence, all on the increase in the last few decades — examples that did come up in the discussion following the presentation.

First, as was noted by Msgr. Caffarra, abortion is a form of family violence — one that exists at the center of the family. Although I believe the studies remain to be done, I would expect that abortion increases the chances of other later violence in the family; that a circle of violence speads from abortion throughout the rest of the family.

There is also the recent phenomenon on battered parents. (Statistics are available from the U.S. Census Bureau.) Hundreds of thousands of American parents are unable to physically control their teenage children. Psychologists agree that the central problem has been the loss of parental authority, especially that of the father. Particularly hard to control are adolescent boys, especially if they are involved with drugs. (In fact, a small but significant proportion of murders in this country now involve a child killing his mother or father, one tragic example of which occurred at my university this last week. An 18-year-old freshman killed his mother with a baseball bat in an argument over his grades and his girlfriend. There was no father in the family.)

And, of course, divorce is itself often a severe form of violence against children. The best recent studies show that 35 to 40% of the children of divorce suffer severe long-term depression and other long-lasting psychological disabilities (see Wallerstein & Kelly, 1980). Delayed but violent responses to divorce are common. Hence, the children of divorce more often commit suicide, kill others, get involved in drugs, and they go into crime at a much higher rate than children from intact families. (For a summary of this evidence, see Cochran and Vitz, 1983.)

As I said, "gruesome" is perhaps the only word for the statistics on family violence. As for the good news, these statistics don't provide much, but the studies themselves are an important positive symptom. We are becoming aware of family violence and are just beginning to focus on some of the causes and possible remedies. In any case, the first step in solving a problem is to become aware of it and, however painful, the very awareness of it is still good news.

Another family problem is well described by Msgr. Fahey and by Dr. Soldo in their chapters on aging, in particular, on the "Third Age" in a person's life, roughly the 20 to 30 years after retiring from work or after a couple has raised their children. The existence of this Third Age is primarily the consequence of the enormous increase in life expectancy, something that is becoming a worldwide phenomenon. Here I think the good news isn't hard to find. In this case, the good news is that the problem exists — people are living longer and healthier lives. Saints be praised! It is clear that the Church has much to learn about dealing with the problem, and Fahey provides a very helpful analysis of the issue. In a similar vein, Dr. Soldo very interestingly describes and interprets the challenges of the three or four generation family. She points out the increasing variability in family life and its greater complexity — much of it coming from increased longevity. But the longevity "problem" is basically a good one and I'm optimistic about the Church's ability to contribute to the lives of its older members and, in turn, to benefit from their extra years. I like to think of the Third Age as the time of wisdom and spiritual depth; certainly the world can use as much of these two virtues as it can find. So I look forward to the Church's positive responses to the challenge of aging, in particular, to the suggestions and reports of Dr. Soldo and Msgr. Fahey and the Fordham University Third Age Center.

Professor Destro briefly described many of the important general issues involved in family law and family policy. A central point for the Church is to be aware that government intervention into family life has often been motivated by interests opposed to the functional integrity of the family. The Church needs to develop clearer awareness of its own position on and potential contribution to the national debate over family policies.

Dr. Janice D'Avignon's paper very nicely identifies the problem of loss of parental confidence in their ability to raise children, a loss brought on by the rise to prominence of child-rearing experts. The real problem, as she notes, is to use discernment in selecting experts. Their knowledge can be very useful, but sound judgement is needed to avoid those whose expertise is embedded in false and anti-Christian philosophy. Here, I would like to fully support D'Avignon's rejection of Values Clarification. Unfortunately, the Values Clarification position has deeply affected much Catholic religious education material, and some very substantial changes in religious education will be needed in the future. I also very much agree with D'Avignon's and Clayton Barbeau's suggestion that parents themselves be directly consulted as experts — for in many respects that's what they truly are.

Mario Paredes showed us another family problem: the special stresses faced by the many new Hispanic families that have come here in recent years. Again, we see families struggling with the anti-family climate of this country's dominant, thoroughly hedonistic, secular culture. America's individualism, our tendency to value things over people, our flabby tolerance of divorce, all hurt and undermine the newly-arrived Hispanic family. Their conflict is especially painful for they often came from the older, preindustrial family and village life. They are caught very sharply in the clash of two very different historical eras.

Obviously, in view of the Hispanics' deep Catholic understanding of much of the family, the Church should do everything possible to welcome and protect them, and to expand their influence in this country. Since many of their values were formed in a preindustrial world, they may well be helpful and wanted as

Americans try to develop a new *post*industrial, *post*modern family life — one that may be able to recover some of the strengths of the earlier period.

In any case, it is quite clear that other religious groups are well aware of the need for family ministry to our new Hispanic arrivals. The rapid growth of various Protestant groups in the American Hispanic community has been extensive and shows no sign of slowing. A major key to this growth has been the ability of these groups to reach out to support the Hispanic family. (I will return briefly to this issue later.)

One related point here is that the Church must develop a positive evangelistic response if it hopes to keep up its membership. The policy of counting on immigrant families and large Catholic families of second or third generation immigrants will no longer do. The Church is losing many of the Hispanics and it has already lost almost a whole generation of young American Catholics. Active evangelization among the un-churched, among the large ex-Catholic population and among those no longer satisfied with their own church's theology is now needed. The old passive posture of the Church with respect to converts will no longer suffice.

I turn now to the less problem-centered, more theoretical chapters. Chapter One by Dr. McCready presented a big picture — an historical overview, along with interesting specific details. The three major ages of the family identified by McCready are the preindustrial, community/family centered around agriculture and small town life; the more recent institutional family created in the bureaucratic and corporate period; and now in the U.S. the just-developing postmodern or pluralistic family. I generally agree with McCready's analysis here, although I think the last stage — pluralism — may be a transition family prior to a new, still unclear, and more stable social environment.

Now the bad news is that a period of transition from one era to the next is always one of great stress in which the family is destabilized. Clayton Barbeau gave us insightful but distressing examples of these changes in American life over the last 50-100 years. In this country most of the family change is currently from the modern, urban institutional family to the postmodern pluralistic family. Elsewhere in the world, the first transition, from community family life to the modern, urban, industrial way of living still involves millions of families. (The older style Hispanics who come to this country are to some extent encountering all the possible transitions at once, including the usual stress of sometimes directly moving from premodern to postmodern.)

I would like to underscore a number of McCready's points. Programs to help the family must not cost it still more time or money — instead these programs should serve a real family need, such as day-care centers, meals on wheels, etc. I also agree with McCready and with Barbeau that the mentality of the postmodern family is indeed increasingly determined by images, the media and personal experience. Above all, the theology of the Church — propositional knowledge according to McCready — very much needs to be translated into the language and experience of the family. I firmly believe — indeed I know from family experience — that the Catholic propositions are true, but the linkage to daily experience and knowledge has not been made. In part, to remedy this situation I would like to emphasize a new point, the need for support for new Catholic art and especially support for sound Catholic media, e.g. the Eternal Word Network.

The good news — what might that be? Even 20 or 30 years ago our knowledge of the history of the family was quite limited. In recent years historical knowledge has increased greatly and we are at least becoming knowledgeable about the central importance of the family and what it is that effects the family. The Church in those countries still moving into the urban, industrial phase has a chance to learn from earlier mistakes, for example, to learn from the failure of the Church in 19th century Europe to address the needs of the working class family. Today, the urban working class family is being destabilized — even destroyed — by the permissive consumerism so effectively pushed by TV, as well as by many other social forces. Perhaps the Church in those countries which have yet to feel the impact of the postmodern changes will be fore-warned and better prepared when these changes begin to effect their families. Again, awareness of the problem is a necessary, though not sufficient, precondition for any positive response to it.

Fr. Preister, also in a theoretical vein, begins by noting that we are in a transition from a modern, industrial period with its emphasis on the autonomous individual, to some kind of post-modern society. He makes the significant point that whatever this new period or third stage will be like, it already shows strong signs of rejecting autonomous individualism in favor of a new emphasis on interdependence, connection, and systems of people. Certainly such a change should be good news for Catholicism with its long history of emphasis on the family and community and its opposition to individualism. Here with Preister we start with the good news, for such a new third stage would be ripe for an acceptance of the Catholic concept of family. Preister goes on to show that the Catholic theory or model of the family has been clearly articulated by the Vatican, especially by our present Holy Father. In short, the centrality of family for the contemporary social situation has been well understood by the Church. Indeed, I don't know of any other major organization that has anything like the Church's grasp of the family and its problems.

And yet — and here is the bad news — we all know that with a few exceptions, the Church so far has been unable to articulate its ideal effectively. Somehow the all-important practical implementation of the model Catholic family in response to the present situation has yet to be developed.

Msgr. Caffarra's Prologue moved us from statistics and history to the more abstract world of the theological and philosophical basis of the Christian family. He gave us a part of the Church's general theoretical understanding of the family by beginning with a philosophical understanding of the nature of a person. Next, he identified a man and woman united in marriage as the proper locus for the creation, with God, of a new person; and it is with a child that there is fulfillment of the nature of the family. Once the new person (not individual!) has arrived, the function or purpose of the family is, in cooperation with the Church, to nurture the developing child. The family as a nurturing environment, as a little church, is the "spiritual womb" for the new life, and this purpose expresses itself in the mission of the family, namely to develop the child's capacity for Christian love.

Finally we come to Fr. Ashley's theoretical review, one that so richly ties in with the preceding talks. Again we have a summary (from Shorter) of three types or stages of family development —

the traditional, the industrial, and the new, mostly unformed, postindustrial family. Ashley clearly identifies how both of these two earlier types of family fall far short of a true Christian concept of the family. These earlier findings should always be kept in mind, since there is a tendency to overidealize the family of the past. In fact these earlier versions of family life were, generally speaking, far from wonderful. So some of the "good news" is that today's family failures are to some extent nothing but business as usual.

Fr. Ashley also spells out Pope John Paul II's understanding of the family, one that develops and articulates the Church's earlier positions. This model, as I've already mentioned, gives the Catholic a true vision of the future, for it corrects the weaknesses and keeps and transforms the strengths of the two earlier models of the family. In terms of some of the language used in this volume, one can see the traditional family as authoritarian, the industrial family as individualistic, and the still-to-be-formed postmodern family — in its ideal form — as authoritative and interdependent: based on truth and love. Such a new family grounded in the true nature of person, and in the family as the system for developing the person, remains to be tried on any large scale. It is a new model, a new vision. It is a model that will fit with what we can see coming of the new system-oriented, less individualistic society. Finally, it is clearly a Gospel model of family. It is thus, like the Gospel, the true Good News for all the bad news about today's family.

PART II

I would now like to add some observations of my own, and make some suggestions for dealing with the family crisis. First, however, let me note that I will speak frankly — perhaps too frankly. If I am impolite I apologize in advance and you can blame my preconversion, pre-Catholic secular past.

I will start — once again — with the bad news. In reflecting on the nature of the family crisis in this country, I have become convinced that behind it lies another, deeper crisis. It is a crisis that Fr. Ashley clearly alluded to, but one that otherwise has received little attention here and almost no attention anywhere else. The deeper crisis I refer to is quite simply a crisis of American manhood — that is, a crisis in what it means to be a man, and above all, in what it means to be a father; most particularly, in what it means to be a Christian father.

This crisis has developed because the concepts of manhood and fatherhood have been under relentless attack throughout the modern period, an attack that has become acute in recent years.

Let me describe the situation in which the Christian father finds himself today. He is — if you will — the point man, leading his family as best he can like a small patrol through a hostile and anti-Christian society. He is being shot at from all sides. The world of business and the professions doesn't really give a damn about a man's family or his function as father. They want one thing: commitment to the job, to the business, and the more time and energy you give to that the better. A family is a kind of luxury that shouldn't get in the way. To have three or more children is often seen as a statement of lack of full commitment to your job, your company, your career. It certainly takes time — and that will often cost the father promotions and raises. The result is that the man who needs more money gets less. There is certainly no longer any real status in our society to being a father. And, of course, for decades, corporations have assumed a father will move his family whenever his skills can be used elsewhere, or even leave his family on a few months of special assignment because of the corporate need. If he turns down the "opportunity," this is often seen as evidence of lack of full commitment.

Meanwhile, the new world of sexuality and pornography has placed another aggressive anti-family force in the corporate-business world. Everywhere the Christian father gets the message: look out for yourself, forget fidelity, be a James Bond or a Hugh Hefner, grab all the gusto you can. And now there are all the new sexual temptations and pressures from so many women working in the business and professional worlds. No wonder divorce is rampant. We care more about our individual rights and salaries, about our personal pleasures, than about anything else.

Then there is our pluralistic culture, a culture that increasingly mocks Christianity and very openly makes fun of Christian values. The net effect of all these pressures is to make the Christian father look like — and often feel like — some kind of chump, some kind of fool, even a drudge. No wonder there are so many families without fathers!

From a different side come the shots of the feminists, and the shooting has been pretty heavy from that direction for twenty years now. They have provided a constant, strident attack on men for being men — or for not being the men *they* want men to be. About all this movement has consistently expressed an intense hatred for the very concept of manhood and fatherhood and its adherents actively work for the suppression or removal of these important, distinctive realities.

This long-term, multifaceted attack from all sides on men, especially on fathers, has had enormous impact. American men increasingly seem to fall into two categories. Many remain men but cease caring much for others. They devote their energy, strength and intelligence exclusively to their own individual well-being, to their careers, to looking out for Number One. They distance themselves from women who are seen as sex partners, while marriage is understood as something to be avoided or as just a current arrangement to be temporarily maintained until something or someone better comes along.

However, many other men, often unconsciously, cease being men at all. They become nice androgynous creatures, but they are also indecisive, unreliable and weak. Very briefly, men are opting for one of two ways of being: The strong man who leads and exploits, or the weak man who is ineffectual but nice. Recently, it seems like the latter is the fastest growing category. We all know "the Great American Wimp." He feels uncomfortable around men, because men sense he is squishy. The wimp needs to be loved at all costs, and the typical cost of this need is the truth. In particular, the truth of manhood embarrasses him and therefore he acts as though it doesn't exist. This new type of American, "the Wimpman," was at first welcomed by many women. But, by now the complaints are coming in loud and strong. The wimp, like the macho, fundamentally avoids commitment to others, he can't be counted on, often he is still too dependent, too much like a child — a Peter Pan. Hence both the macho man and the wimpo man avoid true commitment to women — and, of course, women know it. The final result is that a good man becomes even harder to find. All this only increases the disappointment, frustration, bitterness, and anger of many women, which only leads them to further attacks on men and manhood, which further pushes men away. What a vicious cycle.

Now, so much for the bad news. The answer to all this — let me suggest — is the Christian man, the man who is fully a man in the natural sense: He leads, he has energy, zeal, but he puts his manhood in the service of God and of others — his family, employees, or community. Here is the man who truly enjoys his God-given masculinity, because he is using this gift for others. Thus does grace perfect nature. He is a man with true strength, without the macho's selfish insecurity, without the secret cringing and insecurity of the wimp.

I could go on at length about the crisis of manhood in our society, and about the Christian man devoted to servant leadership as the answer. Instead I will conclude this topic by pointing out that this model of manhood is functioning quite well in those religious groups most actively growing, and in particular in those challenging the Church today. I have a good number of evangelical and pentecostal friends. Through them I have seen or heard how they work. The pentecostal groups who are converting former Catholics by the thousands are almost always led and energized by devoted men. Indeed, one of the distinctive features of these groups is the masculine energy and zeal found in them. Furthermore, the women in these groups are — as far as I can see — delighted with the situation. The men are energetic, happy, and provide true male leadership and, of course, in the process, role models for their sons. The men are *there*, busy serving the needs of others without exploitation or selfishness. The woman in such a group is freed from the debilitating anxiety of trying to be both a mother and a father — an impossible and thankless task; she is freed of anxiety about men who can't be counted on; she is free to be a woman and to develop the great natural strengths of her own womanhood.

This energetic maleness so typical of the successful, rapidly growing challenge to the Church should make it clear that further moves toward androgynous Church organization has little evidence to recommend it in the real world of the religious competition. (I won't even bother to discuss this issue with respect to Islam.)

My specific suggestion to you is to support and joyfully celebrate — at least once every year — the Christian concept of manhood and fatherhood. And also let me say personally, as one kind of Christian father — a natural father — to each of my readers who is a spiritual and ecclesiastical father — that you and your priests are the best, the clearest, and the most fundamental, representatives of Catholic manhood in our society. Don't forget!

Make no mistake — to attack the basic concept of fatherhood is to attack God the Father; it is to attack Jesus who came to do his Father's will and who gave us only one prayer, the *Pater Noster.* It is even to challenge the Holy Spirit who is one with the Father and Son.

Now to a new subject and, much more briefly this time, the bad news. Even if in the future, God willing, the father and the family are restored to better health (the perfect family we will see only in heaven!), the fact is, right now there are millions of people out there who are suffering from the failure of their family. For many, the pain comes from a father who left them, or who abused them; for others it was an unloving, preoccupied, and manipulative mother, and there are, of course, countless other possibilities. The immediate issue is how to deal with the large number of the "walking wounded" that we all meet every day. Here, you might expect a psychologist to recommend greatly expanded psychotherapy, all kinds of fancy and expensive programs — but I won't for the simple reason that I don't think they would do much good. I do recommend some increase in sound Christian psychotherapy, for in a substantial number of cases I think this can really help. Primarily, however, I would like to suggest something else, something that should be pretty familiar to all of you. The essential problem for so many people has been the failure of their natural family to provide adequate love and support when they were young. The loss of this love in most respects can never be replaced. It is simply a terrible fact. However, there is one very important answer to the failure of the natural family and that is the Holy Family. The most important healing answer to the loss of natural love in one's childhood is the gain of supernatural love in one's adulthood. Here it is that I think traditional Catholic devotions and spiritual practices can be of great help for many people.

Let's say that a teenage boy is suffering from an absent father and a poorly developed sense of his own masculinity. His father was not abusive, just absent. There is evidence that such young men often benefit from devotion to God the Father. A young woman who has been physically abused by her father or step-father may be unable, at least for awhile, to approach God the Father; she may however be very positively served by worship of her "brother," Jesus, or by devotion to her "mother," the Blessed Virgin Mary. For Catholic fathers struggling with family life, I suggest devotion to St. Joseph. For those needing integrated love, a sense of family, there is contemplation of the Holy Trinity, or the life of the Holy Family. Therefore, my message is basically very simple. Traditional Catholic piety and spiritual practices represent a very sound kind of family psychology, a spiritual psychology that will comfort and support many people today whose own families have been defective, and for whom there is no other possible answer. One further point, the practice of these devotions in small groups is also something that has much to recommend it for it brings in a direct sense of family closeness.

Well — you may be thinking — so you suggest support for Christian and Catholic manhood — and the recovery of Catholic devotions centered on God the Father, and the Holy Family, the Trinity, and the Saints. But, aren't today's family and social problems more enormous and complex than the Church can deal with, given its over-extended and terribly limited resources? I do agree, yet I am an optimist on this. Part of my optimism is based on the good news, already mentioned, including the great historical changes now underway, changes that I think are working in a pro-Christian, even pro-Catholic direction.

Certainly many cycles seem to be coming to an end. The 1000 year cycle of Western Europe is coming to an end; the 500 year cycle of the Renaissance, the 250 year cycle of the Enlightenment and Industrialization, the 125 year cycle of the modern city, the 60 year cycle of the secular, liberal state, and its associated consumer-oriented prosperity. These cycles no doubt are oversimplified, but the end of the modern period — at least in Western Europe and North America — and the start of a still ambiguous new period does seem underway. This new period will probably reject much of modernism. Fr. Preister suggests that people will move toward integration, synthesis and coordinated systems, and away from

282

autonomy, analysis and independent units. Certainly in the long run such a new era bodes well for Catholicism, but in the short run, I grant you, we may find ourselves in severe trials.

About four years ago I had an interesting talk with a French philospher who was describing the intellectual life of Paris. He concluded by saying "Marxism is dead, existentialism and Sartre are dead, structuralism is dying — for the first time in France in over 200 years the door is open." We looked at each other and then agreed to pray that it would be Christ who would walk through the door. I do not know if that has been the case, but about two years later Cardinal Lustiger showed up in Paris and is now part of French intellectual life, so at least one of our Lord's representatives has come through the door. Like Lustiger, I think the Church is still very young — if not in it's infancy, at least still in its childhood — and so, like him, I'm optimistic about the coming third millenium. The pathologies of modern life are clear to many people today and as an ideology modernism is now playing itself out — but the Church goes rolling on. And with the newly clarified Catholic understanding of the nature of the person, the nature and purpose of the family, with the developing understanding of manhood and womanhood, we have a vision of what the next era could be. Of course for such a vision to occur, for a Catholic Restoration to take place, we will need much new help. For that, more than anything else, we must pray. In the last analysis, as we all know well, we can do nothing of ourselves. We can sense the coming of new Catholic life, we can begin to notice the arrival of a new group of young, saintly, prayerful, loving Catholics — new Catholics who will be able to bring their faith to the postmodern world and its troubled families. Perhaps many new religious orders are waiting to be born. Perhaps there will be a new family apostolate, perhaps an order of the Holy Family.

But for any of this to happen we must pray for the Catholic father, we must pray even more for the whole Catholic family, but most of all we must pray for the coming of a new reality, one that will be called a true Catholic Restoration — a restoration brought about by a new generation of saints.

Bibliography

Cochran, R. F., Jr., & Vitz, P. C. (1983). "Child protective divorce laws: A response to the effects of parental separation on children." *Family Law Quarterly, 17,* 327-363.

Wallerstein, J., & Kelly, J. (1980). *Surviving the breakup: How children and parents cope with divorce.* New York: Basic Books.

Index

Pope John Center Publications

The Pope John XXIII Medical-Moral Research and Education Center has dedicated itself to approaching current and emerging medical-moral issues from the perspective of Catholic teaching and the Judeo-Christian heritage. Previous publications of the Pope John Center include:

THEOLOGIES OF THE BODY: Humanist and Christian, by Benedict M. Ashley, O.P.; An historical, philosophical and theological approach to a non-dualistic anthropology, as a foundation for Christian ethics; 1985, 770 pp., $20.95.

MORAL THEOLOGY TODAY: Certitudes and Doubts, Proceedings of 1984 Bishops' Workshop in Dallas, 355 pp., $17.95.

SEX AND GENDER, A Theological and Scientific Inquiry, edited by Mark F. Schwartz, Sc.D., Albert S. Moraczewski, O.P., Ph.D., James A. Monteleone, M.D., 1983, 420 pp., $19.95.

TECHNOLOGICAL POWERS AND THE PERSON, Nuclear Energy and Reproductive Technologies, Proceedings of the Bishops' Workshop for 1983, Dallas, 520 pp., $15.95.

HANDBOOK ON CRITICAL SEXUAL ISSUES, edited by Donald G. McCarthy, Ph.D., and Edward J. Bayer, S.T.D., 1983, 230 pp., $9.95.

HANDBOOK ON CRITICAL LIFE ISSUES, edited by Donald G. McCarthy, Ph.D. and Edward J. Bayer, S.T.D., 1982, 230 pp., $9.95.

MORAL RESPONSIBILITY IN PROLONGING LIFE DECISIONS, edited by Donald G. McCarthy and Albert S. Moraczewski, O.P., 1982, 316 pp., $9.95.

HUMAN SEXUALITY AND PERSONHOOD, Proceedings of the Bishops' Workshop in Dallas, February, 1981, 254 pp., $9.95.

GENETIC COUNSELING, THE CHURCH AND THE LAW, edited by Albert S. Moraczewski, O.P., and Gary Atkinson, 1980, 259 pp., $9.95.

NEW TECHNOLOGIES OF BIRTH AND DEATH: Medical, Legal, and Moral Dimensions. Proceedings of the Workshop for Bishops in Dallas, January, 1980, 196 pp., $8.95.

A MORAL EVALUATION OF CONTRACEPTION AND STERILIZATION, A Dialogical Study, by Gary Atkinson and Albert S. Moraczewski, O.P., 1980, 115 pp., $4.95.

ARTFUL CHILDMAKING, Artificial Insemination in Catholic Teaching, by John C. Wakefield, 1978, 205 pp., $8.95.

AN ETHICAL EVALUATION OF FETAL EXPERIMENTATION, edited by Donald McCarthy and Albert S. Moraczewski, O.P., 1976, 137 pp., $8.95.

These books may be ordered from: The Pope John Center, 186 Forbes Road, Braintree, Massachusetts 02184. Telephone (617) 848-6965. Prepayment is encouraged. Please add $1.00 for shipping and handling for the first book ordered and 25¢ for each additional book.

Subscriptions to the Pope John Center monthly newsletter, *Ethics and Medics,* may be sent to the same address. Annual subscriptions are $12.00.